United to Improve
America's Health®

D0562328

edge ware

insights from complexity science
for health care leaders

Brenda Zimmerman, Ph.D.
Curt Lindberg
Paul Plsek

VHA Inc.
Irving, Texas

edgeware

Printed in the United States of America.

ISBN 0-9667828-0-1

Edgeware
Table of Contents

Welcome

I. Primer

II. Principles

III. Tales

IV. Aides

V. Bibliography

VI. Glossary

Index

edgeware

# welcome

edgeware

Welcome to *Edgeware*
Complexity resources
for health care leaders

Complexity. It is a concept that is imposing in its very name. In fact, even the idea of explaining complexity (making complexity simple) is, at its heart, paradoxical. This raises intriguing questions: Must an approach to complexity be complex? How should a resource book for complexity science be structured? It is questions such as these that *Edgeware* seeks to answer.

So, how does *Edgeware* address complexity? You will soon discover that *Edgeware's* very structure models the principles it is addressing. This holds implications for you, the reader (or, to use a more accurate term, the participant):

Edgeware is nonlinear.

Those of you who are strictly left-brained and orderly may find your preferences challenged. Edgeware is not a book to be read from beginning to end. Instead, it is a collection of aides, ideas and resources that allow people with different learning styles and in different contexts to explore this fascinating science from multiple angles. Start at the beginning. Start at the end. Pick a page at random. It doesn't matter – you will soon find your way.

Edgeware offers multiple points-of-entry.

Whether you are new to complexity science, or you are further along in the lifelong journey of exploring its intricacies, there are several portals through which you can access *Edgeware*. The following pages of this Welcome section will assist you in taking the first step.

Edgeware is unsettling.

Complexity may require that you disassemble some of your old mental models about organizations and the world around you. Old beliefs about control and management, for example, look very different when viewed through a lens of complexity. Resist the temptation to dismiss the difficult lessons of complexity; it's good to be somewhat unsettled. (This, in itself, is a concept consistent with complexity.)

Edgeware honors the old.

There's no need for you to throw out everything you know.

Complexity science is not about bulldozing over old concepts and theory. Rather, it helps illuminate what has worked in the past, and why. One of the beauties of complexity science is that it is cross-disciplinary. It is built on patterns that can be observed in the economy, in a vegetable garden, in global organizations ... even in the structure of clouds. In fact, the roots of complexity science are thousands of years old.

Edgeware is a thinking approach.

This is not a program that you roll out in organizations, with banners and coffee mugs. It's a new way of thinking and seeing the world – and, hence, a new way of working with real organizational and health care issues.

Edgeware offers multiple voices.

You may notice that *Edgeware's* personality is somewhat fragmented. Its tone and approach shift frequently. Its perspectives vary. In fact, many voices are represented here, including several leading thinkers in complexity science and many health care leaders who are putting complexity-inspired approaches to work.

Edgeware is a family of tools.

This book is only one of the resources available to you. Please join us online to review our comprehensive library of complexity resources and to receive news of upcoming events. To visit us, go to: *http://www.vha.com*

Also, the comprehensive *Edgeware* binder contains all of the material in this book, as well as more in-depth articles and tools.

Most important of all, remember that *Edgeware* thrives on your learnings, your experiences, your energy. It is more than this book; it is an active community of learners. Your participation, in whatever fashion, holds the potential for tremendous change.

What is in *Edgeware?*
Edgeware is divided into six chapters.
They are:

I. Primer

Before you begin a painting project, it's a good idea to first lay down a coat of primer. This prepares the surface, so the paint will go on better. The same is true in learning. This introductory paper prepares your mind with a context and a base-level understanding of complexity science. Later, the more challenging concepts are much more likely to stick.

This chapter is a good place to start if you prefer a scholarly and scientific overview of the field of complexity.

II. Principles

"Theory is fine. But what am I supposed to do?" Good question. That's where the Principles chapter comes in. Here you will find summaries of nine specific, action-oriented heuristics (or rules of thumb) for leading in a complex environment. Each principle is accompanied by insights from some of the leading thinkers in complexity theory.

III. Tales

Stories are powerful. They explore truth and nuance in a way that makes it real. For the student of complexity, stories answer the important question, "What does this look like in practice?" These are true tales of organizations facing issues – most in health care – viewed through a lens of complexity. (You may even find several that deal with challenges similar to yours!)

If you are one of the many people whose learning style favors association and illustration, you may wish to begin your journey of learning here.

IV. Aides

Complexity theory is challenging – not just to learn, but to practice. Sometimes it's nice to have a little help. That's what this chapter is for. Unlike tools, which conjure an image of a machine that cranks out results, these are aides – relational, flexible resources that can empower you on your journey through a complex environment. Review them, apply them, adapt them … and make these aides your own.

V. Bibliography

Plenty of books and articles are available for those who wish to delve deeper into particular complexity concepts. This bibliography is selective, including only the best. Instead of a dry list approach, the bibliography includes reviews, observations and comments to help you find the right book or article – whether you're looking for something scientific and academic, or a simple, usable approach. Happy reading!

VI. Glossary

Be prepared to stretch your vocabulary. Complexity theory is loaded with multisyllabic terms that are probably new to you. (One reason for this is the cross-disciplinary nature of complexity theory. It draws upon biology, physics and computer science, just to name a few disciplines.) As you encounter new terms throughout *Edgeware*, you can find their clear explanations here.

Navigating *Edgeware*

If you need to get from one corner of your block to the other, you follow the sidewalk. There's no need to deviate from the linear path.

But what if you are on a weekend hike in the woods? Certainly there is much pleasure to be found in exploring in a nonlinear fashion: The sound of a distant waterfall prompts you to veer off to the left; a less-followed trail suddenly reveals itself, branching off to the right. You make these choices spontaneously, and in the process learn your way around the landscape.

Aides
•*Metaphor*

Edgeware is not designed to get you to the corner. Instead, it is a companion for exploring a challenging and exciting new landscape: complexity science.

The problem with new landscapes is that it is easy to get lost. That's why *Edgeware* features simple navigational tools to facilitate your free exploration. If you are familiar with the hyperlink method of finding your way around the Internet, then *Edgeware* will feel familiar to you. The Internet hyperlink metaphor was central in organizing these materials.

How to navigate using margin icons

Throughout *Edgeware*, you will see icons alongside the text, located in the margins. These icons represent chapters of the book. (You just reviewed these icons on the previous two pages.) The icons will link you to further definitions, illuminations or illustrations of the concepts described at that point in the text. For example, the "exploring the woods" concept above is an example of metaphor. Right there in the margin is an icon of the Aides chapter of *Edgeware*, pointing the way to an aide called "metaphor." To find it, simply turn to the Aides chapter of *Edgeware*. (The chapters are easy to find, since they are clearly marked with "tabs" that bleed to the edge of the right page.) In most cases, a table of contents will direct you to specific topics.

Where do I begin?

Still following the sidewalk? That's OK. Sometimes, it helps to have a little push to get started. Here are two ways to get moving:

1. Jump right in.

Principles
•*Clockware/
swarmware*

Sometimes, the best way to get started is just to dive in. Begin anywhere. Just pick a page. Any disorientation you feel will be temporary. You will quickly find your way around, thanks to the hyperlinking. Free yourself from the need to take it in order, and allow your relationship with the material to take on a life of its own. (Note that this approach is an example of swarmware. The principle of "Clockware/swarmware" is represented by an icon in the margin. If you wish, turn to the Principles chapter, and locate "Clockware/swarmware" in its table of contents to learn more about this concept.)

2. Identify what you need.

Below, the six chapters are identified on two dimensions: their level of mastery (new to these concepts, or experienced); and their outcome (learning or doing). For example, if you're looking for in-depth learning, you might begin exploring the Tales chapter. For some more approachable ideas for action, try the Aides chapter.

	Mastery		Outcome	
	New	Experienced	Learning	Doing
Primer	●	○	●	○
Principles	●	○	●	●
Tales	●	●	●	●
Aides	●	○	○	●
Bibliography	●	●	●	○
Glossary	●	●	●	○

Acknowledgments

Edgeware was truly a collective effort. As authors, we worked as a team to create the concept, content and style of the book. But the book also relied upon our network of complexity scientists, organization theorists, journalists, business executives and, of course, health care leaders. Some researchers and journalists contributed directly as authors or co-authors of sections of chapters. Others contributed indirectly as a source of ideas and inspiration, and their work is quoted extensively throughout this book. The health care leaders shared their stories, frustrations, passions and lessons. They were both our teachers and students of complexity.

We have listed below the direct contributors to this book. The list of indirect, but no less significant, contributors is far too lengthy to note here. We extend our thanks to all who helped shape our ideas for this book.

- Ken Baskin, Ph.D., *Baskin Consulting*

- Jeffrey Goldstein, Ph.D., *Adelphi University*

- David Hutchens, *iconoclast communications*

- Roger Lewin and Birute Regine, *Harvest Writers*

- Jeff Posey, *VHA Inc.*

- Susan Scott, *Scott Cartoons Ltd.*

- James B. Webber, *Sages in Bloom*

- Janet Biedron, R.N., *director of admissions, Muhlenberg Regional Medical Center*

- James Dwyer, D.O., *vice president, Medical Affairs, Memorial Hospital of Burlington County*

- Tom Irons, M.D., *president, HealthEast*

- Mary Anne Keyes, R.N., *vice president, Patient Care, Muhlenberg Regional Medical Center*

- John R. Kopicki, *president and chief executive officer, Muhlenberg Regional Medical Center*

- James Roberts, M.D., *senior vice president, VHA Inc.*

- Linda Rusch, R.N., *vice president, Patient Care, Hunterdon Medical Center*

- James Taylor, *president and chief executive officer, University of Louisville Hospital.*

- Deborah Zastocki, R.N., *senior vice president, Chilton Memorial Hospital*

**primer**

edgeware

A Complexity Science Primer
What is complexity science and
why should I learn about it?

This chapter is called a "primer" because it is intended to be a first step in understanding complexity science. In house painting, the primer or prime coat is not the finished surface. A room with a primer on the walls often looks worse than before the painting began. The patchy surface allows us to see some of the old paint, but the new paint is not yet obvious. It is not the completed image we want. But it creates the conditions for a smoother application of the other coats of paint, for a deeper or richer color, and a more coherent and consistent finish. As you read this primer, keep this image in mind. This paper is not the finished product. Ideas and concepts are mentioned, but only given a quick brush stroke in this primer. You will need to look to the other parts of this book to get a richer color of complexity.

Complexity science reframes our view of many systems that are only partially understood by traditional scientific methods. Systems as apparently diverse as stock markets, human bodies, forest ecosystems, manufacturing businesses, immune systems, termite colonies and hospitals seem to share some patterns of behavior. These patterns provide insights into sustainability, viability, health and innovation. Leaders and managers in health care organizations are using complexity science to discover new ways of working.

Why would health care leaders be interested in complexity science? In a recent research project with VHA members, we uncovered two inter-related reasons for the interest: frustration and resonance.

There is a frustration with some of the traditional clinical and organizational interventions in health care. Health care leaders in the study said they no longer trusted many of the methods of management they had been taught and practiced. They didn't believe in the strategic plans they wrote because the future was not as predictable as it was depicted in the plans. They saw intensive processes of information-

> "At first, learning about complexity science and what it suggested about leadership was confusing, even stressful. Once I began to learn it, to understand it, and to discuss it with other professionals, it began to make sense. ... I really believe in it. ... In complexity science, I'm learning that leaders of modern organizations have got to take on a different role – especially in this health care revolution."
>
> John Kopicki, CEO,
> Muhlenberg Regional Medical Center,
> Plainfield, N.J.

gathering and consensus-building in their organizations in which nothing of substance changed. They were working harder and feeling as though much of their hard work had little or no effect. Complexity science offered an opportunity to explore an alternative world view. Complexity science held a promise of relief from stress, but also suggested options for new interventions or ways of interacting in a leadership role.

The second hook for health care leaders was resonance. Complexity science resonated with or articulated what they were already doing. It provided the language and models to explain their intuitive actions. By having a theory to explain what they already knew, they felt they could leverage their intuitive knowledge and use it more confidently.

Although we are in the early days of deliberately applying complexity science to health care, we are gathering evidence of leaders using the ideas in general management and leadership, planning, building health care systems, clinical quality improvement, community health improvement and new service development. Some of the application projects have generated positive results, while others are still works in progress. Complexity science promises to become an important influence on health care.

Comparing complexity science with traditional science

Complexity science addresses aspects of living systems that are neglected or understated in traditional approaches. Existing models in economics, management and physics were built on the foundation of Newtonian scientific principles. The dominant metaphor in Newtonian

Aides
• *Metaphor*

science is the machine. The universe and all its subsystems were seen as giant clocks or inanimate machines. The clocks or machines can be explained using reductionism – by understanding each part separately. The whole of the machine is the sum of the parts. This clockware perspective has led to great discoveries by focusing on the attributes and functioning of the parts – whether of a human body or a human organization. The parts are controlled by a few immutable external forces or laws. The parts are not seen to have choice or self determination. The machines are simple and predictable – you need only understand the few guiding external rules that determine how the parts will behave. There are limits to this perspective when understanding living systems, and in particular human organizations. Clearly, humans are not machine parts

Principles
• *Clockware/ swarmware*

without individual choice, and so clockware is a necessary but not sufficient way of understanding complex systems.

The Newtonian perspective assumes that all can be explained by the careful examination of the parts. Yet that does not work for many aspects of human behavior. We have all experienced situations in which the whole

MECHANICAL UNIVERSE

is not the sum of the parts – occasions in which we cannot explain the outcomes of a situation by studying the individual elements. For example, when a natural disaster strikes a community, we have seen spontaneous organization for which there is no obvious leader, controller or designer. In these contexts, we find that groups of people create outcomes and effects that are far greater than would have been predicted by summing up the resources and skills available within the group. In these cases, there is self-organization in which outcomes emerge that are highly dependent on the relationships and context rather than merely on the parts. Stuart Kauffman calls this "order for free" and Kevin Kelly refers to it as "creating something out of nothing."

Complexity science is not a single theory. It is the study of complex adaptive systems – the patterns of relationships within them, how they are sustained, how they self-organize and how outcomes emerge. Within this science there are many theories and concepts. The science encompasses more than one theoretical framework. Complexity science is highly interdisciplinary, including biologists, anthropologists, economists, sociologists, management theorists and many others in a quest to answer some fundamental questions about living, adaptable, changeable systems.

Tales
- *Learn as you go*
- *Emerges from the fabric*
- *Wizards and CEOs*
- *Make it or let it*

Bibliography
- Kauffman: *At Home*
- Kelly: *Out of Control*

From physics envy to biology envy

There has been an implicit hierarchy of sciences, with physics as the most respectable and biology as the conceptually poor cousin. Physics is enviable because of its rigor and immutable laws. Biology, on the other hand, is rooted in the messiness of real life and therefore did not create as many elegantly simple equations, models or predictable solutions to problems. Even within biology there was a hierarchy of studies. Mapping the genome was more elegant, precise and physics-like, hence respectable, whereas evolutionary biology was softer, dealing with interactions, context and other dimensions that made prediction less precise. Physics envy was not only evident in the physical and natural sciences, but also in the social sciences. Economics and management theory borrowed concepts from physics and created

COMPLEXITY UNIVERSE

THE PATTERNS OF RELATIONSHIPS BETWEEN THE PARTS

organizational structures and forms that tried (at some level at least) to follow the laws of physics. These were clearly limited in their application and exceptions to the rules had to be made constantly. In spite of the limitations, an implicit physics envy permeated management and organization theories.

Recently, we have seen physics envy replaced with biology envy. Physicists are looking to biological models for insight and explanation. Biological metaphors are being used to understand everything from urban planning, organization design and technologically advanced computer systems. Technology is now mimicking life – or biology – in its design. The poor cousin in science has now become highly respectable and central to many disciplines. Complexity science is a key area in which we witness this bridging of the disciplines with the study of life (or biology) as the connecting glue or thread of common interest.

For health care leaders, the shift from physics envy to biology envy provides an opportunity to build systems that are sustainable because of their capacity to live. Living organizations, living computer systems, living communities and living health care systems are important because of our interest in sustainability and adaptability. Where better to learn lessons about sustainability and adaptability than from life itself.

> "Some people really want to stop controlling, but are afraid. Everywhere things are changing, creating high degrees of uncertainty and anxiety. And the more anxious you are, the more in control you need to be. Making all this even worse, we've bought into the myth that leaders have all the answers. Managers who accept this myth have their levels of anxiety ratcheted up again. ... If complexity theory can begin freeing managers from this myth of control, I think you'll see people a whole lot more comfortable."
>
> Linda Rusch
> vice president of Patient Care
> Hunterdon Medical Center
> Flemington, N.J.

Complexity questions

The questions asked by complexity scientists in the physical, natural and social sciences are not little questions. They are deep questions about how life happens and how it evolves. These questions are not new. Indeed, some of the answers proposed by complexity science are not new. But in many contexts, these answers were not explainable by any theory. They were the intuitive responses that were known by many but appeared

"I used to have physics envy, then I embraced unpredictability and developed complexity cravings and a lust for living systems."

illogical or at least idiosyncratic when viewed through traditional scientific theories. Complexity science provides the language, the metaphors, the conceptual frameworks, the models and the theories that help make the idiosyncrasies nonidiosyncratic and the illogical logical. For some health care leaders who are studying complexity, the science is counterintuitive because of the stark contrast with what they had been taught about how organizations should operate. Complexity science describes how systems actually behave rather than how they should behave.

Complexity science provides more than just explanations for some of our intuitive understandings. It also provides a rigorous approach to study some of the key dimensions of organizational life. How does change happen? What are the conditions for innovation? What allows some things to be sustained even when they are no longer viable? What creates adaptability? What is leadership in systems where there is no direct authority or control? What does strategic planning mean in highly turbulent times? How do creativity and potential get released? How do they get trapped? Traditional management theories have focused on the predictable and controllable dimensions of management. Although these dimensions are critical in organizations, they provide only a partial explanation of the reality of organizations. Complexity science invites us to examine the unpredictable, disorderly and unstable aspects of organizations. Complexity complements our traditional understanding of organizations to provide us with a more complete picture.

That is the good news about complexity science. There is also some bad news. Complexity science is in its infancy. It is an emerging field of study. There are few proven theories in the field. It has not yet stood the test of time. But it has become a movement. Unlike some other movements in the management arena, the complexity science movement spans almost every discipline in the physical, natural and social sciences. There is often a huge schism between those who study the world using quantitative approaches and those who use qualitative methods. Complexity has created a bridge or a merger of quantitative and qualitative explanations of life. It has attracted some of the world's greatest thinkers, including some of the most respected organizational theorists and Nobel and MacArthur prize winners in many fields. It has also attracted poets, artists and theologians who see the optimism implicit in the science. By examining how life happens from a complexity perspective, we seem to have increased our reverence for life

Bibliography
• Waldrop:
  Complexity
• Lewin:
  Complexity

> "Out of nothing, nature makes something. How do you make something from nothing? Although nature knows this trick, we haven't learned much just by watching. ... [Life's] reign of constant evolution, perpetual novelty and an agenda out of our control ... is far more rewarding than a world of clocks, gears, and predictable simplicity."
>
> Kevin Kelly,
> "Out of Control," pages 468-472

– the more we understand, the more we are amazed.

The next two sections of this chapter almost need a warning label. They are filled with the new jargon of complexity science. Each term is given a quick brush stroke here, but is explained in greater detail in other parts of this book. For the reader new to the field of complexity, read the next two sections to get an overall sense of complexity science. You do not need to understand every term at the outset to start the journey into understanding complexity.

Definition of complex adaptive system

Glossary

Complex adaptive systems are ubiquitous. Stock markets, human bodies, forest ecosystems, manufacturing businesses, immune systems and hospitals are all examples of CASs. What is a complex adaptive system? Each word is significant. "Complex" implies diversity – a great number of connections between a wide variety of elements. "Adaptive" suggests the capacity to alter or change – the ability to learn from experience. A "system" is a set of connected or interdependent things. The "things" in a CAS are independent agents. An agent may be a person, a molecule, a species or an organization, among many others. These agents act based on local knowledge and conditions. Their individual moves are not controlled by a central body, master neuron or CEO. A CAS has a densely connected web of interacting agents, each operating from their own schema or local knowledge. In human systems, schemata are the mental models an individual uses to make sense of their world.

Description of complex adaptive systems

CASs have a number of linked attributes or properties. Because all the attributes are linked, it is impossible to identify the starting point for the list of attributes. Each one can be seen to be both a cause and effect of the other attributes. The attributes listed are all in stark contrast to the implicit assumptions underlying traditional management and Newtonian science.

Tales
• *What we could be doing*
• *Worldwide complexity*
• *Make it or let it*
• *Wizards and CEOs*

CASs are embedded or nested in other CASs. Each individual agent in a CAS is itself a CAS. In an ecosystem, a tree in a forest is a CAS and is also an agent in the CAS of the forest, which is an agent in the larger ecosystem of the island, and so forth. In health care, a

> "The tendency of people in positions of power is to believe that they can control, and they believe in the power of 'Let us figure it out. Let's hire the experts, let us sit in a room, figure it out and then it'll happen.' That is a common theme, and it's one that I just don't believe in."
> James Taylor
> president and CEO
> University of Louisville Hospital
> Louisville, Ky

"As a physician, I learned to think from a biological perspective. When I went into management, traditional organizational theory seemed artificial, foreign to my experience. So when I started studying complexity through the VHA project, I was stunned. Here was a way of thinking about organizations that compared them to living things. That makes sense to me, intuitively."

Richard Weinberg, M.D.
vice president of Network Development
Atlantic Health System
Passaic, N.J.

physician is a CAS and also an agent in the department, which is a CAS and an agent in the hospital, which is a CAS and an agent in health care, which is a CAS and an agent in society. The agents coevolve with the CAS of which they are a part. The cause-and-effect is mutual rather than one-way. In health care, we see how the system is coevolving with the health care organizations and practitioners, which make up the whole. The entire system is emerging from a dense pattern of interactions.

For a CAS to be sustainable, there must be diversity, which is a source of information or novelty. As John Holland argues, the diversity of a CAS is the result of progressive adaptations. Diversity that is the result of adaptation also becomes the source of future adaptations. A decrease in diversity reduces the potential for future adaptations. This is why biologist Edward O. Wilson argues that the rain forest is so critical to our planet. It has significantly more diversity – more potential for adaptation – than any other part of the planet. The planet needs this source of information and potential for long-term survival. In organizations, diversity is becoming seen as a key source of sustainability. Psychological profiles, which identify individuals' dominant thinking styles have become popular management tools to ensure a sufficient level of diversity, at least in terms of thinking approaches, within teams in organizations. Diversity is seen as a key to innovation and long-term viability.

Bibliography
- Holland: *Hidden Order*
- Wilson: *Diversity*

Many of us were taught that biological innovation was due in large part to random genetic mutations. When these random mutations created individuals that fit the environment better than their predecessor, their attributes had a higher chance of being retained in the gene pool. Adaptation or innovation by random mutation of genes explains only a small fraction of the biological diversity we experience today. Crossover of genetic material is a million times more common than mutation in nature, according to John Holland. In essence, crossover suggests a mixing together of the same building blocks or genetic material into different combinations. Understanding this can lead to profound insights about CASs. The concept of genetic algorithms is paradoxical in that building blocks, genes or other raw elements that are recombined in a wide variety of ways are the key to sustainability. Yet the process of manipulating these blocks occurs only when they are in relationship to each other. In genetic

Principles
• *Chunking*

terms, this means the whole string on a chromosome. Holland argues that "evolution remembers combinations of building blocks that increase fitness." It is the relationship between the building blocks that is significant, rather than the building blocks themselves. The focus is on the interrelationships.

In organizational terms, this suggests it is not the individual that is most critical, but the relationships between individuals. We see this frequently in team sports. The team with the best individual players can lose to a team of poorer players. The second team cannot rely on one or two stars, but instead must focus on creating outcomes that are beyond the talents of any one individual. They create outcomes based on the interrelationships between the players. This is not to dismiss individual excellence. It does suggest that individual abilities is not a complete explanation of success or failure. In management terms, it shifts the attention to focus on the patterns of interrelationships and on the context of the issue, individual or group.

CASs have distributed control rather than centralized control. Instead of a command center that directs all agents, control is distributed throughout the system. In a school of fish, there is no boss that directs the other fishes' behavior. The independent agents (or fish) have the capacity to learn new strategies and adaptive techniques. The coherence of a CAS's behavior relates to the interrelationships between the agents. You cannot explain the outcomes or behavior of a CAS from a thorough understanding of all of the individual parts or agents. The school of fish reacts to a stimulus, for example the threat of a predator, faster than any individual fish can react. The school has capacities and attributes that are not explainable by the capacities and attributes of the individual agents. There is not one fish smarter than the others that is directing the school. If there were a smart "boss" fish, this form of centralized control would result in a school of fish reacting at least as slow as the fastest fish could respond. Centralized control would slow the school's capacity to react and adapt.

Distributed control means that the outcomes of a complex adaptive system emerge from a process of self-organization rather than being designed and controlled externally or by a centralized body. The emergence is a result of the patterns of interrelationships between the agents. Emergence suggests unpredictability – an inability to state precisely how a system will evolve.

Bibliography
• *Kauffman:*
    At Home

Rather than trying to predict the specific outcome of emergence, Stuart Kauffman suggests we think about fitness landscapes for CASs. A CAS, or population of CASs, is seen as higher on the fitness landscape when they have learned better strategies to adapt and coevolve with their environment. Being on a peak in a fitness landscape indicates greater

> "In the past, when managers have tried to implement change, they'd find themselves wasting energy fighting off resistors who felt threatened. Complexity science suggests that we can create small, nonthreatening changes that attract people, instead of implementing large-scale change that excites resistance. We work with the attractors."
>
> Mary Anne Keyes, R.N.
> vice president of Patient Care
> Muhlenberg Regional Medical Center
> Plainfield, N.J.

success. However, the fitness landscape itself is not fixed – it is shifting and evolving. Hence a CAS needs to be continuously learning new strategies. The pattern one is trying to master is the adaptive walk or capacity of a CAS to move on fitness landscapes toward higher, more secure positions.

The coevolution of a CAS and its environment is difficult to map because it is nonlinear. Linearity implies that the size of the change is correlated with the magnitude of the input to the system. A small input will have a small effect and a large input will have a large effect in a linear system. A CAS is a nonlinear system. The size of the outcome may not be correlated to the size of the input. A large push to the system may not move it at all. In many nonlinear systems, you cannot accurately predict the effect of the change by the size of the input to the system.

Weather systems are often cited as examples of this phenomenon of nonlinearity. The butterfly effect, a term coined by meteorologist Edward Lorenz, is created, in part, by the huge number of nonlinear interactions in weather. The butterfly effect suggests that sometimes a seemingly insignificant difference can have a huge influence. Lorenz found that in simulated weather forecasting, two almost identical simulations could result in radically different weather patterns. A very tiny change to the initial variables, metaphorically something as small as a butterfly flapping its wings, can radically alter the outcome. The weather system is very sensitive to the initial conditions or to its history.

An example in an organizational setting of nonlinearity is the immense effort put into a staff retreat or strategic planning exercise in which everything stays the same after the big push. In contrast, there are many examples of one small whisper of gossip – one small push – that creates a radical and rapid change in organizations.

Nonlinearity, distributed control and independent agents create conditions for perpetual novelty and innovation. CASs learn new strategies from experience. Their history helps shape the path they take. Newtonian science is ahistorical – the resting point or attractor of the system is independent of its history. This is the basis of neo-classical economics and is the antithesis of complexity.

Complex adaptive systems are history-dependent. They are shaped and influenced by where they have been. This may seem obvious and

Bibliography
• Lorenz: *Chaos*

trivial. But much of our traditional science and management theory ignore this point. What is good in one context is assumed to make sense in all contexts. Marketers talk about rolling out programs that were effective in one place and hence should be effective in all. In traditional neoclassical economics, there is an assumption of equifinality – it does not matter where the system has come from, it will head toward the equilibrium point. Outliers or minor differences in the starting point or history of the system are ignored. The outlier or difference from the normal pattern is assumed to be dampened and hence a blip is not important. Brian Arthur's work in economics has radically altered this viewpoint. For example, he cites evidence of small differences fundamentally altering the shape of an industry. The differences are not always dampened but may indeed grow to reshape the whole. Lorenz referred to this in meteorology as sensitive dependence to initial conditions, which was discussed earlier as the butterfly effect. In economics, in nature, in weather and in human organizations, we see many examples for which understanding history is key to understanding the current position and potential movement of a CAS.

Bibliography
• Arthur:
Increasing Returns
• Lorenz: *Chaos*
• Waldrop: *Complexity*

CASs are naturally drawn to attractors. In Newtonian science, an attractor can be the resting point for a pendulum. Unlike traditional attractors in Newtonian science, which are a fixed point or repeated rhythm, the attractors for a CAS may be strange because, while they may have an overall shape and boundaries, one cannot predict exactly how or where the shape will form. They are formed in part by nonlinear interactions. The attractor is a pattern or area that draws the energy of the system to it. It is a boundary of behavior for the system. The system will operate within this boundary, but at a local level – we cannot predict where the system will be within this overall attractor.

A dominant theme in change management literature is how to overcome resistance to change. Using the concept of attractors, the idea of change is flipped to look at sources of attraction. In other words, to use the natural energy of the system rather than to fight against it. The nonlinearity property of a CAS means that attractors may not be the biggest, most obvious issues. Looking for the subtle attractors becomes a new challenge for managers.

"Well clearly I'm experiencing emergence – this outcome is far greater than the sum of my parts."

Tales
• *Emerges from the fabric*

Principles
• *Tune to the edge*

CASs thrive in areas of bounded instability on the border or edge of chaos. In this region, there is not enough stability to have repetition or prediction, but not enough instability to create anarchy or to disperse the system. Life for a CAS is a dance on the border between death by equilibrium or death by dissipation. In organizational settings, this is a region of highly creative energy.

Why is complexity science relevant now?

The seeds for complexity science have been around for a long time. The founding parents of complexity science were often far ahead of their time. Why is now the right time for complexity science? More specifically, why is this the time for complexity science studies of human organizations? Turbulence, change, adaptability and connectedness are not new to the late 20th century. There are at least four reasons why now is the time for complexity science:

1. the limit of the machine metaphor
2. the coming together of biology and technology
3. the connections between studies of micro and macro phenomena
4. the apparent compressions of space and time

The first three reasons are outlined briefly in this section. The last reason, the compression of space and time, is described in the next section.

Complexity science is a direct challenge to the dominance of the machine metaphor. Since Newton, the machine metaphor has been used as the lens to make sense of our physical and social worlds, including human organizations. The machine metaphor has been a powerful force in creating manufacturing, medical and organizational advances. However, its limits are now becoming more obvious. It is as if we have collectively learned all we can from the machine metaphor and will continue to use that knowledge where appropriate. But we have more and more instances for which the machine metaphor is simply not helpful. For example, it does not explain the emergent aspects of an organization's strategy or the evolution of an industry. Complexity science, with its focus on emergence, self-organization, interdependencies, unpredictability and nonlinearity provides a useful alternative to the machine metaphor.

In addition to changing the metaphor for interpreting events, complexity science is gaining momentum because of the coming together of biology and technology. Biologists are using technology to understand biology, for example, in biotechnology. Computer technologists are using biology to create computer software that has some lifelike characteristics. Without the technological advancements, due in part to the machine metaphor, we would not be able to replicate nature's fractal forms, or understand the implicit process rules that allow flocks of birds to move as one, or explain the chaotic heart rates of healthy humans. Complexity science is understandable to us now because of both the advances in technology and the increased respect for biological lessons.

> "It is a curious thing … at least for me it has been. It is both mind-expanding because of new notions, but it also seems like it is affirming of stuff you already know. It is quite paradoxical."
> James Roberts, M.D., senior vice president VHA Inc., Irving, Texas

Complexity science brings together the two solitudes of microstudies and macroanalysis. For example, the micro studies of the human genome and the macro studies of evolutionary biology are coming together with complexity science. The lessons from the micro studies are informing the macro analysis and the lessons from the macro studies are informing the micro. This second learning – the macro informing the micro – has been underplayed in our search for applying Newtonian scientific thinking to life. A Newtonian perspective suggests that the parts can explain the whole. Therefore, the quest is to study the parts in greater and greater detail. Complexity science suggests that the whole is not the sum of the parts. Emergent properties of the whole are inexplicable by the parts. In complexity, studies of natural and human systems are explained by both kinds of analysis – micro (or analysis of the parts) and macro (or holistic analysis).

Bibliography
• Gell-Mann: *Quark*
• Wilson: *Consilience*

Murray Gell-Mann, a Nobel Prize winner, discovered and named the quark – clearly a study of micro parts. But his journey of discovery into the tiniest parts led him to a path of holistic understanding and an appreciation for ecology. His book, *The Quark and the Jaguar,* exemplifies this coming together of the appreciation of the micro and macro analysis. Edward O. Wilson, a renowned biologist, argued that we are seeing the confluence of the two major foundations of biology: (1) the molecular basis of life, and (2) the evolutionary basis for human (and ecosystem) behavior. This profoundly influences both clinical and organizational aspects of health care. Some health care interventions are seen to be context dependent – we cannot explain the micro functioning without understanding the macro context. Community health affects the well-being of the individuals within the community. Complexity provides us with the opportunity to look at problems with multiple perspectives, studying the micro and macro issues and understanding how they are interdependent.

This section provided some explanations for the complexity science movement in the physical and natural sciences. But there is an additional explanation for its power in social systems – the compression of time and space. The next section describes this seemingly esoteric issue. Some readers may not feel the need to understand the roots of complexity from this perspective and may skip ahead to the section that addresses the paradoxes of complexity.

The compression of time and space

One of the signature qualities of the late 20th century is the apparent compression of space and time. Why should health care leaders care about something as seemingly esoteric as the compression of space and time? Most of the models of organization, methods to improve performance and measurement concepts that dominate the management field today were created with the implicit assumption of space and time lags. In other words, they were designed for a world that in many ways no longer exists. When these approaches are tried in contexts in which there is this space-time compression, the results are often frustration, stress and lack of improvement. This section demonstrates the compression of space and time using examples from manufacturing, banking and health care.

Dee Hock, the founding chief executive officer of Visa International, refers to the major effect the compression of time has had in financial markets. In the past, there was an expectation of a time lag (or float) between the initiation and completion of most financial transactions. For example, if you purchase an item on credit there is a time lag between when you make the transaction and when the cash is paid to the supplier. We have elaborate systems designed to take advantage of this float. This luxury of float disappears with the use of debit cards or equivalent systems of real-time transfer of funds.

Hock argues this same reduction of time lags happens today with information. We used to have the luxury of a time lag between the discovery of an idea and the application into practice. This time lag is now almost nonexistent in many aspects of society. In health care, medical research is reported on (often in sound bites on the news). The public access to medical research has often created a push to put the ideas into application immediately.

An example of a time lag reduction that has had a remarkable influence on manufacturing around the world is the idea of just-in-time inventory systems. The idea was a simple one, eliminate the need for storing, financing and managing inventories by creating real-time order and delivery systems between suppliers and producers. When the concept was first introduced there were many skeptics. Yet in a very short period of time, this was standard practice in many (perhaps most) manufacturing industries. Just-in-time inventory changed the relationship between suppliers and producers. It was both facilitated by the improvement in technology and shaped new improvements in

Bibliography
• Waldrop:
  Trillion

> "I found a lot of what we did [in management] was really dumb. It was very impersonal. We treated people as if they were one-dimensional. If you figure them out, give them strict rules, put money in front of them, they will perform better ... it was very linear."
>
> James Taylor
> **President and CEO**
> **University of Louisville Hospital**
> **Louisville, Ky**

I. Primer

technology to get the most benefit from the concept. Boundaries became blurry between what was in the organization and what was outside of it. Networks were created to minimize the potential problems if a supplier could not provide the needed goods on time. The definition of success for a supplier was altered, and new skills and flexibility were needed in the employees and the physical production systems.

In terms of compression of space, we can now bypass many of the intermediaries in our society. Intermediaries play the role of a bridge between organizations or individuals. When we can access the organization or individual directly rather than through an intermediary, we are again witnessing a compression of space.

The financial service industry is another for which this compression of time and space can be demonstrated. Technology has allowed us to bridge huge distances and create connections that permit simultaneous creation and dissemination of information. We see this reduction of time lags for banking in that the currency float of a few years ago has become virtually nonexistent. Money can be transferred instantly between individuals, organizations and countries. The increased degree of connectedness aided by technology has eliminated some of the intermediaries in our society. One of the banks' prime roles was to be the intermediary between those who had money to loan and those who had need to borrow money. For a price, the banks would match the players. Today, this is becoming less significant. When the information of who has money and who needs money is more widely available, many corporations are bypassing the intermediary role of the bank. This is not happening only in financial services. Because of technology that allows increased connectedness, in many industries one can go directly to the source of the information, product or service.

In our organizations, intermediaries are often layers of management or supervision. Part of their jobs is to bridge the gap between the providers of service, or front-line workers, and upper management. Bridging the gap creates time lags in our organizations. These lags provide the information float and hence the luxury (and sometimes the frustration) of time delays. But these intermediary positions are being eliminated in many industries, including health care, through downsizing. If the positions are eliminated but the role of intermediation and the expectation of float still exist as old mental models, we will simply see overworked employees trying to fulfill the same roles but with fewer resources and less success.

Intermediaries also imply external designers of a system. The designers are at a distance from the deliverers of the service. This is a separation of thought and action in both space and time. The planners plan, and others implement – a separation in space. The plans are created first and predetermine the action steps to take – a separation in time.

Complex adaptive systems have the capacity to adapt and evolve without an external designer. They self-organize without either external or centralized control.

In highly interconnected contexts, in which there is a compression of time and space, the assumptions of float, intermediaries and external designers are problematic. Many management models, such as traditional strategic planning processes, are built on these assumptions. When they hold, the models are relevant and useful, and can improve the effectiveness and efficiency of organizations. When the assumptions are invalid, these models can lead to an illusion of control, but an actual loss of effectiveness and adaptability.

Tales
• *Learn as you go*

Some of the paradoxes of complexity

Complexity science is highly paradoxical. As you study the world through a complexity lens you will be continually confronted with "both-and" rather than "either-or" thinking. The paradoxes of complexity are that both sides of many apparent contradictions are true.

The first of these paradoxes is that the systemic nature of a CAS implies interdependence, yet each interdependent element is able to act independently. Interdependence and independence coexist.

Another paradox in complexity is that simple patterns of interaction can create huge numbers of potential outcomes. Simplicity leads to complexity.

CASs operate in a context that is frequently unpredictable; not merely unknown but unknowable. Yet it is the agents' propensity to predict, based on schema of local conditions, that allow them to act in an apparently coherent manner.

Complexity science is the study of living systems but living systems die. As a metaphor associated with life, it needs to encompass all aspects of the life cycle. Death is part of this cycle. The traditional management literature's depiction of the life cycle begins at birth and ends at decline. Complexity also includes the study of death and renewal.

Tales
• *Another way to think*

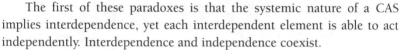

Aides
• *Stacey matrix*
• *Wicked questions*
• *Min specs*
• *Ecocycle*

Principles
• *Paradox*

Bibliography
• Hurst/ Zimmerman: *Ecocycle*

Complexity is a metaphor

A recent article in a popular magazine argued that we need to distinguish between complexity researchers who use the theory from those who use the metaphor. What that statement missed is that all science is metaphor, as Gareth Morgan argues. It is metaphor that shapes our logic and perspective. Metaphor influences the questions we ask and hence the answers we find. A powerful metaphor becomes deeply rooted

Bibliography
• Morgan: *Images*

in our ways of understanding, and is often implicit rather than explicit. In biological terms, a metaphor is the schema by which we make sense of our situation.

Complexity science presents a contrast to the dominant scientific and organizational metaphor and thereby challenges us to see what other questions we can ask about the systems we are studying or living within. The metaphor of systems as mechanical or machine has shaped our studies in physics, biology, economics, medicine and organizations. Complexity is about reframing our understanding of many systems by using a metaphor associated with life and living systems rather than machines or mechanical systems. Viewing the world through a complexity lens means understanding the world from biological concepts.

Aides
• *Metaphor*
• *Reflection*

Principles
• *Complexity lens*

SAT NITE AT CLUB CHAOS

The inquiry continues

It is normal to finish a chapter like this with a conclusion – to end with a summary of the key points and implications. Yet consistent with both the science of complexity and the state of its development, it seems more appropriate to end with questions. The questions can be viewed from five levels of analysis:

1.   health care sector
2.   regional health care system

3. institution or organization
4. division, department or work group
5. individual person

Some of the questions listed here are aimed at one of these levels, but most can be used for any level. We invite you to participate with us in this inquiry as it applies to health care.

- **The overall question is, how can complexity science improve health and health care?**

Some other questions to ponder as you read through this book are:

- *How does coevolution affect the role of a health care leader? If everything is changing and I am part of that change, how do I plan?*

- *How can complexity science help us form regional health care systems that are more likely to make a difference?*

- *If a CAS self-organizes, what is the job of manager or leader of a CAS?*

- *Can we use ideas of self-organization to unleash the full potential of our staff?*

- *What is the role of a hospital in the emergent health care system? Can we create the conditions for emergence?*

- *What do we have to change to improve the quality of our health care system and reduce costs? Can complexity science provide us with any insights to this question?*

- *How can complexity science improve clinical interventions? For example, how can understanding genetic algorithms improve clinical decision-making?*

- *If a hospital is a CAS, what does this imply about strategic planning?*

- *Can we use insights from CASs to improve community health and well-being?*

- *If the edge of chaos is the area of greatest innovation, how do we stay on the edge of chaos? What are the risks of staying on the edge?*

- *What organizational structures, designs and processes are consistent with a complexity science perspective? How would implementing these complex ideas improve health care?*

- *How can we ensure complexity science enhances and complements proven clinical and management approaches? Where and when does complexity science add most value? Where are traditional approaches more appropriate?*

principles

Nine emerging and connected organizational and leadership principles
Some introductory thoughts

Our study of the science of complex adaptive systems and our work with health care organizations in VHA has led us to propose some principles of management that are consistent with an understanding of organizations as complex adaptive systems. In the spirit of the subject matter, there is nothing sacred or permanent about this list. However, these principles do begin to give us a new way of thinking about and approaching our roles as leaders in organizations.

We are not the first to propose such a list. Our intent here is to capture practical principles that emerge from the science of complexity in language that resonates with management issues. Furthermore, astute readers will also observe that our list of principles, and CAS theory itself, has much in common with general systems thinking, the learning organization, total quality, empowerment, gestalt theory, organizational development and other approaches. It has much in common with these, but it is not any of these. CAS theory clarifies and pulls together many aspects of good thinking from the past. An understanding of CAS is an understanding of how things work in the real world. That others in the past have also understood these things and put them into various contextual frames should not be surprising. An understanding of CAS simply provides a broader, more fundamental, potentially unifying framework for these ideas.

II. Principles

The Nine Principles:

1. View your system through the lens of complexity.

2. Build a good-enough vision

3. When life is far from certain, lead with clockware and swarmware in tandem

4. Tune your place to the edge

5. Uncover and work with paradox and tension

6. Go for multiple actions at the fringes, let direction arise

7. Listen to the shadow system

8. Grow complex systems by chunking

9. Mix cooperation with competition

View your system through the lens of complexity

In addition to the metaphor of a machine or a military organization

Bibliography
- Morgan: *Images*
- Hoagland: *Life*

Aides
- *Metaphor*
- *Reflection*

The predominant metaphor used in organizations today is that of a machine. Almost equally popular is the metaphor of a military operation. If an organization is a machine, then we simply must specify the parts well and make sure that each part does its part. If an organization is a military operation, then command, control and communication needs to be hierarchical; survival is key; and sacrificial heroes are desired (although no one really wants to be one themselves). Most of today's organizational artifacts – job descriptions, rank-and-file employees, turf battles, strategic plans and so on – emerge from these largely unexpressed and undiscussed metaphors. If you buy into these metaphors, then the traditional actions of management make sense and should work.

The basic problem with these metaphors when applied to a complex adaptive system is that they ignore the individuality of agents and the effects of interaction among agents. Or worse, they simply assume that all this can be tightly controlled through better (read: more) specification. While there are many situations for which the machine and military metaphors might be useful – for example, routine surgical processes – there are also many situations for which these metaphors are grossly inadequate. When we view our system through the lens of complexity, we take on a new metaphor – that of a CAS – and, therefore, are using a different model to determine what makes sense for leaders to do.

Viewing the world through the complexity lens has been a marvelously stress-reducing experience for the health care leaders in VHA. Many have come to see that the massive sea changes they have experienced and agonized over recently – the failed Clinton health care reform plan, the rise of managed care,

> "All theories of organization and management are based on implicit images or metaphors that lead us to see, understand and manage organizations in distinctive yet partial ways ... the use of metaphor implies a way of thinking and a way of seeing that pervade how we understand our world. ... One of the most basic problems of modern management is that the mechanical way of thinking is so ingrained in our everyday conceptions of organization, that it is often very difficult to organize in any other way."
>
> —Morgan

the AIDS epidemic – are natural phenomena in a complex adaptive system. Such things will happen again, each will leave its mark on the health care system. Predicting when and where the next one will come is futile. Learning to be flexible and adaptable is the only sustainable leadership strategy.

"To see life as a whole – to observe what all life has in common – requires a shift in the way we normally look at things. We must look beyond the individual insect or tree or flower and seek a more panoramic perspective. We need to think as much about process as we do about structure. From this expanded viewpoint, we can see life in terms of patterns and rules. Using these rules, life builds, organizes, recycles and recreates itself."

–Hoagland

II. Principles

edgeware

Build a good-enough vision
Provide minimum specifications, rather than trying to plan every little detail

Tales
• *Emerges from fabric*
• *Worldwide complexity*
• *Make it or let it*
• *A leap into uncertainty*
• *What we could be doing*
• *A complexity tool box*

Bibliography
• Morgan: *Images*
• Stacey: *Unknowable*
• Waldrop: *Trillion*

Aides
• *Min specs*
• *Generative relationships*

Since the behavior of a CAS emerges from the interaction among the agents, and since the detailed behavior of the system is fundamentally unpredictable, it does little good to spend all the time that most organizations spend in detailed planning. Most organizational leaders have participated in very detailed planning, only to find that assumptions and inputs must be changed almost immediately after the plan is final. Complexity science suggests that we would be better off with minimum specifications and general senses of direction, and then allow appropriate autonomy for individuals to self-organize and adapt as time goes by.

The science behind this principle traces it roots back to a computer simulation called "Boids," developed in 1987 by Craig Reynolds (and available on many Internet software bulletin boards). The simulation consists of a collection of autonomous agents – the boids – in an environment with obstacles. In addition to the basic laws of physics, each agent follows three simple rules: (1) try to maintain a minimum distance from all other boids and objects; (2) try to match speed with neighboring boids; and, (3) try to move toward the center of mass of the boids in your neighborhood. Remarkably, when the simulation is run, the boids exhibit the very lifelike behavior of flying in flocks around the objects on the screen. They flock, a complex behavior pattern, even though there is no rule explicitly telling them to do so. While this does not prove that birds actually use these simple rules, it does show that simple rules – minimum specifications – can lead to complex behaviors. These complex behaviors emerge from the interactions among agents, rather than being imposed upon the CAS by an outside agent or an explicit, detailed description.

"The principle of min specs [minimum specifications] suggests that managers should define no more than is absolutely necessary to launch a particular initiative or activity on its way. They have to avoid the role of 'grand designer' in favor of one that focuses on facilitation, orchestration and boundary management, creating 'enabling conditions' that allow a system to find its own form."

—Morgan

In contrast, we often over-specify things when designing or planning new activities in our organizations. This follows from the paradigm of "organization as a machine." If you are designing a machine, you had better think of everything, because the machine cannot think for itself. Of course, in some cases, organizations do act **MIN SPEC** enough like machines to justify selected use of this metaphor. For example, if you are having your gall bladder removed, you'd like the surgical team to operate as a precision machine; save that emerging, creative behavior for another time! Maximum specifications and the elimination of variation might be appropriate in such situations.

Most of the time, however, organizations are not machinelike; they are complex adaptive systems. The key learning from the simulations is that in the case of a CAS, minimum specifications and purposeful variation are the way to go.

This principle would suggest, for example, that intricate strategic plans be replaced by simple documents that describe the general direction the organization is pursuing, and a few basic principles for how the organization should get there. The rest is left to the flexibility, adaptability and creativity of the system as the context continually changes. This, of course, is a frightening thought for leaders classically trained in the machine and military metaphors. But the key questions are: Are these traditional metaphors working for us today? Are we able to lay out detailed plans and then just do it with a guaranteed outcome? If not, do we really think that planning harder will be any better?

The quintessential organizational example of this principle of good-enough vision and minimum specifications is the credit-card company, Visa International. Despite its $1 trillion annual sales volume and roughly half-billion clients, few people could tell you where its headquarters are or how it is governed. Its founding chief executive officer, Dee Hock describes it as a nonstock, for-profit membership corporation in which

MAX SPEC

members (typically, banks that issue the Visa cards) cooperate intensely "in a narrow band of activity essential to the success of the whole" (for example, the graphic layout of the card and common clearinghouse operations), while competing fiercely and innovatively in all else (including going after each other's customers!). This blend of minimum specifications in the essential areas of cooperation, and complete freedom for creative energy in all else, has allowed Visa to grow 10,000 percent since 1970, despite the incredibly complex worldwide system of different currencies, customs, legal systems and the like. "It was beyond the power of reason to design an organization to deal with such complexity," Hock explained. "The organization had to be based on biological concepts to evolve, in effect, to invent and organize itself."

> "Managers therefore cannot form a vision of some future state toward which the business can be moved; the futures open to the system are too many, and the links between a future and the actions leading to it are too obscure. Chaotic dynamics lead us to see strategy as a direction into the future that emerges from what managers do. In chaotic conditions, strategy cannot be driven by pure intentions. Instead, it represents the unintentional creation of order out of chaos."
>
> —Stacey

When life is far from certain, lead with clockware and swarmware in tandem

Balance data and intuition, planning and acting, safety and risk, giving due honor to each

Clockware

"Clockware" is a term, coined by Kevin Kelly, that describes the management processes we all know that involve operating the core production processes of the organization in a manner that is rational, planned, standardized, repeatable, controlled and measured. In contrast, Kelly's term "swarmware" refers to management processes that explore new possibilities through experimentation, trials, autonomy, freedom, intuition and working at the edge of knowledge and experience. Good-enough vision, minimum specifications and metaphor are examples of swarmware that we have already seen. The idea is to say just enough to paint a picture or describe the absolute boundaries, and then let the people in the CAS become active in trying whatever they think might work.

In an informed approach to complexity, it is not a question of saying that one is good and the other is bad. The issue is about finding an appropriate mix for a given situation. Where the world is certain and there is a high level of agreement among agents (for example, the need for consistent variable names and programming language syntax in a large software system, or the activities in the operating room during a routine surgery) clockware is appropriate. In a clockware situation, agents give up some of their freedom and mental models to accomplish something they have collectively agreed upon. The CAS displays less emergent, creative behavior, and begins to act more like a machine. There is nothing wrong with this.

However, where the world is far from certainty and agreement (near the edge of chaos) swarmware is needed with its adaptability, openness to new learning and flexibility. Swarmware is also needed in situations for which the old clockware processes are no longer adequate for accomplishing the

> "For jobs where supreme control is demanded, good old clockware is the way to go. Where supreme adaptability is required, out-of-control swarmware is what you want."
>
> –Kelly

Tales
- *Wizards and CEOs*
- *Another way to think*
- *A complexity tool box*
- *Emerges from the fabric*
- *Make it or let it*

Bibliography
- Kelly: *Control*
- Stacey: *Unknowable*

Aides
- *Stacey matrix*

II. Principles

purpose, in situations for which the purpose has changed or in situations in which creativity is desirable for its own sake.

> "Cohesive teams are needed for day-to-day issues. Spontaneous learning networks that have open conflict and dialogue are vital to handling strategic issues."
>
> —Stacey

Swarmware

Tune your place to the edge

Foster the "right" degree of information flow, diversity and difference, connections inside and outside the organization, power differential and anxiety, instead of controlling information, forcing agreement, dealing separately with contentious groups, working systematically down all the layers of the hierarchy in sequence and seeking comfort

II. Principles

Theoretical studies of complex adaptive systems suggest that creative self-organization occurs when there is just enough information flow, diversity, connectivity, power differential and anxiety among the agents. Too much of any of these can lead to chaotic system behavior; too little and the system remains stuck in a pattern of behavior.

Again, we can look to biological sciences for a dramatic illustration of this principle. Dr. Ary Goldberger is a cardiac specialist at Harvard Medical School who has done much research in the role of complexity in physiologic systems such as the beat-to-beat record of a healthy heart. It shows an irregular, wrinkly appearance – not a smooth, regular tracing. Furthermore, when this tracing is magnified, there is even more wrinkly detail. This complex pattern of irregular fluctuations is a fractal. Surprisingly, if you were to view an equally detailed heart-rate tracing of a patient before cardiac arrest, you would probably not see more chaotic activity, as you might expect, but rather virtual consistency and regularity. Thus, predictable and regular activity can lead to a heart attack; unpredictability and fractal (chaotic-like) variability are associated with health and stability. (Note that this pattern can also be observed in other biological systems: in sleep, chaotic patterns have been shown to produce restful sleep and extreme regularity may indicate a coma; and in muscles, chaos indicates healthy functioning and stability indicates seizure or degenerative disease.)

Tales
- *Another way to think*
- *Power of information*

Bibliography
- Kauffman: *At Home*
- Waldrop: *Complexity*
- Stacey: *Creativity*
- Goldberger: *Nonlinear dynamics*

Aides
- *Wicked questions*
- *Metaphor*
- *Stacey matrix*
- *Generative relationships*
- *Reflection*

Of course, the trick in a human CAS lies in gauging the "right" amount of information flow, diversity,

connectivity, power differential and anxiety among the agents. Since the predominant metaphors of organizational life are those of a machine and military operation, most organizations today have too little information flow and diversity, and too much power differential. The degree of connectivity and anxiety can go either way. This is a general observation that could of course be different in any specific context. If you are in a CAS, you will have your own mental model about such things, as will the other agents in the system.

Since the detailed behavior of a CAS is fundamentally unpredictable, there is no way to arrive analytically at an answer for what amount of information flow, diversity, connections inside and outside the organization, power differential and anxiety among the agents is proper. You can have more- or less-correct intuitions, and some sense of general direction, but that's inherently the best you can do. You'll just have to try tuning up or down the various factors and reflect on what happens.

Aides
• *Reflection*

Reflection is, therefore, a key skill for anyone in a CAS. Good leaders in a CAS lead not by telling people what to do, but by being open to experimentation, followed by thoughtful and honest reflection on what happens.

"At the ideal number of connections, the ideal amount of information flows between agents, and the system as a whole finds optimal solutions consistently ... which in a rapidly changing environment allows the whole to persist."

–Kauffman

"Living systems are very close to the edge of chaos phase transitions where things are loose and fluid. ... Systems that are most adaptive are so loose they are a hairbreadth away from [being] out of control."

–Waldrop

"The emphasis on managing long-term specific outcomes is completely misplaced. They cannot be managed, but it is possible to influence control parameters ... managers still need strategic plans; however, they relate not to outcomes and actions to achieve them, but to methods of affecting anxiety, power, difference and connectivity."

–Stacey

Uncover and work with paradox and tension

Do not shy away from them as if they were unnatural

Because the behavior of a CAS emerges from the interaction among agents, and because of nonlinear effects, "weird" stuff seems to happen. Of course, it is only weird because we do not yet have a way to understand it.

ALICE IN CREATIVELAND

In a CAS, creativity and innovation have the best chance to emerge precisely at the point of greatest tension and apparent irreconcilable differences. Rather than smoothing over these differences – the typical leadership intuition from the machine and military metaphors – we should focus on them and seek a new way forward.

An organization in which tension and stresses are quickly smoothed over or even denied is one that isn't learning or adapting very efficiently. Consider an organization embroiled in internal conflict over some kind of change, in which one group wants radical change and the other is holding steadfastly to the status quo. There may be a temptation for leaders to compromise, try to deliver to both groups, or prematurely stand by one position while discounting the other. How might you work with paradox and tension in this case? The approach one leader took was to mix the two warring factions (the "radical change" people and the "status quo" people) into a single group and give them the task of finding a "radical way to hold on to the status quo." This is a paradox; it makes no sense according to the prevailing mental models.

> "The chaos manager must recognize these 'forks in the road' and create a context supporting the new line of development by finding interventions that transcend the paradoxes or make them irrelevant. ... The task hinges on finding new understandings or new actions that can reframe the paradox in a way that unleashes system energies in favor of the new line of development."
>
> —Morgan

Tales
- *Make it or let it*
- *Unleashing people*
- *A complexity tool box*

Bibliography
- Morgan: *Images*
- Zimmerman: *Fractal*

Aides
- *Wicked questions*

II. Principles

However, working on it placed the group at the edge of chaos and increased the likelihood that creative approaches would emerge.

Here are some other paradoxical questions to consider. Can you think of others that are relevant to your context?

- How can we give direction without giving directives?
- How can we lead by serving?
- How can we maintain authority without having control?
- How can we set direction when we don't know the future?
- How can we oppose change by accepting it? How can we accept change by opposing it?
- How can a large organization be small? How can a small one be large?
- How can we be both a system and many independent parts?

Another way to uncover paradox is to ask "wicked questions." These are questions that have no obvious answers, but expose our assumptions. For example, in an organization that was trying to build a more-enabled environment, one leader asked, "Are we really ready to put responsibility for the work on the shoulders of the people who do the work?" Perhaps you can sense the discomfort in such a question. But challenging the sacred cows is an activity that can put you at the edge of chaos, and begin to reveal the hidden assumptions.

> "Clearly leadership has to do with the sustaining of creative tension in organizations. Creative tension is derived through strategic imbalance, which occurs when operating at the limits of organizational consensus or the boundaries of the organization. Innovation takes place on the edges of the organization where the potential for far-from-equilibrium conditions is optimal."
>
> —Zimmerman

Go for multiple actions at the fringes, let direction arise

You don't have to be "sure" before you proceed with anything

As we have already noted, in a CAS it does little good to plan the details. You can never know exactly what will happen until you do it. So, allowing the flexibility of multiple approaches is a very reasonable thing to do. Of course, such a flexible approach is unreasonable when we view the situation through the metaphor of a machine or military organization. A machine can work only one way, and an old-style military organization must follow procedures and regulations.

The science that supports this principle of CAS behavior comes primarily from the study of gene pools in evolutionary biology. David Ackley points outs that, "Researchers have shown clearly and unequivocally how populations of organisms that are learning (that is, exploring their fitness possibilities by changing behavior) evolve faster than populations that are not learning." We do not think it strains the metaphor here to suggest that our managerial instincts to drive for organizational consensus around a single option might be equivalent to inbreeding in a gene pool. And we all know the kinds of dysfunction that inbreeding in nature can spawn. We are personally struck by the fact that even though the words "organization" and "organism" have a common root, we have learned to think about them in such remarkably different ways.

The fringes that we are referring to here are the issues that are far from the zone of certainty and agreement. Recall that we pointed out that it was not a question of the machine metaphor being wrong and the CAS metaphor being right, nor is it about throwing out clockware and replacing it with swarmware. Neither approach is inherently right or wrong; but either approach can be inappropriate and ineffective in a given context. The leadership skill lies in the intuition to know which approach is needed in the context one is in. The degree of certainty and agreement is a good guide.

However, when we do find ourselves in situations far from certainty and agreement, the management advice contained in this principle is to quit agonizing over it, quit trying to analyze it to certainty. Try several small experiments, reflect carefully on what happens and gradually shift time and attention toward those things that seem to be working the best (that is, let

Tales
• *Worldwide complexity*
• *Learn as you go*

Bibliography
• Kelly: *Control*
• Stacey: *Unknowable*
• Nohira: *Action*
• Morgan: *Images*

Aides
• *Reflection*
• *Min specs*
• *Stacey matrix*

II. Principles

> "A healthy fringe speeds adaptation, increases resilience and almost always is the source of innovations."
>
> –Kelly

direction arise). These multiple actions at the fringes also serve the purpose of providing us with additional insights about the larger systems within which every system is inevitably buried.

A concrete example of this principle is the health care organization that is trying to come up with a new financial incentive plan for physicians. There are many options, with success and failure stories for each one. Therefore, we are far from certainty and agreement. Rather than meeting endlessly over it trying to pick the right approach, experiment with several approaches. See what happens, see what seems to work and in what context. Over time, you may find a right way for you, or you may find several right ways.

> "Successful experiments can go a long way in creating a foothold in a new reality. In particular, they offer important insights on the feedback loops and defensive routines that sustain a dominant attractor pattern and what can be done to help a new one to emerge."
>
> —Morgan

Listen to the shadow system

That is, realize that informal relationships, gossip, rumor and hallway conversations contribute significantly to agents' mental models and subsequent actions

Complexity theorist Ralph Stacey points out that every organization actually consists of two organizations: the legitimate system and the shadow system. Everyone in an organization is part of both. The legitimate system consists of the formal hierarchy, rules and communications patterns in the organization. The shadow organization lies behind the scenes. It consists of hallway conversation, the grapevine, the rumor mill and the informal procedures for getting things done. Most traditional management theory either ignores the shadow system, or speaks of it as something leaders must battle against (as in, "overcome resistance to change" – it's that military metaphor again).

Stacey further points out that because the shadow system harbors such diversity of thought and approach, it is often the place where much of the creativity resides within an organization. While the legitimate system is often focused on procedures, routines and the like, the shadow system has few rules and constraints. The diversity, tension and paradox of these two organizations that coexist within one can be a great source of innovation if leaders could just learn to listen to, rather than battle against, the shadow.

One health care executive entered the shadow system when he joined a group of doctors and nurses talking in the cafeteria one day. He was so fascinated by their discussion of improving the process for delivering anti-coagulants, he soon became part of this underground ad-hoc team. In doing so, he quietly sidestepped the difficult, formal process for approving quality improvement projects instituted by the hospital. The resulting work was so successful, it led to a close re-examination of the approval process that had been unintentionally discouraging such innovation.

Tales
• *What we could be doing*

Bibliography
• Stacey: *Creativity*

Aides
• *Reflection*

II. Principles

When we see our organizations as CASs, we realize that the shadow system is just a natural part of the larger system. It is simply more interconnections among agents, often stronger interconnections than those in the legitimate system. Leaders who lead from an understanding of CASs will not have a need to discredit, agonize over, or combat the shadow systems in their organizations. Rather, they will recognize and listen to the shadow organization, using the interconnections it represents as another avenue for tuning information flow, diversity of opinion, anxiety, and power differential (see "Tune your place to the edge," page 31).

"When the legitimate and shadow system operate against each other, an organization is in the phase transition at the edge of chaos; it is only here that it is changeable, because it is only here that it is capable of double-loop learning. ... When an organization is in this state, at least some of its members play by engaging in exploratory dialogue, utilizing analogies and metaphors, and employing self-reflection to develop new knowledge. ... If this change is then amplified throughout the organization to become the dominant schema of the organization, potential innovation has occurred."

–Stacey

Grow complex systems by chunking

Allow complex systems to emerge out of the links among simple systems that work well and are capable of operating independently

Question: Who built the Internet?

That's an easy one. The answer, we all know, is no one. Not Bill Gates or any other computer genius. The Internet is our most visible and oft-cited example of emergent phenomena, an elegant case study of how a complicated and vastly diverse system can self-organize ... in this case, almost overnight. On close examination, we see that the Internet evolved in chunks – like a set of building blocks – with components being integrated into the system only after they had been individually refined, proven and accepted by a collective, systemic jury.

Complex systems are ... well, complex. They are not easily understood or built in detail from the ground up. Chunking means that a good approach to building complex systems is to start small. Experiment to get pieces that work, and then link the pieces together. Of course, when you make the links, be aware that new interconnections may bring about unpredicted, emerging behaviors.

This principle is the basis upon which genetic evolution proceeds. Building blocks of organism functionality (for example, webbed feet on a bird) develop and are combined through crossover of genetic material with other bits of functionality (for example, an oversized bill more suitable for scooping fish out of the water) to form increasingly complex organisms (a pelican). The good-enough genetic combinations may survive and are then available as building blocks for future combinations.

Tales
• *What we could be doing*

Bibliography
• *Waldrop: Complexity*
• *Holland: Hidden*
• *Kelly: Control*

Aides
• *Reflection*

II. Principles

> "Interesting, beguilingly complex behavior can emerge from collections of extremely simple components."
>
> —Waldrop

> "A scan of history shows that technical innovations almost always arise as a particular combination of well-known building blocks."
>
> —Holland

The UNIX computer operating system is another good example of an ever-evolving complex system that was built from chunks. The basic – and at the time it was introduced, revolutionary – principle behind the UNIX system is that software functions should be small, simple, stand-alone bits of code that do only one thing well, embedded in an environment that makes it easy for each such function to pass its output on to another function for further processing.

Applying this principle to team-building in a mid-sized organization, for example, would suggests that leaders should look for and support small natural teams. We might provide coaching and training for these teams. Then, when these teams are functioning well, look for ways to get the teams to work together and involve others. These new links may result in weird behavior; with a CAS, this is to be expected. The leaders should be open to doing some adapting of their own. Rather than insisting on pressing forward with the training, ground rules, or procedures that worked so well in the first teams, the leaders should understand that the interconnections among teams has resulted in a fundamentally new system that may need new approaches.

> "The only way to make a complex system that works is to begin with a simple system that works. Attempts to instantly install highly complex organization ... without growing it, inevitably lead to failure. To assemble a prairie takes time – even if you have all the pieces. Time is needed to let each part test itself against all the others. Complexity is created, then, by assembling it incrementally from simple modules that can operate independently."
>
> –Kelly

Continual reflection and learning are key in building complex systems. You cannot reflect on anything until you do something. So start small, but do start.

Mix cooperation with competition
It's not one or the other

Nature competes. If you have ever glimpsed a lion stalking and devouring an elk on a PBS program before quickly changing the channel, you know this to be true.

Bibliography
• Axelrod:
  Cooperation
• Waldrop:
  Trillion
• Goodwin:
  Leopard

Nature cooperates, too. Observe members of an ant colony working together to produce intricate ant-mound societies.

These dynamics are not mutually exclusive. Natural and biological systems display both cooperation and competition. And so can corporate, business and sociological systems.

Perhaps no one has explored this paradox with more vigor – or success – than Dee Hock, former chief executive officer of Visa International. The corporation's growth averages around 20 percent annually; it serves around a half-billion clients in more than 200 countries; sales volume is now passing $1 trillion.

In the massive, sprawling Visa system, the cooperation-competition paradox is a fundamental part of the structure. Fierce competition occurs among member institutions and banks that issue Visa cards, set prices and develop services … all while going after each other's customers. But these institutions must also cooperate: for the system to work, merchants and vendors must be able to accept any Visa card anywhere in the world, regardless of who issued the card. This mixture of cooperation and competition has allowed the system to grow globally, seemingly immune to traditional constraints of language, culture, currencies, politics or legal codes.

One popular expression of the competition-cooperation paradox is the "tit-for-tat" strategy. It came about when political scientist Robert Axelrod tested a variety of competitive strategies using computer simulations. Time and again, the simplest strategy of all took the prize in this complex contest: University of Toronto psychologist Anatol Rapport's "Tit-for-Tat" program started out by cooperating on the first move, and then simply did exactly what the other program had done on the move before. The program was "nice" in the sense that it would never defect first. It was "tough" in the sense that it would punish uncooperative behavior by competing on

> "We are used to thinking about competitions in which there is only one winner, competitions such as football or chess. But the world is rarely like that. In a vast range of situations, mutual cooperation can be better for both sides than mutual defection. The key to doing well lies not in overcoming others, but in eliciting their cooperation."
>
> –Axelrod

II. Principles

the next move. It was "forgiving" in that it returned to cooperation once the other party demonstrated cooperation. And it was "clear" in the sense that it was very easy for the opposing programs to figure out exactly what it would do next. Thus, some have proposed the heuristic that "nice, tough, forgiving and clear guys finish first."

In his 1984 book, *The Evolution of Cooperation*, Robert Axelrod showed the profound nature of this simple strategy in its application to all sorts of complex adaptive systems – trench warfare in WWI, politics and even fungus growth on rocks. Commenting on this strategy, Waldrop said, "Consider the magical fact that competition can produce a very strong incentive for cooperation, as certain players forge alliances and symbiotic relationships with each other for mutual support. It happens at every level of, and in every kind of, complex adaptive system, from biology, to economics, to politics."

> "It's against the interests of either predator or prey to eliminate the enemy. That's clearly irrational, yet that is clearly a force that drives nature."
> —Ehrlich

A good leader would be one who knows how to, and prefers to, cooperate, but is also a skillful competitor when provoked to competition (that is, a nice, forgiving, tough and clear person). Note that this strategy rejects both extremes as a singular strategy. While much is said these days about the importance of being cooperative and positive-thinking in business dealings, the always-cooperative leader may find his or her proverbial lunch is being eaten by others. Similarly, while sports and warrior metaphors are also popular in some leadership circles, the always-competitive leader may find himself or herself on the outside looking in as alliances are formed.

> "[A] concept that is deeply ingrained in biology is competition. This is often described as the driving force of evolution. ... However, there is as much cooperation in biology as there is competition. Mutualism and symbiosis, organisms living in a state of mutual dependency ... are an equally universal feature of the biological realm. Why not argue that cooperation is the great source of innovation in evolution?"
> —Goodwin

Conclusion

Our existing principles of leadership and management in organizations are largely based on metaphors from science that are hundreds of years old. It is time that we realized that science itself has largely replaced these metaphors with more accurate descriptions of what really happens in the world. Science is replacing its old metaphors not because they are wrong, but because they only described simplistic situations that progress has now moved us well beyond. Similarly, our organizations today are not the simple machines they were envisioned to be in the Industrial Revolution that saw the birth of scientific management. Further, people today are no longer the compliant "cogs in the machine" that we once thought them to be. We have intuitively known these things for many years. Management innovations such as learning organizations, total quality, empowerment and so on were introduced to overcome the increasingly visible failures of the simple organization-as-machine metaphor. Still, as we have pointed out, the metaphor remains strong.

The emerging study of complex adaptive systems gives us a new lens through which we can now begin to see a new type of scientific management. This new scientific management resonates well with more modern, intuitive notions about what we must do to manage increasingly complex organizations today. More importantly, the new thinking in science provides a consistent framework to pull together these heretofore intuitive notions. Now, for example, advocates of open communications and empowerment can claim the same firmness of ground that advocates of structure and control have been claiming exclusively. Science can now say rather clearly that structure and control are great for simple, machine-like situations; but things such as open communication, diversity and so on are needed in complex adaptive systems – such as those in modern organizations. The new scientific management will, no doubt, revolutionize organizations in the coming decades much as the old scientific management changed the world in the early decades of this century.

Nine emerging and connected organizational and leadership principles
From the study of complex adaptive systems

Principle (shorthand)	Full statement of principle	Further explanation or contrast to the traditional approach
1. Complexity lens	View your system through the lens of complexity …	… in addition to the metaphor of a machine or a military organization.
2. Good-enough vision	Build a good-enough vision and provide minimum specifications …	… rather than trying to plan out every little detail.
3. Clockware/ swarmware	When life is far from certain, lead from the edge, with clockware and swarmware in tandem …	… that is, balance data and intuition, planning and acting, safety and risk, giving due honor to each.
4. Tune to the edge	Tune your place to the edge by fostering the "right" degree of: information flow, diversity and difference, connections inside and outside the organization, power differential and anxiety …	… instead of controlling information, forcing agreement, dealing separately with contentious groups, working systematically down all the layers of the hierarchy in sequence, and seeking comfort.
5. Paradox	Uncover and work with paradox and tension …	… rather than shying away from them as if they were unnatural.
6. Multiple actions	Go for multiple actions at the fringes, let direction arise …	… rather than believing that you must be sure before you proceed with anything.
7. Shadow system	Listen to the shadow system …	… realizing that informal relationships, gossip, rumor and hallway conversations contribute significantly to agents' mental models and subsequent actions.
8. Chunking	Grow complex systems by chunking …	… by allowing complex systems to emerge out of the links among simple systems that work well and are capable of operating independently.
9. Competition/ cooperation	Mix cooperation and competition …	… it's not one or the other.

II. Principles

tales

e d g e w a r e

Tales of complexity

As part of our ongoing learning about the dynamics of complex adaptive systems, we must make a conscious effort to see the world and our work within it through a different lens. Reflection, journaling and storytelling are integral to using this complexity lens effectively.

Principles
•*Complexity lens*

Storytelling is verbal or written communication that describes a context and the observable events within that context. The storyteller might also choose to add interpretations of the events through an explicitly identified lens, the thinking process of the storyteller and the lessons learned from the story.

Good storytelling is a two-way process. Stories have value for both the teller and the receiver. Telling a story helps clarify one's thinking. The act of recounting a story often helps the storyteller see patterns and connections more holistically. Receivers benefit both from the shared learnings and from the opportunity to offer their own reflections. There are always multiple points of view, lenses and mental models that can be applied to a collection of events. Good storytellers are, therefore, never defensive about their stories and their interpretations; rather, they encourage dialogue and welcome the reflections of others.

Aides
•*Reflection*

The stories in this chapter were compiled by a variety of people based on their own reflections through the complexity lens. These pioneers have graciously agreed to share their learnings with others. These tales represent some of the first efforts in health care to tap the wisdom of complexity; as such, they are early stories and some are unfinished. Even so, the learnings are compelling.

The tales are listed and cross-referenced on the following pages. Dates in parentheses are the time frames in which the tales occurred.

III.Tales

Minimum specs for the tales

We saw no need to impose a common format on the tales in this chapter of the book. Consistent with the complexity approach, our minimum specifications for the stories were only that:

Aides
•*Min specs*

- they provide an early hook to the reader in the form of a provocative title or first sentence

- health care-based readers should be able to identify in some way with the people or issue in the story

- the story should clearly indicate a complexity principle or aide (the tie-in can be in either a positive or negative sense)

- the story should contain explicit, honest reflection (multiple lens and reflectors welcomed; stories in which the storyteller is all-wise and everyone else is stupid are not welcomed)

- the people in the story are comfortable having the story told, and the storyteller was comfortable sharing the reflections

Other than these few specs, we have encouraged storytellers to be as diverse as they wish in telling their stories and sharing reflections.

The tales are in no particular order. You can read them in any order you wish. Recognizing the diversity of learning styles that people bring to a topic such as complexity, we will not be surprised to hear that some people consider the tales a stand-alone centerpiece of this book; while others find them helpful only because they illustrate the principles and aides in the other chapters of the book. Use them in whatever ways are helpful to you and the people around you.

Aides
• *Reflection*

Each tale is told mostly through a complexity lens, with references to other lenses as appropriate. The tales are primarily examples of hindsight reflection, as defined in the Reflection section of the Aides chapter; although there are some aspects of insight reflection in tales that report on works in progress, and some aspects of foresight reflection in some comments about what the storyteller might do in the future.

You might not agree with the reflections offered, or you may see additional things. That is the beauty of stories. They are filled with meaning. The lens and mental models we bring to a story determine what we see in it. The reflections offered here are just one way of seeing things.

A Guide to the tales

Basic information on the tales in this chapter, designed to help you find stories that may be most helpful and relevant.

Wizards and CEOs: The Oz factor . . . . page 55

Birute Regine and Roger Lewin

A story from John R. Kopicki, president and chief executive officer, Muhlenberg Regional Medical Center, Plainfield, N.J. (1996-'98).

One person becomes the catalyst for sweeping organizational change. Further insights are drawn from a delightful metaphor: "The Wizard of Oz."

Illustration of: •emergence •self-organization •coevolution •phase transition •clockware/swarmware •generative relationships •wicked questions •multiple actions •tune to the edge

Emerges From the Fabric:
Working inside and outside . . . . page 69

Ken Baskin, Brenda Zimmerman and Curt Lindberg

A story from Linda Rusch, R.N., vice president, Patient Care, Hunterdon Medical Center, Flemington, N.J. (1996-'97).

Establishing the context and conditions to foster new community health improvement initiatives and creative approaches to inpatient nursing care.

Illustration of: •complexity lens •clockware/swarmware •wicked questions •minimum specifications •conditions for emergence •good-enough vision •metaphor

III. Tales

III. Tales

A story from James Roberts, M.D., senior vice president, VHA Inc., Dallas, Texas (1997-'98).

A complexity approach creates a learning network of physician leaders, and illustrates an approach for assessing projects based on the Stacey matrix.

Illustration of: •emergence •self-organization •good-enough vision •Stacey matrix •clockware/swarmware •paradox •complexity lens

A story from Federal Metals, Canada (1989).

A company that created a complexity-informed plan to strategy.

Illustration of: •emergence •wicked questions •creating conditions •reflection •metaphor •tune to the edge

Wizards and CEOs
The Oz factor

Birute Regine and Roger Lewin

A story from Muhlenberg Regional Medical Center, Plainfield, N.J.

Illustration of:

- emergence
- self-organization
- coevolution
- phase transition
- clockware/swarmware
- generative relationships
- wicked questions
- multiple actions
- tune to the edge

The first thing you notice when you approach the entrance to Muhlenberg Medical Center is Jimmy. Jimmy, predictably and contagiously convivial, cradles the elbow of an elderly woman, gently guiding her to an awaiting cab. "So how are you feeling, beautiful?" he says flirtatiously and sincerely. She giggles girlishly and gives his hand a nudge with her elbow. You would never guess that Jimmy has worked at the hospital for 42 years. His mischievous eyes and quick wit suggest someone far younger than his years. His current position is official greeter for the medical center, which is in Plainfield, New Jersey. But he also assists those leaving the hospital – maneuvering wheelchairs and making sure people have a ride home – all of which has made for more speedy and facile discharges. The hospital could operate without Jimmy; some might think him to be a luxury; but he so impresses everybody that comes through the door – making people welcome, setting a friendly tone – that it overrides the fact that he is an unmeasurable benefit. This says a lot about Muhlenberg – a medical center that values good relationships with its customers, right from the start.

The entrance to the medical center is a kind of solarium, with ficus trees, a fountain with its inevitable coins, scattered pots of poinsettias. Inside the foyer, on the left, is a waiting area that resembles a living room. On the mantel of a false fireplace are photos that you might find at grandma's house. Nearby stands an information table with hospital services on display. To the right of the living room is the extremely successful Express Admissions facility; and further on is the circular information desk – quiet, open, friendly. Nearby is a hallway of offices, one of which belongs to chief executive officer and president of Muhlenberg, John Kopicki. In late 1997, Muhlenberg began the process of merging with the nearby Kennedy Hospital, to form the Solaris Health System – one of many such mergers provoked by the current turmoil in the health care industry. So, in addition to being head of Muhlenberg, John is also the executive vice president of Clinical Delivery Systems for Solaris.

When you step into the reception area to John's office, you'll be greeted by his assistant Lou Ciganenko, whose graciousness and efficiency leaves you knowing you are in good hands. Multicolored sticky notes decorate the front edge of her desk, reminding John of an appointment tomorrow morning, a phone call to return by the end of the day. If you ask to see John, it's unlikely he'll be there. During this time of transition, he's spending more and more time at Kennedy doing what he does best – building relationships. John doesn't network; he takes seriously the task of developing trust through support, dialogue and consensus-building. Even though the Muhlenberg staff understands that they have to take charge as he forges new links with their new and more powerful partner, they miss him. The merger has everyone on edge – anxious about their jobs, excited about the possibilities, curious about the outcomes – and John's presence is a comfort for many. But transitions are never easy, and this one is no exception. Muhlenberg is fortunate to have John navigating the turbulent waters of change – because he's been there before.

Command and control

The time in question was not a merger, but not unlike a merger either. It, too, was a time of transition for Muhlenberg, one that John had not expected to be part of, because he was planning to leave the hospital. In 1990, after a brief spell as Muhlenberg's chief operating officer, John had an opportunity to join a management culture that was closer to his own style, and so he handed in his resignation. It just so happened that, at the same time, Muhlenberg's Board of Governors was coming to a major decision of its own: it felt the hospital needed a change of direction, a change of leadership. So, too, did the medical staff. As a result, two days before John was set to leave, the board asked him to stay and become the president and CEO. John accepted, knowing that what lay ahead would be one of the biggest challenges he had ever faced.

Fran Hulse, vice president of Medical Affairs, who has worked at Muhlenberg since 1971, is one of the living memories of the center. She remembers the time prior to John's appointment as CEO this way:

"It was a very uptight culture. People were extremely reserved and cautious about what they were going to say openly. The CEO's view of management was very controlling – things had to work the way he said they would. Period. What tended to happen was that even senior people felt they couldn't challenge him and expect to survive. Top management felt they had to be tightly on top of every single thing that happened, and had to OK everything. This created a climate that was anything but open as far as inviting feedback and comment – positive or negative. And negative had a lot of risk attached to it – if you spoke negatively about the wrong thing, you might just shorten your career at this institution. There was a pervasive sense of oppression, and as a result employees felt constrained and very reluctant to express their ideas and opinions openly. And the medical staff were frustrated. Their patience was wearing thin because the administration was giving lip service to medical staff issues and doing nothing to address them."

When the medical staff heard of John's resignation, they literally revolted. They called a special meeting among themselves, and passed a vote of no confidence in the administration. Once the sleeping giant woke, it wielded a lot of power. The medical staff started lobbying board members, pleading their case. The doctors felt that John understood their problems, and that he could work with them. John was the kind of person they felt they could trust, could relate to, who cared about what they said. The board listened, and offered John his greatest challenge.

Implicit in this account of Muhlenberg's management culture, and common to all command-and-control cultures, is a story of disconnection. People disconnect from themselves – what they really think and feel – as a way of keeping their jobs and surviving the culture. They are disconnected from each other through silence, by not giving or receiving genuine feedback: that's fertile ground for festering complaints. They are disconnected from their purpose, forgetting why they are there, becoming complacent and "just doing my work," because they are preoccupied with and living in an atmosphere of fear and suspicion. Command-and-control leadership generates disconnection; and disconnection empowers command-and-control leadership. A vicious circle.

Shifting worlds

The command-and-control style of management was not unique to Muhlenberg. Generally, it is more the rule rather than the exception in modern American organizations. It is in the tradition of scientific management, with roots that go back to Frederick Taylor in the early decades of the century. It is a highly analytical, mechanistic view of the work place, and is based on linear thinking, hierarchical structures and solutions imposed from the top down. Organizations are viewed as

Principles
• *Clockware/ swarmware*

III. Tales

machines, and people as the working parts of the machine that need to be controlled for maximum efficiency. But with the shift from the industrial age to the information age, this approach has reached its limit. Certainty has given way to uncertainty in the business world, just as it has in the world of science.

In science, a mechanistic view of the natural world has given way to an appreciation of the world as being dynamic and complex, nonlinear and creative. Some realms of the world are mechanistic and predictable, of course, such as the orbiting of the planets. But most are not. Most are complex networks of interacting components that produce rich patterns that cannot be predicted from even the most detailed information about the components. Biologists, for instance, are beginning to embrace the new science of complexity theory as a means of understanding the complex dynamics of life at all scales, from the simplest ecosystem, such as a pond, right up to the global ecosystem: each scale rich in nonlinearity, unpredictability and creativity. Taking their cue from complexity science, managers are beginning to recognize that business organizations are much more like organisms than machines. Each organization is a complex network of interacting components, and each is embedded in successively larger webs of interconnections, right up to the global economy, just like ecosystems. Nonlinearity and unpredictability therefore characterize the world of modern business, not comforting linearity and predictability.

Being a successful leader these days therefore requires a recognition that the world is not the way it used to be, or the way it used to be perceived. And no more so than in health care, where uncertainty and unpredictability can no longer be denied or dismissed, where leaders find themselves under extraordinary pressure to provide health care that is both cost-effective and high-quality. During this time of crisis and ambiguity, a top down approach to management comes up short. Leaders cannot command outcomes – the business environment is too complex, too fast-changing. Faced with the reality that change cannot be stopped, leaders have to change how they think about change. Once, setting a goal and planning each step to achieve that end was regarded to be good change strategy, and sometimes worked well. Now, adaptability and flexibility are the hallmark of a robust organization, which calls upon different leadership skills.

Principles
- *Tune to the edge*
- *Complexity lens*

Leaders in the new environment need to understand how to tap into people's creativity in the midst of chaos, rather than control their behavior. Leaders need to maintain a steadfast confidence that order, although unpredictable, will emerge, rather than feigning a certainty. Leaders need to embrace the complexity of the world, not fight to control it. As John Kopicki says: "If you're an autocratic manager, you're going to have a very difficult time operating in this chaotic environment. You just can't tell people what to do and think they're going to do it. It just doesn't work that way anymore." Complexity theory gives managers guidance for how to navigate in today's chaotic environment, how to unleash the creative and adaptive talents of their people, by relinquishing the control mode of traditional management. In other words, it shows managers how to make their organizations more efficient and capable of appropriate change.

However, it is not an easy path for managers who find comfort in control – or at least in the illusion of control. It is not easy even for a leader whose innate management style resonates with the complexity approach and who is dedicated to making it work, as John's story shows. But when it works, the dividends are great, and not just in material terms. This approach involves valuing people for themselves, as human beings. A culture emerges in the work place, in which people feel that their efforts are recognized, and are therefore prepared to go the extra mile to meet extraordinary challenges. This is both a rewarding and powerful management practice, as John recognizes. "Sadly, we are living in a non-affirming society," he says. "People hunger for recognition, and when they receive it they are extremely motivated, and fulfilled."

A controlling style of management wasn't John's nature. True, he was trained in a traditional MBA program at The George Washington University, but he wasn't interested in being a traditional manager. Rather, his leadership style is more intuitive, his reasons to lead more idealistic rather than egoistic. As the son of a funeral director, John learned early on to have a tremendous respect for people. Perhaps that is why he's attracted to managing organizations that take care of people – as his father, he also services people in a time of need. When John became Muhlenberg's CEO, he faced an enormous uncertainty – how his style of leadership would affect the existing culture. How could he shift a culture of command and control, where predictability reigned king, to a culture in which there was an acceptance of uncertainty and change? How could he open up a closed system whose lines of communication had shut down? And how to bring people along in this transition, knowing that this was the organization's only recourse for survival, given the harsh economic circumstances that lay ahead?

The science of complexity has a language and concepts for analyzing the transition of complex systems from one state to another, often called a phase transition. In Muhlenberg's case, it was a shift in cultures, from the established command-and-control culture to a more flexible, adaptable culture that would flow from John's different style of leadership. We could talk in complexity theory terms about how this transition was engendered – through changing the rules of behavior, with new emergent properties – but sometimes scientific theories don't capture the richness of the experience. Instead we'll turn to a classic folk story, "The Wizard of Oz,"

III. Tales

which is rich with metaphors and archetypal characters, and offers many insights into organizational life. We'll focus on the Wizard (as portrayed in the book, not the film), a character that lends itself to a deeper understanding of the world of the CEO in a command-and-control culture.

The Wizard of Oz

As you recall, Dorothy found herself in a strange land, and wanted to go home. She was told by the Good Witch of the North to see the almighty and powerful Wizard of Oz, who would surly be able to find a way to send her back to Kansas. Along the way she gathered three companions who also wanted help from Oz – the Scarecrow, the Tin Man and the Lion. After many adventures, they found themselves in the audience of Oz, who, in a display of plumes of fire and a thundering voice, proceeded to terrify them and, instead of helping them, ordered them to kill the Wicked Witch of the West. Only when her broomstick was in his hand would he help them out, he proclaimed. Against all odds, Dorothy and her companions managed to do just that.

Dorothy was furious when, on her return to the Emerald City, the Wizard dissembled and failed to keep his promise. The Lion roared, to frighten the Wizard. The roar had more effect on Toto, Dorothy's dog, who jumped in fright, and accidentally knocked down a screen, exposing a little old man with a bald head.

"Who are you?" they asked incredulously.

"I am Oz, the Great and Terrible," he said in a trembling voice. "But don't strike me – please don't – and I'll do anything you want me to do."

Dorothy and her friends were shocked, having believed him to be a great Head, a terrible Beast, a ball of Fire.

"No, you are all wrong," said the little man meekly. "I have been making believe. I'm just a common man." And so we learn that among his tricks is ventriloquism, which enabled him to throw his voice onto the illusions he created.

This moment of personal conversion, when a man steps out from behind the screen of illusion, when apparitions of power are dispelled (by none other than a dog, which archetypally symbolizes intuition) and a common man is revealed, is perhaps every CEO's dream and nightmare. But how did the Wizard find himself behind a screen of illusion in the first place? And why is it so frightening for him to reveal himself as a common man? The Wizard of Oz, as CEO, gives rich insight into the complex dynamics and collusion that occurs in a command-and-control culture.

Like Dorothy, Oz also landed in this strange land by accident, and like John Kopicki, ending up where he never expected. Seeing Oz descend from the clouds in his balloon, the people of the strange land thought he must be a great Wizard. And, of course, he let them think that, tantalized by the privileges associated with power. Because the people were afraid of him and would do anything he wished, he ordered them to build a city and a Palace, "just to amuse myself and keep the good people busy." In this way, he became the CEO of Emerald City. He ruled with a fearsome hand, a true command-and-control type. But his story of leadership is not that simple, for Oz is an ambiguous, paradoxical character: he is both a perpetrator and a victim of control.

To be idealized by your people can be very seductive to a leader. To be idealized is to be adored and feared, but not seen – the paradox of enormous visibility as an image and simultaneously invisibility as a person. Oz's high visibility was captured across the land in the myth of his omniscient powers. On the other hand, his invisibility was quite literal. Once the people built him the palace, he shut himself up and would not see anybody. And he did this for reasons no one would have imagined – out of fear: fearful that the witches would discover that he was not more powerful than they, and fearful that they would surely destroy him. And he feared that if he went out of the Palace, his people would discover he was not the Wizard that they thought he was. As he says, "then they would be vexed with me for having deceived them. And so I have to stay shut up in the rooms all day, and it gets tiresome." In this way, Oz controls and is controlled by his position. And so we have the portrait of a leader who projects a power he does not feel, who is inaccessible out of fear of being found out, who is isolated and out of touch with his people, who lives a lonely life. And he is also someone who has become somewhat comfortable with the illusion, as Oz states, "I have fooled everyone so long that I thought I should never be found out."

But, not surprisingly, he is found out. And the discovery of his true identity exposes a collusion between Oz and his people. Both propagate his illusion of power. His people need him to be omniscient, which perpetuates a parent-child relationship. In every organization there are people who just want to be told what to do; who need to think there is someone more powerful than themselves, who wish for another to take care of everything. They endow powers on their leaders that the leader does not possess. And they project their own longing for power onto him. And, like Oz, there are leaders who allow it. Still, there is a vulnerability with this type of power, as Oz despairingly notes, "How can I help being a humbug when all these people make me do things that everybody knows can't be done?"

Even when Oz acknowledges his failings and admits he can't keep the promises he made to the foursome, they in a sense don't allow him to stand on grounds of mutuality. He points out to them that they don't really need what they are asking for. The Scarecrow doesn't need brains; he needs experience. The Lion doesn't need courage; he needs confidence. And the Tin Man, well, Oz can't imagine why he would want a heart, when it can so easily be broken. But they insist that he bestow these traits to them anyway. And so he ceremoniously gives them what they already have. As a result, they enter a phase transition in which two systems, two different realities, paradoxically coexist.

John recognized a similar paradoxical time in his own organization during the phase transition of his new leadership. "There are times when people will come to you and want that control decision. I mean, that's the incredible thing about it. You're all going along as a team, and then suddenly everybody will be looking at you, and you better not disappoint them. They want you to say, 'By God, it's going to be this way.' Sometimes people say, 'We've done this as far as we can. All we want is your final blessing.' At that point they don't want to hear me saying, 'Well, geez, what do you want to do?' They really want to have that final blessing from me, that final approval. I don't understand it. It's way beyond me."

Yes, it is way beyond John. It has more to do with the psychological residue of people used to being controlled than it has to do with John. When people work in an environment day in and day out where they are used to being told what to do, are rarely asked what they think, are used to perceiving themselves as weaker, used to a parental type relationship with the leaders, it has its effects. They develop a fear of freedom. Ingrained behavior doesn't just disappear. It takes time, patience and guidance. The transition from a command-and-control culture to a culture of change and adaptation requires a dual conversion, of the leader and of the organization. Both engage in a process of parting veils of illusion, and in particular, the illusion that the leader has complete control and has all the answers. It is finding a ground of mutuality, adult-adult relationship based on a common humanity.

For Dorothy and Oz, that moment occurred when Dorothy, realizing his promises would not be kept, said to the wizard, "I think you are a very bad man."

"Oh, no, my dear," said Oz. "I'm really a very good man; but I'm a very bad wizard, I must admit."

Letting go

Although control and command is contrary to John's nature, giving up control is not an easy practice – even for him. He talked about it this way. "I think unconsciously, you always want to maintain your control. You really have to fight against that. It's the toughest thing for senior management to do, to give it up. Even when you recognize that you have to just give it up – it's hard to have that flexibility, to have that patience. You have to create a new discipline in yourself. For instance, I had to have the courage to let my VP, Mary Anne, go ahead and spend money for which she couldn't demonstrate the payback. That doesn't mean I'm frivolous; that means that I have to make hard choices when it's impossible to know the outcome. At other times, when I've let go, I'll think, 'What the hell has this proven?' But I never say it."

John's struggle to let go of control is rooted in his MBA training at The George Washington University, which inculcated the conventional management model that leaders are controllers. But for men generally, letting go is difficult, because traditional roles, and the definition of masculinity, demand that men be in control. Traditional roles put enormous pressure on men to perform, produce, to be the answer man – a very mechanistic orientation. Leadership would then naturally be associated with fixing problems, providing solutions, enabling what's disabled, leveraging – also a mechanistic view. And because masculinity is heavily associated with autonomy, it is also about being the Lone Ranger, as John points out: "You know, CEOs don't talk to one another. Did you ever hear a group of CEOs saying, 'How's everything going?' 'Are you fine?' Never. At a meeting once, there were a couple of them saying, you know, 'I'm so tired of making decisions. Being the CEO, it's so hard.' And what I've been able to do is say 'Yes, it is chaotic; we're out of control. The best we can do is rely on our instincts.' And they seem to respond to that."

Personally and professionally as hard as it is, this less-directive, less-controlling style of leadership enhances an organization's performance, in many ways. For example, until recently, Muhlenberg was rated from the mid- to lower-range in patient satisfaction, according to the Press Ganey survey. The hospital's management committee had recognized the importance of improving these ratings, but had failed to shift them. As John's open, growth-nurturing style of management began to permeate Muhlenberg, extraordinary organizational achievements began to be made by recognizing that front line workers are the ones closest to the problem and are therefore likely to be able to reach solutions, such as reducing admission time from 24 hours to just one hour (see Unleashing People Potential). The same approach to the stubborn problem of patient satisfaction brought similarly dramatic improvement: within a year, the scores started to climb, and for the last two quarters of 1997, Muhlenberg's ratings were well into the 90th percentile range, superceded only by Hunterdon Medical Center.

It is probably no coincidence that much of the management culture at Hunterdon embraces a complexity, bottom-up, human-centered approach. As Jeffrey Pfeffer, of Stanford's Graduate School of Business, demonstrates so cogently in his recent book *The Human Equation*, human-centered

Tales
• *Unleashing potential*

Bibliography
• Pfeffer: *Human Equation*

III. Tales

management practice consistently leads to enhanced organizational performance, including the financial bottom line. It can be seen through John's experience at Muhlenberg. It is evident at Hunterdon. And it is manifest in surveys of more than a thousand business organizations in the United States and Europe. The fact that complexity-guided management theory leads to human-centered management practice leads to the most readily understood reason for why CEOs might want to throw over the (illusionary) certainty of control in favor of the uncertainty of lack of control: it is good business.

Faces of transition

The practice of letting go (and it is a practice, since no one is perfect) initiates a different personal journey and a profound struggle between the common man and the Oz factor – between openness and secrecy, vulnerability and omniscience, honesty and illusion. It is this conversion within the CEO, and through his example, that guides the conversion in the culture. It is not so much about a different way of doing as it is about a different way of being.

When we examine the conversion of Oz (or CEO) from Wizard to man, what emerges as pivotal to this change is a different way of being in relation to one's people. Similarly, when John and his people recounted powerful moments that affected them and the existing culture, we see that it is John's way of being with them that instigated the change. Specifically, there are four behaviors: be open, be straight, be human, be in relationship. These behaviors proved very effective in convincing a skeptical culture that things could and would be different. These ways of being may sound simple, but as John and others will attest, although ultimately life is simpler, it's hard to do.

Be open, not controlling

Why should a leader be open to his people? Because openness gives him access to information about the problems, solutions, the reality of the organization. Fran Hulse, Muhlenberg's vice president of Medical Affairs, recounts an early event that illustrates the power of openness.

Aides
• *Wicked questions*

Principles
• *Tune to the edge*

"Early on we started to bring management groups together informally, away from the hospital, to try to get to know each other more on a personal level. The first time we did it, there was a roomful of people, around 45, and we asked the questions: What are we doing wrong? What do you think? How can we make it work? Nobody said a word. Here we were putting out all these direct questions, and all you could feel was the silence and the tension in the room. By the third time we got together some of the barriers were coming down. It was incredible to see people relax a little bit. People had to build trust. They had to feel this wasn't just more lip service. I think it was less about trusting us and more about how shell-shocked they were. Because they had no reason not to trust us. It wasn't until you saw the reactions of those people that you really appreciated how bad it must have been to work here."

To be open means to allow things to unfold. Allow it to be. Allow it to be silent. Being open means restraining the impulse to take control and make something be what you want it to be, rather than allowing it to be. Being open means getting teams involved, drawing people out, getting them to sit down and solve problems – being open to them as problem-solvers.

Be straight, not secretive

John made it clear in the beginning that it was going to be different under his leadership And people had to decide if they could change – become team players, be experimental, be straight. Being straight builds trust in an organization – people know where they stand. When there's trust in an organization, people are more efficient and take greater risks, which spurs creativity.

Fran recalls John being straight with her:

"It makes me think about the fact that we were conditioned by the previous leadership to do business in a way that was kind of calculating. I mean, not that we were necessarily by our natures calculating and devious. But I think without even realizing it we were conditioned about a certain way of doing business, where you had to strategize things in the back room so that a certain thing would play out a certain way. But there were players that never had the whole picture of what was really going on. When you do business in a calculating way, you're doing it and you don't realize you're doing it because it is what you do to keep things going and how you survive. And I think literally John cut through that right in the beginning. He used to do that with me and say, 'You know, you don't have to do that Fran. Just talk to them. Don't worry about telling them. We're not holding anything back here.' He had to keep reminding us that we're not going to keep secrets here. That we can't do that anymore; it doesn't get you anywhere."

Fran also remembers a powerful moment when John was straight with the organization:

"John came right out in the open on some real big issues with the staff. At employee meetings held periodically through the year, John would get up and tell people what was going on. 'Here's the story, guys,' he'd say. 'And you've got to know this because we can't deal with this without you. I'm not keeping anything from you.' People listened and they questioned. Several years ago we were in a financially bad position. We had cuts and it was looking bad. John had to tell them that he was going to have to freeze wages; no raises for that year. He had a full house, standing room only, people sitting in the aisles. He pulled out all the charts, presented all the finances, took them through it step by step. He explained why; he told them what we were going to do. He told them how great they've been. They applauded at the end of the meeting! We sat there and said, 'Can you top that?' Usually you get, 'Nobody appreciates me,' or 'Why am I only getting 2 percent?' They applauded!"

If you are straight and bring people along, what emerges is a sense of inclusion. The resilience of people is often underestimated. People can accept very difficult situations if they feel they are part of the process, even when this includes no raises or even leaving their jobs.

Be human, not omniscient

People want to care about their leaders. It gives them a sense of community. People who feel a sense of community speak of being more willing to adapt and be flexible. When people see their leaders as human, it's easier to care for them. And when their leaders can be human, it gives people permission to be human. COO Phil Brown recounts a time with John:

"John and I talk about personal issues from time to time. For instance, John stopped in last night. He came in to talk about how he was feeling about a family matter and things that were going on. And that gave me an opportunity to say back to him about how I see him, about who he is. I mean, I could understand, given the difficulties and challenges he was facing at the time, if it had been played out as anger and bitterness at work. But in fact he did just the opposite, coming to me, telling me about his concerns strengthened our relationship. I said, I understand now some more about why you are so caring, and giving, and patient. I haven't often had those types of relationships in work setting, where those kinds of conversations get going."

John recognizes that his own frailties actually bind him to his staff:

"This management team puts up with me when I go off the deep end. Everybody has got to go off the deep end sometime. Somewhere we've developed a tolerance where we don't hold grudges. It's also about the ability to have failure in an organization where people don't jump all over you, blaming and screaming. This gives permission to change. I heard a CEO recently admit he was wrong. He said, 'I pushed my people too hard. We failed. We didn't understand this field, and we're going to take some hits and lumps.' I guarantee you they're going to figure this out. He accepted blame. They're going to come out of this OK. When the leader takes responsibility during a crisis, he gives permission for the team to regroup. What normally happens in a crisis is the leadership is replaced or they blame someone else. How many times has a CEO of a company come in and said 'I'll take that responsibility?' I don't see that a lot."

Be in relationship

A control culture sees people as opponents and relationships as hierarchical. A changing culture sees people as part of a web of connections and relationships as connections to build. So much of what John accomplishes and inspires stems from his way of being in relationship to others, which engenders a sense of mutuality and respect. It even reframes the meaning of charisma and power.

Principles
• *Generative relationships*

People associate charisma with being slick, razzle-dazzle, a powerful attractiveness, interesting. Much like the all and powerful Oz. John's charisma, on the other hand, is not a screen of projection, like Oz, that lights up the place. Instead, it arises from his sincerity and honesty as a person, and the way he deals with people. Charisma with him is an emergent property – it comes through in his relationship to others. As Fran states, "If anything, you would say he's not that comfortable a public speaker. But then you find that out and it becomes his strength because he's real; he's not a phony. It works in a completely different way."

Similarly, when power is in the context of a mutual relationships it is power with another rather than in the command-and-control approach of power over another. If there are two phrases that capture the spirit of this culture of change and mutuality at Muhlenberg, at all levels, it's "just, try it" and "work with me." It is John's way of being in relationship to people that defines him as a leader, not his position.

A culture of change and care

A culture of change, adaptation and action did emerge at Muhlenberg, as John hoped it would. And care. Care for the patients, as exemplified by Jimmy's warm and reassuring greeting at the front door, so important to people who are sick and often disoriented. It's no coincidence that patient-satisfaction scores have gone way up. "I'm very proud of that," John says. And care for the people who work there, too. Mary Anne Keyes, vice president of Patient Care, says she has the best team she has ever had. "It's an incredible experience to come in every day, to believe in what you're doing with people, to enjoy the relationships – that's worth a lot." That's just what John wants to hear. "If we can't come here every day being happy, there's no reason to come here at all," he says.

Principles
• *Multiple actions*

III. Tales

But no one should imagine the process – this transition from one culture to another – is quick and easy. It demands dedication, constant vigilance, constant practice – and a lot of patience. "You have to keep trying," says John, "and you have to be prepared to get things wrong, because you will. You have to be prepared to fail at things." But, slowly, the culture starts to shift – a little here, a little there, building toward a critical mass. At that point, what was previously dominant in the culture – that is, the residue of command and control – is rapidly eclipsed by the newly emergent culture, a culture of change and care. The phase transition is upon you, unplanned, unanticipated. "It just happened," remembers Dr. Bob Bayly, "as opposed to if we had tried to sit down and design it."

Nor should it be assumed that this flexible, adaptable management practice is for everyone. It is no surprise that several senior managers left soon after John became CEO – some voluntarily, and some otherwise – because they had no stomach for even the prospect of a very different form of management. They were what John calls "culture casualties." And even now, seven years later, there are those who don't fully embrace the new culture, which demands cooperation and teamwork to be successful.

Complexity theorists know that complex systems – such as business organizations – are very sensitive, very responsive. If positive influences are present, the system can become highly creative – new ideas flow to overcome problems or exploit opportunities. Equally, if negative influences are present, the system can become inhibited – politicking replaces openness, for instance. As Raymond Robinson of nuclear medicine observed: "Things feed off each other. One person does it, so another person does it. Where hatred can be infectious, so can good emotions like care be infectious." There's an important lesson here for managers who pursue principles of complexity theory: just as you can't sit back and hope for good things to emerge out of chaos, so, too, you have to be tough with people in the organization if they threaten the health of the culture. Culture casualties are inevitable.

Now that the culture at Muhlenberg has found some stability within itself, and people are more adept at riding the roller coaster of change, they are embarking on a merger with Kennedy Hospital, where initially the management practice appears to be different. Two different cultures face each other, with unease on both sides. "I think everyone's anxiety level here [at Muhlenberg] is high," says John. "But people have consistently said, 'Let's just get on with it. Let's find out how it turns out.' It's kind of an acceptance of life and what is going on in the world. It's incredible." And what about John himself? He continues to do what he does best, investing himself in a whole new set of relationships. What will his way of being, his style of management bring to this new transition? Not even a Wizard could know. ℰ

Emerges from the Fabric
Working inside and outside

Ken Baskin, Brenda Zimmerman and Curt Lindberg

A story from Hunterdon Medical Center, Flemington, N.J.

Illustration of:
- complexity lens
- clockware/swarmware
- wicked questions
- minimum specifications
- conditions for emergence
- good-enough vision
- metaphor

Principles
- *Complexity lens*

Linda Rusch, vice president of Patient Care, Hunterdon Medical Center, believes complexity theory can help health care professionals do more than improve their hospitals' operations. By focusing on interconnections, it can help them understand the health care system that is now emerging.

"When President Reagan fired striking air traffic controllers," she explains, "many of the results arose at the family level, in higher suicide rates, broken marriages and domestic violence. Or think about drug abuse and teen-age pregnancy. Are these social issues? Or health care issues? Complexity theory tells us it's foolish to draw a sharp line between the two. They're interconnected; they affect each other.

"So what we need is a model of health care that emerges from the fabric of the community," Rusch says. "As consumers continue to revolt against the excesses of managed care, that kind of system will emerge. Already, nurses in the maternity unit collaborated with the prosecutor's office to provide an educational program on domestic violence. Complexity theory tells me that will happen, if we allow forces to run their course without trying to control it."

Unlike some of the participants on VHA's complexity task force, such a hands-off approach to management was second-nature to Rusch. Her graduate school training in psychiatry emphasized systems theory.

"I learned family therapy," she notes. "You don't direct family therapy. You create conditions, expose paradoxes and watch the dynamics play out. The healing occurs as you let people work out their problems. All these ideas are at the heart of a complexity approach to management." Even though she was used to thinking this way, Rusch at first found herself confused by complexity theory.

"About two years ago, Curt [Lindberg] was putting together the complexity task force and wanted to include nurse executives," she says. "I volunteered, but was really confused at first. We were bombarded with a barrage of new concepts, like clockware and swarmware. It was like nailing Jell-O to the wall."

But after a while, Rusch recognized that most of these ideas were "really systems theory." Now she finds many of the concepts from complexity theory indispensable, both for doing her job and teaching others to do their jobs more effectively.

Aides
• *Wicked questions*

"I loved learning to use the wicked question," she offers as an example. "You know. The question everyone is thinking, but no one has the guts to actually say. It helps people understand what's actually going on. Until they do, it's hard to resolve any problem."

Principles
• *Clockware/ swarmware*

Rusch has also become fond of the terms "clockware," those routine tasks that require careful adherence to standard procedures, and "swarmware," those for which precise outcomes are unlikely, and creativity and innovation are valuable.

"My staff goes around saying, 'We're swarming now!'" she says with a laugh. Still another of her favorite techniques is "minimum specs." The idea is to ask people to take on challenges by giving them only one or two absolute requirements, the minimum specifications. Rusch has begun working with two nurse managers in one such project.

"I asked both Carol and Pat to pretend they were the CEO of the Marriott Hotel, and write down all the things they saw in their units, but hold off on solutions," Rusch explains. "Carol came back with a three-page list of things she hadn't realized before – from the cluttered appearance of the nurses' stations to the disturbingly high level of noise."

Aides
• *Metaphor*
• *Min specs*
• *Good-enough vision*

"I'm asking Pat and Carol to work with their nurses to transform their units into 'humanistic healing environments," Rusch says. "That's all. I'm convinced that they will create two units that are both very, very customer-service oriented and good places to heal."

A final technique Rusch discusses is releasing control. She talks about it in terms of Gareth Morgan's comment: "Farmers don't grow crops. They create the conditions in which crops grow."

"My training in systems theory ensured that I'd never be a control-freak manager," she says. "But with complexity theory, my role is to set the minimum requirements and then get out of the way. I want my people to have the time to be creative, to experiment and to see what happens. That's not traditional management theory, but I see it working."

Rusch adds that, in teaching others about complexity theory, she's found the desire to drop control more widespread than she'd expected. "Some people really want to stop controlling, but are afraid," she notes.

"Everywhere, things are changing, creating high degrees of uncertainty and anxiety. And the more anxious you are, the more in control you need to be.

"Making all this even worse, we've bought into the myth that leaders have all the answers," Rusch says ."Managers who accept this myth have their levels of anxiety ratcheted up again. So when I tell people about Gareth's [Morgan] rule that we can control only about 15 percent of what's going on around us, many of these managers are enormously relieved. If complexity theory can begin freeing managers from this myth of control, I think you'll see people a whole lot more comfortable."

Rusch adds that the issue of control has also played an unexpected part in the emergence of the new health care system. "On one hand, President Clinton's attempt to impose a new health care system that emphasized control could never have worked," she explains. "On the other hand, it created an enormous amount of second-order change. Everyone in the system began to change more rapidly in response to the impending change."

Rusch also believes that managed care has become a major source of second-order change forming the new health care system.

"Managed care came into the system like an intruder," she says. "It focused on cutting costs without any understanding of what the consumer wanted. Americans are used to choices. Managed care's 'gatekeeper' model is beginning to fail. So managed care helped us get the fat out of the system. Now we're entering a period where the real changes can emerge.

"Complexity theory would suggest that these changes would arise from lots of little interactions, rather than large-scale attempts to control the system," Rusch says. "That's exactly what's happening. The AMA doesn't need to confront managed care. Instead, grass-roots efforts are popping up everywhere, with the consumer saying, I've had enough! Out of this tension between the need for containing health care costs and the demand for choice among quality alternatives, a new system is emerging, with the consumer in the driver's seat."

Rusch is convinced that the new system will emphasize public health by integrating health care professionals with community partners and public policy makers. After all, so many health issues today are also social issues.

"Many of our most costly health problems arise from social issues – violence, drug and alcohol abuse, or sexually transmitted diseases, for example. We can't really address any of these problems by staying in our hospitals and clinics," she says. "Many communities have taken their streets back from drugs and prostitution. We can help them do the work to address their health problems."

One of the major reasons Rusch wants to spread the word about complexity theory to leaders in health care is to help them become involved with this community model of health care.

"Traditionally, health care has been very bureaucratic," she says. "Now we have to break down bureaucracy's departmental silos. Complexity theory can help health care leaders see all the interdependencies. When there's an issue, it teaches us to bring everyone to the table. And as we uncover the tensions and contradictions within the system, we can help a new one emerge."

Another Way to Think

Ken Baskin, Brenda Zimmerman and Curt Lindberg

A story from Chilton Memorial Hospital, Pompton Plains, N.J.

Illustration of:

- metaphor
- tune to the edge
- reflection
- Stacey matrix
- minimum specifications

- clockware/swarmware
- complexity lens
- generative relationships

Principles
• *Complexity lens*

III. Tales

" I've found complexity theory valuable because it can help people develop a different way to think about what we do," says Debbie Zastocki, senior vice president of Clinical Services, Chilton Memorial Hospital. "Most of us learned about management in a world that seemed more stable. Faced with today's rapid change, we need a different approach, like the one complexity gives us.

"For example, as we began to redesign procedures at Chilton Memorial, I was astounded at how hospital staff reacted to the changes we made. It was as if they felt they'd personally failed because we were creating new ways to do our jobs. But once we started talking about some of the ideas from complexity theory, creative destruction, for example, we developed a different framework for thinking about what we were doing.

"Until I realized that forest fires clear the ground for new growth – that new growth is almost impossible without some destruction, I'd always thought of forest fires as purely destructive," she says. "Applying creative destruction to our restructuring helped some staff members refocus on what we were doing to ensure the future of our hospital."

Aides
• *Ecocycle*

Zastocki explains that her interest in this kind of thought had been stimulated before she was asked to work on the VHA complexity task force.

"About two years ago, I attended the Wharton nurse executive program," she says. "We talked about 'managing the space-in-between' – that is, the areas where you can't manage with clear-cut procedures. At the time, most of us understood it was important, but we had trouble getting our minds around what the 'space-in-between' was.

"Working with the complexity task force finally cleared that up for me. Ralph Stacey talks about processes being certain or uncertain and having a high or low degree of agreement about them," Zastocki says.

Aides
• *Stacey matrix*
• *Min specs*

"Processes that are certain with a high degree of agreement are easy to manage with standard procedures. We know what the outcomes have to be and how to reach them. But processes that are certain with low agreement or uncertain with high agreement are – I think – the spaces-in-between."

As an example, she cites the procedural redesign at her hospital.

"We all agreed on the minimum specs – we wanted high-quality, value-added and cost-effective care that met the needs of our patients. We were uncertain about how to perform that redesign. That was the space-in-between, and learning how to manage it has, for me, really been what this work with the complexity task force was about.

"Using what I'd learned with the task force, I began setting up cross-departmental teams to create value as our patients recognized it. We'd always assigned tasks such as drawing blood, handling meal trays or cleaning to people in separate departments. Their work was scheduled by their departments, regardless of how the patients might feel about it. Now," she adds, "we were reorganizing these tasks on the patient care units, working together creatively to serve our patients."

The odd thing, Zastocki points out, is that her staff members seemed to feel intimidated by the new procedures they developed, even when they were far more successful, for both staff and patients.

"Part of the problem seemed to me that most of us, myself included, had such a control-oriented, mechanistic idea of what we were doing," she says. "We were uncomfortable with letting new procedures emerge through self-organization. We really wanted to have every step of the way planned out. Some people even seemed to believe that in letting go of traditional control we were destroying quality.

Principles
• *Clockware/ swarmware*

"Once we'd created an innovative way of doing things, our staff wanted to get out of the space-in-between and return to certainty and agreement. I was surprised it took that pathway. But maybe I shouldn't have been so surprised. There is a need for clockware after swarmware."

Her participation in the VHA complexity task force had given her an advantage in integrating this new way of thinking about how to manage.

Aides
• *Reflection*

"At first, learning about complexity was a mental exercise," she says. "I needed to be challenged to make it more than just theory. As we talked about these issues, like letting go of control, over time, we'd begin asking questions like, 'How are you conducting meetings?' or 'How have you approached projects to encourage self-organization?' And I saw that I was verbalizing the new ideas, but living in the old world. I called what I was doing coaching, but I was actually controlling.

"The lessons I was learning were a form of personal self-emergence and self-organization. I disbanded some meetings and recrafted the way we did things. Now, we've changed nursing and patient care council management. I have a nursing council and a practice council that the staff runs. They're excited. They come up with action items. There's a feeling that they're genuinely excited about what we're doing."

The next step, she believes, is to help community groups engage in this emergent, self-organizing type of behavior.

"We believe we need to build a community-based model of health. Many of the community people we're working at first were looking for bureaucracy and certainty. They wanted us to map out the next 25 steps in the process.

"Of course, it's new territory, so there's no way to map out what will happen. Instead," she says, "we've used the principles of complexity theory to guide our collaboration."

Principles
• *Tune to the edge*

For example, the steering committee pulled together the widest diversity of people possible so that whatever emerged would come from the broadest base in the community. Members included clergy, family practice attorneys, people from the schools and business, others from mental health services, a local college and an insurance company. And because it was both self-selecting and self-organizing, the energy level has continued high and 90 percent of those who started two years ago are still on the steering committee.

Aides
• *Generative relationships*

"Each of the subgroups that has developed from the core group has evolved differently," Zastocki says. "For instance, the group dealing with depression developed a 'gatekeeper' model. They asked who would be likely to know about people in the community with this problem. The answer was that it might be a clergy person or a hairdresser or a bartender. So the group is working on strategies to make resources available to these people.

"What the group is beginning to evolve is the model of health care without walls," she says. "People should be able to draw on health care resources and support wherever they naturally come together. We will need to work in low-certainty, low-agreement activities.

"We'll have to support people who want to know more, to work in alternative modes and see what evolves – that is, we'll have to let community health care self-organize. In the end, we're likely to have a network of interacting agents – consumers, health providers, other resources – and we'll see some very interesting experiments."

The key to making this approach work, Zastocki has come to believe, is the ability of people to continue operating outside a high-certainty, high-agreement area.

"We've had challenges operating in the uncertain areas because people involved found it difficult to stay in this sometimes uncomfortable zone," she explains. "When we've been able to contain the resulting anxiety, we've been able to excite a degree of commitment beyond anything we'd expected. When we haven't, it seems the group needs to stop and regroup almost every time they try something new."

Aides

• *Metaphor*

As a result, Zastocki feels it's extremely important to find techniques for containing the anxiety that's inevitable when they're working outside comfortable, predictable areas. One technique she's found useful is metaphor, such as explaining creative destruction with the metaphor of the forest fire. Another is the spider plant.

"A spider plant doesn't plan or control its growth," she says. "It grows by self-organization until it reaches a point where it's ready to throw off a shoot. Then the shoot grows through self-organization, maybe not exactly the same as its parent, but according to its own way of developing. And the process goes on and on, until you can have a very sophisticated, very complex structure – all without control or planning.

"This is a powerful way of helping people contain their anxiety," Zastocki says. "Whether they're engaged in redesigning hospital processes by evolution or stimulating the emergence of a completely new community model of health care, the spider plant shows that it can happen – that it does happen. And, after all, we're living things, just like the spider plant. So if the spider plant can do it, why can't we?"

Unleashing People Potential
When troublemakers become superstars

Birute Regine and Roger Lewin

A story from Muhlenberg Regional Medical Center, Plainfield, N.J.

Illustration of:
- emergence
- attractors
- complexity lens
- self-organization
- tune to the edge
- minimum specifications
- generative relationships
- wicked questions
- paradox

By the time Mary Anne Keyes came on board in 1992 as the new vice president of Patient Care, nurse manager Janet Biedron had pretty much seen it all at the Muhlenberg Medical Center. She had worked there off and on since 1975, and had had her share of dealing with different management styles. Before John Kopicki came on board as chief executive officer in 1991, it was a heavily command-and-control culture and Janet, like others, had stagnated in that environment. Janet, a straightforward, cut-to-the-chase kind of person, often found herself stepping on people's toes. A free thinker, she couldn't accept a decision just because she was told to: she needed to understand the decision, and it had to make sense to her, or she wouldn't accept it. She took her work seriously and expected others to do the same, so she held people accountable. For instance, when she worked as the supervisor on the weekend shift, if a nurse manager left Friday, knowing that there was only one nurse to take care of 30 patients the next day, Janet couldn't ignore it. She'd pick up the phone and confront the nurse manager. "You knew the situation you left," she'd say, bluntly. "What do you plan to do about it?" Janet wasn't known for mincing her words.

Although she was respected, she fell under mixed reviews with her bosses: some felt threatened by her; others would get annoyed; still others would be upset. Instead of being regarded as a hard worker and a good common-sense thinker, Janet began to be perceived as a troublemaker. And a troublemaker, as someone who challenged the status quo, who recognized what was not working rather than pretending it did, who had courage to stand up for what was right rather than conform to what was expected, was regarded as bad in a command-and-control culture that demanded compliance. With no one telling her that she was doing a great job, which she was, or that the place was running fine, or appreciating that there were no problems, she began to feel perhaps her efforts to improve the work procedures and workplace was a battle not worth fighting. With no one listening, why bother any more? She stopped opening up; she stopped looking for better ways to do things. If she saw something that could be improved, she wouldn't talk about it, or try to do anything to make it better. In essence, she refused to participate. By the time Mary Anne joined Muhlenberg, Janet was out of the loop in many ways; there seemed no opportunities to be creative, no reason to innovative. She did her job of pre-hospital service, supervising eight people, and did it well. But something was missing in Janet, something essential had become dormant – her passion.

At first, Mary Anne Keyes had mixed feelings about working at Muhlenberg. Previously, she had worked exclusively at tertiary hospitals involved with large teaching institutions, and she had grown accustomed to being part of academic circles, where new concepts were discussed and applied. Continuous learning was important to her and so she didn't know how interesting a 396-bed community hospital would be in the long haul, even if it was affiliated with NJ-Rutgers Medical School. She knew she could run a nursing department: that wasn't what interested her. The challenge was figuring out how she could do it better and different each year. It wasn't long before she discovered that Muhlenberg was aswirl with innovative ideas about management that promised a kind of learning she'd never experienced before, no matter how high-powered an intellectual environment she'd been in.

Muhlenberg's CEO, John Kopicki, was participating with senior management in a VHA leadership initiative, headed by Curt Lindberg, that explored something called complexity theory as applied to the work place. Mary Anne hadn't heard of complexity theory, and at first it seemed foreign and a little abstract to her, couched in a new and strange language. But very soon, in the midst of a collective learning experience about the theory, she could see that it wasn't abstract at all. It gave her and her

Principles
• *Complexity lens*

colleagues a new perspective on the day-to-day demands on their jobs, and provided a language that named things that Mary Anne knew intuitively to be right, but that had no external validation. In short, complexity theory gave the group a common language with which to bring their efforts together, and it created a support system for change.

"What I think the language has given us, as we learned some of these things together, is more courage to do things, sometimes scary things," says Mary Anne. "It gives you that willingness to take a leap into the dark, not knowing where you are going to land, but trusting you're going to land safely, and you're going to be okay. For me, that was the most fun – the seat-of-your-pants kind of stuff. Doing what seemed like the right thing to do."

Complexity theory can seem scary in itself, at first, because it says that in complex adaptive systems – and the workplace is such a system – you simply can't predict how things might change, but you can be certain that some kind of order will emerge. Given the right conditions – the right kind of management approach – the order that emerges is going to be beneficial for the work place. To some managers, this lack of predictability, lack of control, is anathema. But to Mary Anne, it was exactly the kind of management style she had come to intuitively on her own: she knew the direction she wanted to go; and she knew she couldn't predict where she would end up; and she trusted it. Validated in her beliefs in trusting that some order will emerge, Mary Anne became, what Kopicki called, "a fearless context changer."

Express admissions

Mary Anne's initiatives for change don't come out of the blue – she listens. She pays a lot of attention to what matters to patients and what matters to her people. Through patient surveys and written responses, and asking around the units, one of the things she heard was that admissions was taking too long. It could take up to 20 hours before a patient received their first dose of antibiotics – that's serious, with someone fighting infection. And the endless waits were distressing for the patients. Mary Anne discovered that this wasn't just a Muhlenberg problem: a VHA study, published at the time she was exploring the issue, showed Muhlenberg to be pretty typical. Mary Anne put herself in the patient's position and asked the question, "What must it feel like to experience her organization as a patient?" Lacking patience in the line of waiting herself, Mary Anne's reaction was outrage. "How could we let that happen?" she demanded of herself, and then of others.

Principles
• *Tune to the edge*

There were several existing committees at Muhlenberg looking at the problem, but none was making any headway. Mary Anne discussed it with the management committee, who suggested integrating prehospital services, which was Janet's job, into other areas – it didn't need to stand alone. But Mary Anne had something else in mind. Maybe Janet could be part of the solution, part of improving the process. Soon after coming on staff, Mary Anne had made it her business to spend time getting to know her people, and they her. When she had met Janet, a seedling of an idea had formed, that here was someone with great potential. So, Mary Anne went to John and asked if she could have a shot at trying something different, to get something going on the admissions problem. "Sure, go ahead and do what you want," he said. "You have until the end of the year."

Aides
• *Min specs*

Aides
• *Generative relationships*

Mary Anne started up a task force, pulling people from all the departments, leaving the project open to anyone who wanted to participate. Among the 20 who joined was Janet, unaware that her job was in jeopardy. This was the first time in Janet's 20-plus years of experience that she attended a meeting chaired by a senior management person. Usually it was middle management that headed these types of task forces. What Mary Anne's presence said to Janet and the rest of the members was that "this woman means business." Although her mostly negative experience with management made Janet guarded at first, she sensed in Mary Anne something different, someone who genuinely cared, who wanted change. The status quo was shifting and Janet began to feel hopeful – there might be a chance to improve something, an opportunity to change and grow. Maybe something would finally get done. Mary Anne began the meeting by simply and directly stating that the current admission time was unacceptable. And she had some ideas on how to change it, something different at the front end.

As Mary Anne began to sketch out her ideas and interact with people on the task force, Janet experienced a chemistry of connection with her that held the promise of transformation. "I thought of it as a new beginning for me," she recalls, still moved by the power of the moment. "It was like coming up from the trenches." The connection was mutual. From the first meeting it was clear to Mary Anne that Janet could not only conceptualize what she, Mary Anne, was trying to do, but Janet was the one who could implement it. Their meeting was synergistic, connecting each of them to their passion, their knowledge and their wealth of experience.

Principles
• *Tune to the edge*

Aides
• *Wicked questions*

Even though she had been told Janet was trouble, that was no trouble for her. "I was looking for someone who could do what was needed to be done," explains Mary Anne. "I didn't worry about the fact that someone was ticked off because Janet disturbed the equilibrium. In fact, that's what I wanted – someone who could shake things up." Mary Anne perceived a troublemaker differently and appreciated rather than devalued Janet's characteristics, because, she was one herself. CEO John Kopicki recognizes these attributes in Mary Anne, and values her for those very qualities. "She drives me nuts," he says with a laugh. "Mary Anne has no satisfaction. She'll ask a million and one questions as to why. She has this constant quest for trying to understand and what can we do about it. Unfortunately, that's not always understood by everyone."

Troublemakers are often misunderstood. Their resistance to buckle under cultural pressure is not seen as a healthy integrity; their challenges are not seen as potentially innovative. They are not seen as envelope pushers. In a command-and-control culture that is invested in predictability and constancy, troublemakers ruffle feathers, rock the boat –

troublemakers need to be put in their place. But in cultures that value adaptation and change, as in Muhlenberg, troublemakers are the movers who push organizations to their creative edges, where new opportunities emerge. So it's not surprising that Mary Anne and Janet would have a powerful connection that would mutually unleash their capabilities, that would set each other off. All the characteristics of a troublemaker that were regarded as bad in a command-and-control culture, now became assets.

As with most task forces, the work quickly devolved to a few people, with Mary Anne and Janet at the helm. Their skills were complementary – Mary Anne had the clout to get things done and Janet knew how to get there. They were on a mission – working alongside each other, determined to make the project a success. In less than two months they were ready to set up a two-week pilot project, with Janet overseeing it and Mary Anne "cheering her on." What emerged was something neither of them could have anticipated or predicted.

The first step was a natural one – to take the fragmented admitting process and do it up front, in a centralized location at the entrance of the hospital. The intent was to have all the paperwork and orders, including radiology, completed before the patient went up to the floor. "It seemed so simple an idea, so obvious," says Janet, "we thought it couldn't possibly be the answer!" But it was. Notably, the project was largely supported by people who weren't directly involved. For instance, assistant vice president Beverly Rolstrum-Blenman recommended two people whom she knew would do an excellent job. Others cooperated by freeing people from their regular duties to participate in the two-week pilot – not a small sacrifice.

Janet knew she had to have the right people for the job, people who could respond to the challenge of being pioneers, people who could come up with ideas of there own, and make them work. Here, Janet's long tenure at Muhlenberg was an important asset: she knew everyone, and she was able to choose carefully. "Had we had the wrong people in the pilot, it may have had a different turn," Janet admits. There were lots of possibilities for things to go wrong, for other departments to get in their way – but instead they got cooperation, such as X-ray squeezing patients in for them. The project was a huge success. In less than three months, admission time was down to 80 minutes. And much of it was due to Janet, who deftly navigated her way around any obstacle, who never doubted the success of the project. Uncertain how it might happen, yes. But doubtful, never.

Departments quickly saw the benefits of upfront admission, and support for the project grew. The management committee quickly approved full implementation. Janet insisted on not rushing the project – she wanted to do it right from the start. "We'll be up and running when we're ready," was Janet's answer to "When is it starting?" Again, she recruited carefully for the expanded unit. Her approach was to have each person be an expert in one of the skills needed in the unit, from secretary to lab person. Then she cross-trained them. Given that no cross-training courses existed, she developed her own. It took a year for the staff to go from being an expert in one thing to being expert in everything. Staff members were happy, because their jobs had expanded, they had learned new skills and their work was more diversified. The staff set up the unit themselves, right down to the adhesive bandages, because, according to Janet, "The way I looked at it was, I'm not going to set up my kitchen and ask you to come cook in it. They had to set it up; they had to make it theirs."

But the project didn't end there; it continued to evolve and grow. As part of preadmission testing and express admission, the unit's staff were doing blood work, electrocardiograms and so forth, and Janet wondered with Mary Anne why they had separate departments unnecessarily duplicating the services? Regular admissions on one hand and emergency room admissions on the other. So the two were consolidated. The unit was doing the registration and preadmission testing, and so was ER and outpatient admission testing. Why wasn't it all one? So they collapsed that too. Since managed care required information from patients prior to actual admission, why not include the financial counseling up front as well? Steadfast throughout, Janet and Mary Anne saw changes as opportunities rather than threats. As a result, express admission was flying.

The ward nurses loved it because all the admission work was done prior to the patient coming to the floor, and they could focus on getting the patient comfortable. The doctors loved it because, it was a "can do" unit – any additional services they requested were always possible. Most of all, the patients loved it. And Janet, director of admissions, now headed a department of 87 people.

Professional growth through relationship

Leadership is obviously critical to the success of any project. So what was it about Mary Anne's way of leading that created conditions for something new to emerge, something extremely successful, both in cost efficiency and in staff and patient satisfaction? What skills did she employ that helped people grow professionally?

We can find an answer here, by looking at it through the lens of complexity theory. In formal terms, the theory says that interesting properties can emerge from a complex system when the components of the system interact in simple but rich ways. Translated to the work place, this means that emergence happens when there is a lot of interaction between individuals who mutually affect one another. Interaction between individuals are relationships; and when people mutually affect one

Principles
• *Complexity lens*

another there is a quality of connection. Complexity theory therefore places positive relationships as central to the creativity, adaptability, achievement and effectiveness that emerges in an organization. It is Mary Anne's relational intelligence and her ability to foster connections that she brings to her management style – intentionally, skillfully and strategically. Motivated by her desire for growth in people, she allows the organic unfolding of processes at work within the organization and within people. No wonder John Kopicki calls her a "grower of people." Mary Anne's style of leadership emphasizes four relational skills that encourage organizational change and expand human possibilities: mutuality, acknowledgment, encouragement and presence.

Mutuality

Mutuality in relationships is the shared power to affect and the shared vulnerability to be affected by another person. Mutuality places people on a common ground that allows for new understandings, new knowledge to emerge. For Mary Anne, mutuality manifested in her being influenced by Janet's ideas, just as Janet was by Mary Anne's. As Mary Anne states, "My relationship with Janet is easy for me. I look forward to an appointment with her. It's not a reporting relationship; she's a professional colleague. We get together and try to figure things out together, doing the best we can." Through her relationship with Janet, Mary Anne realized her potential, just as Janet found hers through her relationship with Mary Anne.

Implicit in mutuality is an emergent and fluctuating authority, where expertise shifts from person to person, and where people recognize a dependence on each other for knowledge and information in order to achieve the best outcome. With their wealth of work experience, their education, fluctuating authority came naturally to Mary Anne and Janet. Generally, Mary Anne minimizes status differences in her interactions with staff, which allows her to learn from others and allows others to have an affect on the organization. "I think you need people to be engaged in the process," says Mary Anne, "and they have to trust that there's a chance that they have some sway over what's going to happen. If they feel like there's no opportunity to influence, then you're wasting everybody's time around the table." In this way, mutuality creates a kind of feedback loop. Mary Anne listens to people's concerns, which influences her focus on what needs to change, which in turn affects the organization, which affects the people in the organization.

Principles
• *Tune to the edge*

Underscoring mutuality of influence and authority is mutual respect – the relational dynamic that nourishes trust, that holds people accountable to each other, that inspires people to reach beyond what they think is possible. And with mutual respect, loyalty emerges. "I have a loyalty to the organization, but even more than the organization I feel a loyalty to Mary Anne," says Janet. "I wouldn't want to let her down. She saw something in me and I wouldn't do anything to jeopardize that. So I go that extra mile."

Acknowledgment

The ability to "see" the capabilities of others and acknowledge not only what they do but who they are is a powerful relational skill that Mary Anne brings to her leadership. Her capacity to see the visible (that is, what she observes) and the invisible (the competencies she brings out) enhances professional growth and achievement in her people. What was visible to some people was that Janet was a troublemaker. What was visible to Mary Anne was that "she was in the wrong spot, doing the wrong kind of things." In Mary Anne's assessment, there aren't any losers, but rather misplaced achievers – people in the wrong context.

Mary Anne also saw what was invisible to many people: "Janet knows what she wants, she's very directed." But seeing without acknowledging it would not be much different from not seeing it at all. Mary Anne speaks of Janet this way: "By the time we got together and I started working with Janet, what she was capable of was much more than she was ever given the opportunity to do. How she's grown in the last three years! Her's is the only self-directed unit we've got here. She's a real star in this organization!" And Janet recognizes and appreciates being seen by Mary Anne. "Mary Anne saw in me what only my mother saw in me," she says, with a peel of laughter. "She sees that I'm an honest player, I call it like I see it. If I believe in it you get 100 percent, 200 percent. If I don't, you get zip."

Mary Anne and Janet's relationship highlights the power acknowledgment has in generating competency, collaboration and a pioneering spirit. Although Mary Anne acknowledges Janet with a sincerity and obvious pleasure in her achievement, this kind of behavior often gets minimized as simply "being nice." Such a view is extremely misguided, because what Mary Anne is displaying here is a highly successful relational skill for creating a team spirit, something that many managers often strive for in vain, by mouthing words such as "empowerment" and "team-building," while still holding a vice grip of control.

Encouragement

Mary Anne encourages people in many ways – she supports, she challenges, she nudges. But what is most striking is just how little it takes. "A lot of people in hospitals just feel they can't do certain things," she explains. "And I say, 'why can't you?' Once you start asking why you can't, pretty soon it's, 'let's go, let's do this.' I mean, you unleash some power. It's just unbelievable. All people need is a little support and encouragement to get them going. People are capable of much more than we give them credit for. People think I have the power to give permission. All I have is the power to encourage. Maybe."

Paradoxical presence

Mary Anne's presence as a leader has a profound influence on the environment of the organization. She validates a different way of knowing – that is, listening and acting on intuition. She intuitively does what is right, which allows others to do the same. As she says, "If it feels right, do it." Again, this might be dismissed as being "fuzzy" or not "rigorous." But it is an important management skill, and it takes courage.

Her presence in the organization embodies many paradoxes. As a leader she gives direction to the concerns of the organization: what issues need to be addressed, what changes need to occur. At the same time she gets out of the way and allows others to act on these concerns. Direction without directives, authority without control. Mary Anne sees the influence of her presence in this way. "One of the things that I think makes this approach to management successful is having the ability to pick out a focus people can grab onto, giving them a little bit of support along the way – it doesn't take much – so that they can do what they need to do."

Principles
• *Paradox*

III. Tales

Janet experiences Mary Anne's presence in this way: "For me, what made her management style successful was that I was given freedom, but also guidance. You have to have both – you can't just have space, independence and freedom without guidance. If she had approached me differently from the way she did, I doubt I would have supported her the way I did." The paradox of structure and no structure is a way of leading that nurtures emergence, self-organization and innovation in the work place. And we learn from complexity, that paradox is a positive sign – the presence of paradox is a hallmark of creativity and its potential.

Aides
• *Min specs*

In addition, Mary Anne's presence, endowed with relational skill, allows people to see things for themselves, in their own terms and in their own time. "Mary Anne is a sounding board for me," says Janet. "I could say, 'this is what I'm thinking,' and with her experience, Mary Anne would know if I'm going down the wrong road, and she'd tell me. But she wouldn't say, 'that's a cliff you are jumping off,' but instead she'd say, 'have you thought about it this way?' She wouldn't say, 'don't do that.' I don't have that kind of relationship with too many people. Talking to Mary Anne helps me organize my priorities."

An outcome of Mary Anne's method of leadership – direction without directives – might be described as the Chinese-cooking style of management:

you spend a lot of time preparing the food, but when you're ready, the cooking goes fast. "I could be the kind of leader who says, 'By God, this is what we're going to do, and this is how it's going to be done," Mary Anne says. "I could make everybody do whatever I decided, but it's not the most effective way of managing people." Instead, argues Mary Anne, it is better to take the time needed to involve people in figuring out what change needs to happen, and how to achieve that change. In Mary Anne's style of leadership, acceptance is the endpoint of a project, not its implementation. With thoughtful and participatory preparation, which takes time, the change then gets done quickly and people are comfortable with it. "Overall, this approach might take longer in the upfront phase than the more traditional approach," says Mary Anne, "But I think it's worth it, because the other way, you spend a lot more time fighting with everybody telling you why it's not working and trying to fix it. You don't have to keep explaining it every six months."

The source of adaptability

The power of these relational skills is not only in their promise to unleash dormant potential in others, but also, by example, demonstrating a different way of working. When Janet talks about managing her people, for example, she manages them much in the same fashion, according to the same relational skills that guide Mary Anne.

Unleashing potential is an obvious management goal. But it is not simple. Practicing mutuality, encouragement, presence and acknowledgment are just that – a practice. And Mary Anne could vow for the fluctuating nature of such a practice – the waters are not always clear, in fact they're more often muddy. But it is practice that recognizes the true source of success. John Howard Jr., the Director of Muhlenberg between 1935-1946, put it this way: "A hospital is a human institution. Its success is not built of bricks or beds or scientific equipment, but of human beings – doctors, nurses, employees, volunteers, patients and the public." The current culture of Muhlenberg, engendered under the leadership of John Kopicki through top managers such as Mary Anne and Janet, has returned the hospital to its roots of care, as expressed by Howard.

Creating work relationships founded on the relational principles we've described not only make for a better work place, but it is also sound business strategy. It is the quality of relationships in organizations that can foster a sense of community. And it is within a community that people have a greater willingness to change and adapt – qualities that can determine whether a health care organization can and will survive these uncertain times.

And whether troublemakers can become stars. So, look around in your own organization and hope to find some troublemakers.

Learn-As-You-Go
Strategic Management
*Forget about the overarching plan
in highly uncertain times*

Brenda Zimmerman and Curt Lindberg

A story from University of Louisville Hospital, Louisville, Ky.

Illustration of:
- emergence
- creating conditions
- action learning
- complexity lens
- reflection
- coevolution
- attractors
- reflection
- multiple actions

The board members of University of Louisville Hospital had just hired a new chief executive officer. One of his early challenges was to create a strategic plan for the next five years and beyond. The board and senior management had already gathered some consultants' proposals from highly respected national and international firms. It was expected that James Taylor, the new CEO, would choose between the proposals and carry out the work.

He struggled with how we was going deal with his new board on this. He decided to be direct.

"The strategic planning idea didn't make any sense in the rapidly evolving health care environment. I told the board that we should put aside the proposals to do a $500,000 strategic plan and get on with addressing the strategic issues themselves. They already had identified the key strategic issues. We knew what they were. I said that I thought we should learn as we go from dealing with those issues if we are going to survive in this strange organizational environment. Let us learn and evolve."

Although Taylor was worried about whether the board would see him as "some kind of weird guy," they accepted his ideas about acting on the strategic issues and learning through the process.

Principles
- *Complexity lens*

He fosters an action-learning, issues-oriented approach. Consultants are hired but only if they agree to work with the team as colearners "to add richness and diversity to our discussion. Consultants who propose to come up with solutions or figure out the process for us" are not considered.

Taylor found that most consultants and managers generally do not understand his request.

"It is hard to get people comfortable with the idea of step-by-step, good-enough-as-you-go, and not falling back into the idea that we can plan our way out of all this or avoiding the real issues by continually studying. The tendency is to get some experts, plan it and avoid talking about what the real issues are."

The hospital made progress on some of the key strategic issues facing the hospital including the relationship with two other hospitals in the city. Collaboration is not implemented on an overall basis but on an issue-by-issue basis to discover what works and what does not work. Mistakes are made. They learn from action.

Aides
• *Reflection*

"I was talking with my board president the other day about some of the difficult strategic issues that we are working our way through. He said that he thought I was the most patient person he had ever run across. I looked at him a bit startled. He said that he meant it as a compliment. He said the unique organizational situation we were facing meant I was not in control. My ability to get things done, as in any complex adaptive system, is dependent upon a lot of others who I cannot command. I guess my view of the way things work makes me seem patient – not always without frustration."

> **Reflection:** *Strategic planning is built on concepts of separation of thought and action, separation of planners and implementors, predictability of the future within probabilities and the capacity to fill a niche or create a new niche. All of these concepts assume a relatively stable environment in which the players in the market are known or at least predictable, the shape of the industry or market is known or knowable and the levers of power or influence are known or predictable. Health care in the U.S. and Canada does not fit these criteria. The one knowable concept is that health care will not look like it does today in a decade. It is not clear who the providers will be or the source of power or which new industries will emerge to assume some of the responsibilities traditionally assumed by hospitals or doctors and nurses.*

The concept of emergent strategy is not new, nor is the idea of the lack of separation between strategy formulation and implementation. However, the traditional approach of senior executives planning the strategy for others to implement still dominates much of the strategy literature and practice in organizations.

Taylor's story does not deal with the identification of the strategic issues. Some were known and some emerged. His concern from experience was that knowing the strategic issues existed was the easy part. Knowing what to do with them was the challenge. His story is about how to address the strategic issues through a layered process of action and reflection – the learn-as-you-go approach.

"It's a more pragmatic, action orientation that says here are the strategic issues so let's address them the best we can. Let's keep our eyes open and find out what we can learn and make sure that we see the new strategic issues as they come or the present ones as they fall away. Let's make sure we create an organizational environment where we can see those things – where we can learn from our actions."

Taylor had the courage and humility to challenge the ideas of strategic planning at his hospital. His ideas of emergence, coevolution and unpredictability are informed by complexity. His choice of interventions, including using minimum critical specifications and finding small actions that connect with the larger strategic issues, are also based on his belief in organizations as complex adaptive systems. However, for the most part he has not brought these ideas explicitly into the open. He has chosen to work with what he believes are the attractors in the system. He works with what will attract people to address a key strategic issue.

Taylor is tackling the hard issues in his organization. For example, he has worked on a collaborative model for a regional cancer care system. But rather than try to reach consensus on topics such as this in which there are politics, little agreement and no certainty, he tries to find small actions and specific topics that they can act on to address the big picture. Lessons from the actions are then fed back as learning for the next loop. It is learn as you go for Taylor. Reflection is important in this process. He uses reflection to recognize the patterns in the interactions between the people and issues. This pattern recognition is an ongoing process. He never assumes he understands it all. It is a never-ending inquiry about himself, the hospital and health care.

Principles
• *Multiple actions*

Aides
• *Reflection*

"It isn't a good expectation for people to think that their leaders can tell what the future is going to be," said Taylor. "We've got to get people past that and not allow that to be an excuse for not stepping up to the hard strategic issues and working through them." 〰

What We Could Be Doing Together

Ken Baskin, Brenda Zimmerman and Curt Lindberg

A story from Memorial Hospital of Burlington County, Mt. Holly, N.J.

Illustration of:
- complexity lens
- generative relationships
- shadow system
- chunking
- good-enough vision

"In the end, complexity theory makes you ask what projects make sense in the world you live and work in," says Jim Dwyer, vice president of Medical Affairs, Memorial Hospital of Burlington County. "As an administrator, I've always gone into planning sessions with a clear idea of what the outcome should be. But since I've been studying complexity, I'm open to more ideas. I don't need to have all the answers, so I'm willing to draw on the experience of anyone who can help ensure the best results."

Principles
- *Complexity lens*

This sense that he didn't have to be in total control, because no one could be, attracted Dwyer to complexity studies from his earliest work with the New Jersey VHA task force.

"It was reassuring to hear people talk about all the things that were out of our control," he says. "After all, in health care we're working with complex systems where the future is sometimes unidentifiable, and relationships aren't necessarily permanent. No one can be fully in control of those kinds of situations, and it made me comfortable to hear a scientific explanation of why that was true."

Dwyer cites the concept of "generative relationships" as one that makes him more flexible and, therefore, more effective.

Aides
- *Generative relationships*

"In the past," he says, "if I were trying to develop a partnership with another physician group, I'd try to bring other people around to the right way – that is, my way – of seeing things. With generative relationships, on the other hand, I begin by showing them what we could be doing together. Then we define what we're both comfortable with and let the relationship grow from there."

As an example, Dwyer points to the discussion his hospital recently had with a primary care group that had a standing relationship with another hospital in the county.

"They initiated the discussion because they were interested in the network of physicians we've been building," he says. "As we talked, they expressed some fears about having to accommodate the management systems and protocols we'd already begun developing. A couple of years ago, I might have tried to convince them that our systems really were the best. But that doesn't seem necessary anymore. So I explained that they didn't have to use our systems, that we could work together in whatever way was best for them.

"Once we demonstrate that we can work together, and they experience how much they have to gain in the process, we can let the relationship grow. Our relationship doesn't have to appear all at once. It's a lot more comfortable for everyone if we let it emerge, let it generate itself."

Principles
• *Shadow system*

Another idea from complexity theory that Dwyer believes has made him more flexible is Ralph Stacey's "shadow system." Stacey notes that most organizations have a dominant system responsible for making day-to-day operations work. They also have a shadow system that plays with innovations that might replace those of the dominant system. Stacey explains that, in markets changing as quickly as health care, it's important for management to be able to tap the potential contributions of the shadow system. Dwyer learned the importance of being able to tap this hidden system with the quality process hospital management put together in 1996.

"We had this formal mechanism for approving quality improvement projects," he says. "We needed it because projects were being pursued without any idea of whether the effort needed for them would be worth the value they produced. Unfortunately, the process became so difficult and took so much time, people were losing their enthusiasm over worthwhile projects." The dominant system was discouraging needed innovation.

"Then, one day, several doctors and nurses got to talking, probably in the cafeteria, about how some of their patients weren't getting anticoagulants quickly enough. So one physician researched the problem and ended up forming a team – I was asked to participate – to study the problem and how other hospitals were handling it. We ended up creating a procedure to ensure that anticoagulants were administered more effectively."

This group was part of the hospital's shadow system. Everything its members did was outside the official quality program. When Dwyer and other members of the dominant quality structure discussed what had happened, they decided to re-examine the official quality program.

"Basically, we decided to turn the structure upside-down," he says. "We created lots of opportunities for people to generate projects and restructured our quality program to support them. As experts, we can help them identify their needs and help them get the data and support they need. But we expect we'll see a lot more important projects because we've found a way to tap the shadow system."

Dwyer's even been able to extend this idea of shadow systems outside the hospital and into his community.

"I'd noticed that managed care had cut down on utilization of our resources, and that many people were suffering because of it," he explains. "At the same time, many people in health care are willing to give their time to help those who were suffering. To connect those with resources and those who needed them, my local parish created a health ministry to catalogue available resources and connect those resources with the people who need them.

"Sometimes it's as simple as pointing people in the right direction or holding their hands. But the idea is straight out of complexity theory: Develop a shadow system to connect the people that the dominant structure has overlooked to resources that this shadow system can now make available," Dwyer says.

In some ways, Dwyer believes this community-based parish effort points to what could be happening to the emerging health care system.

"It's obvious that the system has become too conscious of costs, rather than quality," he points out. "The negative reaction of the public is beginning to reverse this trend, and there are a number of signs about what could emerge.

"A year-and-a-half ago, I was at a VHA session where a consultant, Gus Jaccaci, indicated that we're moving toward a more community-oriented approach that will focus on illness prevention," Dwyer says. "This kind of community-based model would give people a significant role in managing their own health, responsibility would be spread out across the community."

Principles
• *Good-enough vision*

Such a system would favor the kind of generative relationships that Dwyer has begun building.

"The Columbia/HCAs of the world have driven a wave of hospital mergers that have downsides they never thought about," he explains. "Our approach is to serve the community by creating relationships that allow partnering organizations to benefit mutually, yet retain their identities.

"For me, this is the fun part of health care," Dwyer says. "How can we develop relationships that will develop a healthier community, rather than merely a fatter bottom line? I'm convinced that Curt [Lindberg] is right – that we can't plan and create a complete system."

Aides
• *Chunking*

Rather we need to develop it in components, from the bottom. We have to connect and make things more complex and adaptive. "No one organization can do everything. We need to take the best out of each organization and create a network that continues to shift and adapt."

A Leap Into Uncertainty

David Hutchens

A story from HealthEast, Greenville, N.C.

Illustration of:
- tune to the edge
- good-enough vision
- generative relationships
- complexity lens
- attractors
- self-organization

W hat role does courage play in the application of complexity theory? It's not a question that Tom Irons would have thought to ask in the Spring of 1995 when he was named president of HealthEast. Given the task of purchasing medical practices and developing practice management services to increase the educational and referral base of HealthEast's parent hospital and sister medical school, Tom's challenge was one that required keen business insight, fortitude, even political acumen.

But *courage*? No one – including Tom – would have guessed that it would become the central job requirement.

"The pressure was getting intense," reflected Irons, a self-professed cowboy-booted Southern boy whose Carolina drawl masks an intellectual intensity. "On the one side of me were rapidly growing IPAs, eager for capital and posturing against each other, often through me. On the other side was my parent hospital, anxious for me to start linking up with physicians as quickly as possible. And all along, I was getting this sneaking suspicion that I didn't need to be in the business of purchasing practices or working with these IPAs. The practices were too expensive, and the IPAs had their own agendas and no infrastructure."

Flanked by organizational forces that were beyond his scope of influence, Tom began to realize that it was fruitless to try to directly control the direction the system was taking. Perhaps it was time to create something in a new way. The question was, what would that be?

It was time to get courageous.

The leap into uncertainty

Time was passing and the hospital was becoming nervous. Irons had been hired to forge new relationships with physicians, but those relationships weren't emerging. Management services organizations were not an immediate answer. And with the available nonowner relationship structures, there was little incentive for clinical integration or innovation.

Increasingly aware that the old owning-and-controlling model was producing very little, Irons couldn't ignore his intuition any longer. "That's when I made the radical decision," he said. "I decided I would cease working with the IPAs. I would keep positive relationships with them, but there would be no more conversations about financial commitments. As for buying practices, I would do this only in the exceptional cases where there was a competing offer or where physician services in a community were imperiled."

Principles
• *Tune to the edge*

Irons was now in unchartered territory, where terrain was uncertain and direction was unknown. It was in this ambiguous place that he would begin to discover a new way to influence the development of the system.

Aides
• *Generative relationships*
• *Min Specs*

"The first thing I did was get help," Irons recalled. "I began looking for a small group of physicians here in the North Carolina region who I felt were key leaders. Not knowing exactly where I was headed, I selected them based on these four simple criteria:

"One: They must have high clinical credibility.

"Two: they must have absolute personal integrity.

"Three: They must have strong interest in a system of care, in addition to their individual practices.

"Four: They must have this vital shared belief: that whatever we create will improve the health status of the people we serve.

"In retrospect," Irons noted, "I realize how radical this final criterion was. Most health programs only pretend to aspire to that goal. That's their fundamental flaw!"

Tom found four physicians who met the criteria. He convened with the group, offering to compensate them for the time they spent away from their practices. A little tentative, but excited at the prospect of creating something new, all four agreed.

"So, just what is it we're going to actually *do?*" they wanted to know.

Irons confessed: "I don't know. We're going to begin growing this thing before we know what it is." And that's what they did.

An emergence of the new

The plan was almost haphazardly simple: to solicit the support of physicians around the region who were of a like mind with Irons and his team, and find ways to facilitate a mutual coming-together.

But reality soon set in. "At the end of our second session together," said Irons, "we all said *we can't do this*. What would we offer doctors? What would prevent us from doing just what the IPAs were doing – that is, growing and posturing with no real ability to change systems of care? We agreed that what we could do is start from the bottom and build something new – a grass-roots effort that could become a model that the rest of the system may or may not choose to adopt."

So the team agreed upon two central goals: "*We must improve the health status of the people we serve*," and "*Our efforts cannot hurt the hospital or school of medicine, rather, we will support the educational mission of the school and the service mission of the hospital.*"

Principles
• *Good-enough vision*

With those two key parameters in place, the small group of physicians divided into four task forces. ("Each was a task force of one!" Irons recalls bemusedly.) They identified the issues of *structure and governance, information systems, practice reengineering and medical management*, with each task force investigating one issue. The task forces got to work, and by the end of three sessions, they realized these systems in their current state were fragmented, had misaligned incentives and, in short, could not integrate care in such a way as to improve outcomes or increase financial value. So again came confirmation of what they had sensed all along: if they were ever going to get off the ground, they needed to create something new.

Irons reflected: "That was the beginning of a year of extremely difficult work. During that time, the outside pressures never let up! But it became obvious to others that the five of us were determined, and threats and pressures from many sides began to diminish. Still, we were constantly on trial. People were thinking 'This work can't be right – you're spending too much time here while Rome is burning!'"

It was a fearful time, too. "We never stopped feeling unsure, afraid and anxious," Irons confessed. "We knew we could fail. It was a real possibility. But our trust in each other was what finally held us together. In fact, the greatest part of our work was in building lasting, trusting relationships among the five of us."

Confirmation from complexity

It was October of 1997 and the team was hard at work. It was during that time Tom Irons attended a VHA learning network meeting on the subject of complexity – a subject to which he had been introduced only recently.

"It was dramatic," he said. "As I sat there, I could hardly contain myself. I went back the next week and told my team, 'I have marvelous news! I just got tremendous reinforcement that what we're doing is right! Now I understand why we have to do it this way!'

"So I brought three of my teammates to the VHA Complexity and Health Care Conference in December of 1997. After just two hours of presentation, they were stunned. They said *'My God, this is us!'*"

Irons and his team sat entranced over the course of the two-day seminar as they learned the central tenets of complexity management: that systems in which people are far from certainty and agreement can be breeding grounds for creativity and innovation; that order can spontaneously emerge from complex adaptive systems if you nurture it, and don't try to control it; that complexity principles can guide us in creating a new future, even when we don't have a clear vision of what that future should be.

Indeed, Irons and his team realized they had been practicing complexity theory all along. Now they had a language to give shape and confirmation to what they had been doing intuitively. "We immediately wrote down our min specs," said Irons, referring to the principle of *minimum specification*, which indicates that a few simple rules are sufficient for producing amazingly diverse and complex self-organizing behaviors in a system.

"Then we began thinking about our 15 percent," said Irons, referring to another complexity principle that suggests we have the ability to influence only 15 percent of what goes on in our system, and the rest is left up to forces beyond our control. Therefore, by finding and leveraging that critical 15 percent, leaders may produce remarkable, systemwide change. "We said to ourselves, we are the 15 percent!" said Irons.

"We also realized we were creating a new *strange attractor*." (That is, a new model around which activity could organize.) "The old attractors –

the existing systems of structure, governance, practice reengineering and so on – weren't capable of achieving the goals of improving the health status of its people.

"As we listened and participated, a burden lifted from us," Irons said. "We realized we had been dealing with a nonlinear phenomenon all along. We were almost jumping up and down!"

Trust and courage

"I look where we are now, and where we began," Irons said with a laugh. "I thought that by now, we'd have a very clear structure in place and we'd be selling it to our practices. I thought we would create a business, recruit some doctors, the hospital would put up X amount of dollars and people would come. But we just kept putting off bringing in the consultant, because we didn't know yet what we wanted to build. Instead, we discovered we had to let the new system emerge. We couldn't force it. We could only nurture and facilitate it."

Where does the effort stand now?

"Some creative ideas are really beginning to emerge," Irons said. "We're looking at some new ways to merge practices. And we are working on some emerging disease management programs in heart failure, diabetes and more. It's slow going. We're finding that change is incremental instead of sudden and massive. But we are continuing the collaboration necessary to redesign the system.

"The trust we built in our team is expanding to the outside," Irons added. "In the beginning, our hospital partners responded to us with skepticism, and even competed with us for resources and control. They perceived our actions as being control-centered. But we just stayed focused on our min specs, and most of the skeptics are coming to realize we're interested in building bridges – not gaining control. We still have some skeptics, but as others have watched our work emerge, they have caught fire! They've said, 'this is important – not just your goal, but the process you're using.'"

Today, those skeptics see an emerging physician equity model network, in which community hospitals and physicians all have a stake in its success. And it's built around managing *care* rather than costs, with the business structure evolving to accommodate function.

"You know, that trust we built was key," Irons said. "It was hard to get here, but today the trust we have is extraordinary. One doctor on our team was having some problems back in his practice that were making it difficult for him to keep the vision. So each of us met with him often to offer our help. That's the kind of relationship we have.

"Now we call each other almost every day, just to share what we've learned or read. It's very infectious. And it's all the result of creating a new attractor."

Even though he is equipped with the tools and language of complexity theory, Irons is quick to point out that fear is still a real element. "There were many times at the beginning of this work I was tempted just to go back and start buying practices, because it's easier," he admitted. "But now I wouldn't dream of it. My confidence is growing. At its core, a complexity approach is about letting go of control to let a structure self-organize. It's the letting go that's frightening."

"And we could still lose," he added. "But we're building a powerful new attractor, and closing out the influence of other attractors. I don't know quite what's going to happen in the future. But it's going to be good."

So, this is a story still in progress?

"You bet it's still in progress," Irons responded. "And I hope it never gets out of progress. If you build something good, it never stops changing, growing and evolving. This 15 percent is my chance to make a real difference.

"I think I'll be really proud of this someday. How often do you get to say that?"

Worldwide Complexity
*Strategic planning for a
not-for-profit health care organization*

Paul Plsek

A story from the Institute for Health Care Improvement, Boston, Mass.

Illustration of:
*   emergence (application as a planning principle)
*   reflection
*   minimum specifications
*   metaphor
*   complexity lens

The Institute for Healthcare Improvement is a not-for-profit corporation based in Boston. IHI's mission is to "help lead the improvement of health care systems, to increase continuously their quality and value," and it's vision is to be "recognized as a premier integrative force." IHI was founded in 1989 by Donald M. Berwick, M.D. (the current chief executive officer), and has grown in eight years from a grant-funded group of three people to a self-sustaining organization of about 30 employees with a multimillion dollar annual budget. IHI provides courses in improvement technology, annual conferences, publications and "Breakthrough Series Improvement Projects," in which 20 or more health care organizations work collaboratively to generate improvements in targeted areas (reducing c-sections, for example).

I have known Don Berwick for many years and personally played an active role in the early work of the Institute. While I am an independent consultant in health care quality management, I have maintained my friendship with Don and an ongoing association with the Institute.

While IHI's mission statement states "our initial focus is primarily on the health care systems of the United States and Canada," the Institute has engaged in various efforts in other parts of the world. IHI co-sponsors an annual European Quality Forum along with the British Medical Association. IHI faculty have also conducted courses and provided modest consulting help in the Middle East, Norway, Sweden and the Netherlands. These efforts have been largely responsive to personal requests for help from individuals who are friends of Don Berwick.

In early 1997, Don and the organization's chief operating officer, Maureen Bisognano (another person I have known for many years), had concluded, along with a few IHI board members, that there was an opportunity for IHI to expand its work internationally. The thinking at that time was that IHI had a great deal of knowledge on improvement to offer health care organizations in other countries, but that simply responding to requests for help from personal friends was not an effective way to disseminate that knowledge. Preliminary ideas about potentially better ways included setting up branch offices in other countries, establishing franchise agreements with local organizations in other countries, and/or forming a board of directors in Europe with the goal of establishing an IHI-like organization there.

Maureen contacted me in February 1997 to ask if I would take on a part-time, senior leadership position at the Institute to lead an expanded international effort. Specifically, the first task was to sort through the variety of options and produce a business plan for the effort. I agreed to take on this work with a commitment of three to four days per month over the next three years.

Reflection. *The situation is being primarily viewed through a somewhat standard MBA lens. A successful organization wants to grow and there are a variety of existing business models to choose from. Therefore, a business plan is needed to sort the choices and project revenues and expenses. The story could have proceeded from this point with data collection for an environmental scan and an analysis of the strengths, weaknesses, opportunities and threats, leading to quantified benefits and risks associated with the various options.*

Principles
• *Complexity lens*

On the other hand, when viewed through a complexity lens it is clear that there is a massive, multilevel complex adaptive system here. Each country is itself a CAS of health care organizations, leaders, regulators and others. IHI leaders know from their experience that it is hard to plan (in the standard, MBA way) for the evolving needs in the U.S. health care system. This difficulty would now be multiplied as the thinking expands to multiple countries. Viewing the work at hand through the standard MBA lens was not a good way to go. A complexity approach was needed.

At around the time Maureen and I were discussing my potential role at IHI, events were occurring in Sweden that would eventually give us our first test case for an IHI international strategy. Citizen disenchantment with long waits for health care services had led to a piece of national legislation, called the Dagmar Initiative, that mandated improvements in service; specifically, reductions in waits and delays. The Swedish health care service is organized and budgeted at the county level. So, naturally, the mandate to lead the needed improvement effort fell to the Federation of Swedish County Councils, a group in Stockholm that has traditionally provided guidance and knowledge resources to the various county councils throughout the country.

Several members of FSCC, notably the senior director for quality, Margareta Palmberg, had attended several improvement courses and conferences sponsored by IHI. Palmberg is also serving as co-chair for the European Quality Forum, co-sponsored by the IHI and the British Medical Journal. Palmberg and her group, which had been advocating improvement methods in Sweden with modest success for several years, suddenly found themselves in the spotlight with a politically backed mandate to bring about significant improvements. Palmberg e-mailed Don Berwick to tell him what had happened and to ask for help. Don immediately noted that the IHI had just conducted a successful "Waits and Delays Breakthrough Series" that had identified several key "change concepts" that lead to significant reductions in waiting throughout the health care organizations that had participated. It seemed natural that this process might be useful to Palmberg and her group.

Again, all of this was happening at about the same time that Maureen had asked me to help develop a business plan for the IHI international effort. The urgency to organize our thinking to serve the Swedes naturally took precedence over the desire to develop a comprehensive business plan for international efforts.

> **Reflection.** It seems natural to interpret these unfolding events through a complexity lens. They were unpredictable, at least not easily predictable from the IHI's seat in Boston. Even Palmberg and her team were surprised by how quickly they were cast into the spotlight after years of relatively unrecognized struggle. This is indicative of the emergent, nonlinear properties of a CAS.

The details of the Swedish initiative are not important here, except to note these impressions and outcomes:

- The Swedes agreed to a reasonable financial exchange in return for the rights to use the IHI's Waits and Delays Breakthrough Series material to form collaborative improvement groups in Sweden. In other words, this was a good business deal for IHI that never appeared in a formal business plan. This felt good to everyone.

- The Swedes approached their work with great vigor and sense of responsibility. They did not want the IHI to make improvement happen in Sweden for them, they wanted to do it themselves.

III. Tales

This also felt good, because it meant few IHI resources would be required to support the effort. This, in turn, meant that we might be able to work many international venues at once without stretching limited resources too thin.

- While the collaborative is not yet launched at the time of this writing, everyone connected with the IHI who has worked with the Swedish initiative believes that it will be very successful, based on experience in launching the breakthrough series. It feels like a success; it feels right to everyone.

While all of this was happening, time was marching forward. The next quarterly meeting of the IHI Board of Directors was coming up in about six weeks. At its previous meeting, the board had briefly discussed the possibility of an international effort and had agreed to devote more time to it at the next meeting. This was the discussion that led to my being asked to come on board to help prepare the business plan.

But, clearly, we weren't going to get a traditional business plan written in such a short period of time. Instead, I suggested that I could put together a sort of "position paper" that would outline some preliminary thinking; enough to feed a meaty discussion at the upcoming board meeting. Maureen thought this would be fine.

Reflection: Urgency actually works in your favor when you want to use a complexity approach to planning vs. a standard MBA business-plan approach. There was no time to do the analysis that goes into a standard business plan. Qualitative, rather than quantitative, analysis is acceptable when time is short. Qualitative analysis is the stuff of the complexity approach; general direction-setting, metaphor, storytelling, learning from action and so on. In this case, it is fortunate that time pressure came in as it did. But, I guess if I were trying to advocate for a complexity approach to planning, I would be happy to have time pressure (I might even purposefully create it).

Brenda Zimmerman adds her reflection: As I read through this tale, I started to think about the concept of float. Dee Hock talks about the reduction of float in our world – we no longer have cash float, nor do we have information float. The time between thinking and acting, between conceiving an idea and putting it into action is shrinking. Hence the notion of strategic (or business) planning as preceding strategic implementation or actions is problematic. Strategies are not formulated to be later implemented in a world in which there is no float. Strategies are enacted – thought and action are layered and looped. Mintzberg used the term "strategy formation" for some of this idea. The thoughts that precede action are the filters through which we will judge strategic issues. But even these are shaped by actions and are in their own state of evolution. I think Paul's approach here is consistent with this line of thinking. He is not abdicating or shirking responsibility by not writing out a business plan. He is recognizing the need to deal with unknowable, emergent futures in a manner consistent with their nature.

The position paper ended up being a four-page document. Page 1 was an overview of the current situation describing the diverse requests for help that IHI had received from all over the world. Page 2 described the current opportunity, basically, that there was a natural overlap between the knowledge for improvement that IHI had developed over the years and the emerging tension for change in the health systems of other countries.

Page 3 proposed a set of principles to guide IHI's work internationally. The statement that set up the principles was: "Reflection on our interactions to date with groups outside North America has already led us to see a set of principles that we might apply to maximize our impact internationally and avoid distractions." These principles included:

Aides
• *Min specs*

III. Tales

- We should build capacity for improvement locally and only work through legitimate, recognized leaders in other countries.

- We should only work in countries in which there is a clear aim to improve.

- We should only work with groups in other countries that have a legitimate infrastructure to support improvement efforts, the funding sources to see it through and the experience working as a group to make it happen.

- Our international collaborations must always be a two-way street of learning.

- Financial arrangements with international collaborators should always cover IHI costs and return a fair margin to support future efforts.

Page 4 was a summary and a set of discussion questions for the board.

Reflection: *While I saw the principles as a set of minimum specifications for a CAS, I purposefully avoided using the language of complexity. It* *wouldn't have added anything, in my view, and it had a potential downside. I didn't want to turn people off, nor have the focus of the discussion to be on the pros and cons of a complexity approach. My evolving mental model is: It's best to just do a complexity approach and then explain it to people after it works (which, of course, allows you to be silent if it flops). The idea was to state a different approach to business plan development that made sense on its own merits; that it happens to come from a complexity lens is neither here nor there.*

Maureen liked the write-up and the board had a very good discussion based upon it. It helped a lot that this particular board meeting was in Paris just prior to the European Healthcare Quality Improvement conference that IHI was cosponsoring with the British Medical Journal. The board members were keenly aware of the diversity in the various health care systems around the world and how hard it was for Americans to understand all the details of what was going on in these systems. The notion of approaching the issue of IHI's international activities with a set of clear principles with which to judge unfolding possibilities, rather than some semirigid business plan, was appealing.

The board tentatively approved continued activity along these lines. They wanted a timeline of activities for the next year or so, and a bit more discussion about exactly how we would use these principles to identify and act on opportunities.

> **Reflection:** *Luck plays a role in a CAS. The short time frame and the setting in Paris made it easier to gain acceptance for this somewhat unorthodox approach to strategic planning. I did not have to argue against preparing a traditional, analytical business plan. The position paper stood on its own merits as reasonable thinking.*
>
> *Of course, having avoided openly discussing the issue of an analytical business plan vs. an evolving complexity-based approach, there is the danger that at some point someone will say, "OK, so how ya coming on that business plan?" I hope that I am lucky enough to have gotten far enough along the complexity path that I can stop when the question is asked and reveal the new approach as having already been successful in getting us so far. My strategy is to keep doing enough in the language of the old approach to buy time for success to develop. But, who knows?*

The principles (minimum specs) create the environment (container) for emergence. But, how would we know when emergence happens? It seemed to me that the next thing to do was to dramatically increase the information flow in this now worldwide CAS. Up to this point, the information flow was primarily through IHI's CEO, Don Berwick; people in other countries who knew Don would tell him about happenings within their country and ask for IHI help.

Through discussions with various insiders at IHI about the clear need to know more about what was going on around the world in quality improvement, the concept of the "IHI International QI Happenings Data Base" emerged. I generated another "position paper" about this and circulated it among IHI insiders. The metaphor is that of an Internet Web page. The home page would be a map of the world. Click on a country and you can see what's happening in quality improvement there. The Web page would pull together information from three sources: health care demographic databases such as those maintained by the World Health Organization, reviews of articles in the literature written by people outside the U.S. describing quality improvement efforts, and e-mail inputs from people outside the U.S.

Principles
• *Tune to the edge*

The third source, e-mail inputs from people outside the U.S., is key. This is where the interaction among agents within this CAS really occurs. The idea, as of this writing, is to send out an e-mail message from Don Berwick, who is quite well known, to a large number of people internationally. The message will briefly describe IHI's collected knowledge for improvement and then ask for help in compiling an information resource on what is happening in quality improvement around the world (we have a list of specific questions to stimulate thinking).

Based on responses from this initial e-mailing, we hope to establish ongoing communications with many people in the health care QI field around the world. By making the information public (probably as an actual Web site on the Internet), we hope to encourage input, use the dynamic of a public forum to weed out spurious personal opinion from fact, and create a sense of a community working toward a common purpose of improved health care. The idea is to gain information, establish mutually respecting relationships and build a low-cost information network that is continually updating the picture of quality improvement worldwide.

The position paper has stimulated good discussion. Don, Maureen, and several other IHI insiders say, "go for it."

> **Reflection:** *The two key insights that I gained by looking at this through a complexity lens were that (1) information flow was critically important, and (2) I didn't have to "control" the information flow. I firmly believe that once the information begins flowing in this huge CAS, it will self-organize and allow us to see the emerging opportunities for providing services worldwide (the original goal of the business plan that I still haven't written). If we don't get much information back on a particular country, then there is probably not that much interest there and it wouldn't have*

been a very good opportunity anyway. The emerging opportunities for successfully providing IHI's knowledge for improvement will be in countries where the information flow is hot and heavy. We don't need comprehensive information, or even truthful information. We'll simply go where the flow is heaviest, engage in more intense dialogue, see what happens and take steps that seem reasonable as we go.

Of course, the massive e-mail idea might be a flop. If that occurs, we'll just have to think of something else. Increasing information flow in the CAS will still be the theme, the mechanism for doing this may have to be something else. But the cost of doing it this way is a whole lot less than the cost of setting up a branch office or franchise in another country (two ideas that were originally pondered when the thinking was about developing a classic business plan).

In parallel with all of this, there was still the board's request for a timeline and a bit more detail as to how things would go forward. I prepared a two-page addendum to the original position paper. The addendum provided a draft vision statement for the IHI international effort, a one-paragraph summary of the philosophy underlying our next actions, a two-year timeline and a list of goals two years out.

The one-paragraph summary of philosophy finally begins to reveal the complexity lens. It reads:

The principles behind our international effort lead us to take an emergent and opportunistic approach to planning, rather than a more traditional goals-and-strategies approach. In other words, in contrast to a business venture where we might set up branch offices in foreign cities and market our products and services, we want instead to become aware of opportunities where conditions are ripe for natural success in the application of knowledge that we already possess. In such a complex adaptive system, we can plan to build sources of information upon which we can act, but we cannot say a priori where that information might eventually lead us to act.

The timeline that follows this provides milestones for the initial construction of the International QI Happenings Data Base and describes a cycle by which IHI will endeavor to identify two countries per year where emerging conditions compare favorably to the principles (minimum specs). This cycle is tied naturally to IHI's two annual events, the U.S. Forum in December and the European Forum in April; points in time when information flow is particularly heightened and focused. The timeline does not specify exactly where we will form relationships, nor what format those relationships might take; that will emerge from the information flow in the CAS.

> **Reflection:** *I am continuing to walk carefully on the line between a traditional approach to planning and a complexity-based approach. I hope that I am indeed near the edge of chaos where creativity occurs. I am at least conscious of wanting to be there. I know from CAS theory that I must provide a container for anxiety. I hope that that is what I am doing; I hope that I am not being seen as being manipulative. Of course, I don't know if that is how I am being viewed because I am not in the board meetings to hear and see the discussion. Ah-ha! I need to establish an interaction linkage within this CAS so that I can adapt my behavior if needed. I'll ask if I can attend the next IHI Board meeting to discuss the international effort.*

> *I am also conscious of the desire to want to keep multiple options and approaches going simultaneously at the fringes of this effort. I have succeeded thus far in avoiding being clear about whether we are talking about branch offices, franchise agreements, conducting courses, offering assistance on a consulting basis, scheduled conference calls or whatever. In the end, I hope we can experiment and learn from our experiences with all these forms of interaction.*

Principles
• *Multiple actions*

III. Tales

The IHI Board reviewed the new input (vision, philosophy, timeline and goals) at its last meeting just a few weeks prior to this writing and again tentatively approved our moving forward as outlined. Don e-mailed me after the meeting and said that the discussion was good, most of the board is very excited about how this is playing out, but two board members are still not completely comfortable. He said that the discomfort was primarily around not being sure how much IHI effort this would consume over time. He did not mention the complex adaptive systems language I inserted in the material, and neither did I in my response back to him. We agreed that I would work with the IHI staff who had been involved in the successful work with Sweden to document how much IHI time and expense went into this.

> **Reflection:** *I wonder if the two board members are just uncomfortable with this nontraditional approach to strategic planning. At some point, I will have to deal with this openly. But, for now, there is enough time and support to carry on with the emergent approach. To me, we have "good-enough" plans and support.*

This story remains a work in progress.

A Complexity Tool Box

Ken Baskin

A story from VHA Inc., Irving, Texas.

Illustration of:

- emergence
- self-organization
- good-enough vision
- Stacey matrix
- clockware/swarmware
- paradox
- complexity lens

" Edward Wilson talks about biological systems and how centuries of evolution have affected the way we work," explains Jim Roberts, a senior vice president at VHA's Dallas-area headquarters. "Complexity theory gives us a better feeling for those biologically based ways of working together. The more I've studied ideas like self-organization and emergence, the more I've seen them operating in groups at works. So the question, for me, is how these ideas can help us provide better health care service."

Principles
• *Complexity lens*

III. Tales

A physician with experience in measuring quality for The Public Health Service and the Joint Commission of Accreditation of Healthcare Organizations, Roberts came to VHA in part to examine how physicians can be more effective in their leadership roles.

"Physicians serve a variety of leadership roles," he says. "We serve as senior executives, medical directors, vice presidents for medical affairs or senior physicians in member organizations. However, few of us have backgrounds in health system organization or general business, except for our small practices. On top of that, med school gives us a culture of autonomy and individual responsibility, as opposed to the team-orientation we need for many leadership roles.

"What I found from the time I started studying complexity theory with Curt Lindberg about three years ago, is that it gives us a series of tools to help make health care work better."

Specifically, Roberts has been experimenting with complexity theory tools in building a Physician Leadership Network across the VHA system. "The idea, the shared aim that holds us together, has been to create connections so that physician leaders throughout our system can learn

Principles
• *Good-enough vision*

from each other," he says. "What we've found so far is that these tools are effective, that they do seem to reflect the way people work much better than our old bureaucratic ways."

Roberts warns that these tools are less tangible than those provided by Total Quality Management. Control charts, for example, give you formulas for calculating whether systems are in control. The tools of complexity theory are more the products of close observation of the way people and systems behave.

Aides
• *Stacey matrix*

Nonetheless, they've enabled the team working to build the leadership network to make major strides. Some of the tools are relatively simple and concrete. For instance, Roberts has begun mapping projects on Ralph Stacey's four-square grid according to the level of agreement ("close to" vs. "far from") and the degree of certainty ("close to" vs. "far from"), to help think through how they should be addressed.

"One of the challenges physicians in leadership positions face is how to allocate our time," he says. "So, my clinical leadership team has begun mapping tasks on Stacey's grid to get a better idea of which tasks we should focus on.

Principles
• *Clockware/ swarmware*

"For example, tasks in the lower left [close to agreement/close to certainty] are likely to be stable procedures that lead to a product or service in the later stages of its life cycle," Roberts continues. "So it makes sense to delegate those tasks. Tasks in the middle, on the other hand, with a good bit of instability, are likely to lead to a product or service in the earlier stages of its life cycle. So it makes sense for me, as a leader, to pay more attention to issues like customer feedback and what our competitors are doing." Other tools seem more abstract, at first. Roberts recommends the ideas of *coevolution, self-organization* and *emergence* to help managers understand the way groups naturally work together when they need to respond to rapid change.

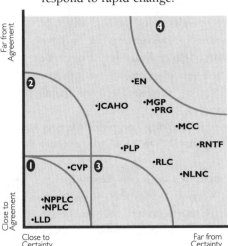

"These terms seemed to refer to separate experiences," he notes. "But the more I saw them in action, the more I realized they combine to describe the same phenomenon." *Coevolution* refers to the way units in a complex adaptive system must continually respond to changes in their environments and, in responding, further change those environments; *self-organization* describes how units in a CAS can respond to changes and cooperate with others without being told what to do; *emergence* refers to the way often-unexpected new developments appear as CASs respond to change.

"When you give a group of people a problem and allow them to self-organize, to solve it in a way that makes sense to them," Roberts says, "they'll explore the environment and decide on an action that will respond to – that is, coevolve with – their environment. In this process, the most amazing, and unexpected, products emerge.

"That's what happened with some members working on our Physician Leadership Network," he says. "They came to the conclusion that we needed a comparative database of physician practices. That need emerged spontaneously. It wasn't in anyone's vision of what we needed. If we had given them detailed instructions on what they were to do, they probably would never have considered it. But because the people working on our needs in this project were self-organizing, free to discover what they needed, they could recognize the unanticipated and let it emerge.

"As they built the database, the relationship between VHA's Dallas headquarters, our regional offices and the physicians we worked with began to change. We all had to coevolve, and we'll continue to coevolve. As long as people have shared aspirations, coevolution will generate new ways of meeting their needs. So products aren't going to have life cycles anymore. The life cycle will be forever."

Aides
• *Ecocycle*

Roberts has also used some complexity theory tools to accelerate the change process. Gareth Morgan's ideas about leveraging paradox as a catalyst for these new, coevolving systems was especially helpful.

Principles
• *Paradox*

"When a group of people begin working on a project, they usually have points of internal conflict," he says. "With these yes/but points, they may, for example, be excited about finding new ways to solve long-standing problems. They may also feel uncomfortable that their solutions will change the ways they've always been successful."

"Morgan suggests the group articulate these paradoxes as quickly as possible, surface them early and honestly. By recognizing their points of discomfort, they can address and defuse them and move ahead more quickly with their solutions," Roberts says.

As an example, he points to the team that recognized the Physician Leadership Network required a database of physician practices. "Our group was looking for the paradoxes that would speed development of the network," he says. "We realized how difficult it would be to connect physicians if we didn't know who they were and what their challenges were. How could we learn this information quickly? The answer that emerged was a strong database. So, by looking for the issue we were most uncomfortable with – the issue it would have been easiest to avoid, as we might have five years ago – we got the leverage to make a major step forward.

"We've even got evidence that the database was the right point to begin from. Since we started working on it, we've continued to get feedback reinforcing how valuable it could be."

Beyond his use of complexity theory to develop a management tool box, Roberts has also found it helpful in thinking about the future of health care and what that can mean for VHA's member hospitals. "It's clear to me that managed health care isn't working," he says. "I heard one HMO executive say, 'Doctors are workers on an assembly line. If they quit, we'll get some new ones.' Health care isn't that easy. People aren't machines. Nobody likes being treated that way.

"So you see a lot of our customers interested in alternative medicine. One senior physician I know is hanging it up. He can't deal with all the angry doctors anymore. It's a real tragedy. This guy makes a major contribution, but he can't take it anymore."

Principles
• *Min specs*

Much of the problem, as Roberts sees it, is the current system's emphasis on the old model of health care as repairing illness. But he sees a new system emerging in the coevolution of a partnership between customers and health care providers. "We need to engage in a partnership with our fellow human beings to serve and improve health, prevent illness and provide comfort," he says. "This idea of coevolving with our customers is one of the most powerful ideas around today. It's forced me to think about the barriers to us really working together, coevolving. How do we blur the distinctions between providers, customers and suppliers? After all, we're all in this together.

"Many of the issues that effect us most – tobacco and alcohol, drugs and violence, for example – are life-style and social policy issues," Roberts says. "Where are the paradoxes that can serve as leverage points for bringing together health care providers and schools, police and social service agencies and government?

"President Clinton's ideas about a strong, centrally run system won't work. It's the right problem, but the wrong solution. It's command-and-control when we need new answers to emerge. And maybe that's the biggest contribution complexity theory can give us – the tools to help tease out a new community partnership model of health care."

Make It Happen or Let It Happen?
A case study of strategy at Federal Metals

Brenda Zimmerman

A story from Federal Metals, Canada.

Illustration of:
- emergence
- wicked questions
- creating conditions
- reflection
- metaphor
- tune to the edge

This case is an excerpt from Brenda Zimmerman's doctoral dissertation, *Strategy, Chaos and Equilibrium: A Case Study of Federal Metals Inc.*, 1991, York University, Toronto, Canada. This version of the case was published in *Strategic Management and Organizational Dynamics,* Ralph Stacey, Pitman Publishing, London, 1993, pages 424-431.

Federal Metals: history and context

Federal Metals, or Fedmet, is owned by Federal Industries Limited, or FIL, a Canadian conglomerate with four industry groups. Fedmet, with revenues of more than one billion dollars in 1988, was the largest of FIL's groups. In 1988 Fedmet accounted for more than 50 percent of the revenue of Federal Industries.

The organization chart of Fedmet is shown in Exhibit 1. With the exception of Manfred Wirth and Carol Besner, the members of the management team attended the formal strategic planning meetings during the 1989 planning cycle.

Federal Metals was primarily a carbon steel distributor that had two main types of steel: flat-rolled, which is used in consumer products; and general line, which has more industrial applications. The Canadian carbon steel industry was approximately 10 million tons in 1988, of which 75 percent was sold directly from the mills to the end-user, and the remaining quarter was sold to service centers such as Russelsteel and Drummond McCall, which were divisions in Fedmet. The percentage sold through service centers had been increasing over the past few years, primarily due to flat-rolled products. The mills were unwilling to cut the flat-rolled into

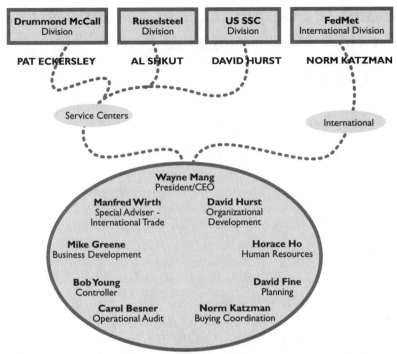

small quantities that the consumer often needed. Fedmet had approximately 20 percent of the carbon steel business in Canada that goes through service centers. They were the largest in the industry with the next three largest making up about 50 percent of the industry volume. In addition to carbon steel, Fedmet also distributed nonferrous products. Fedmet's international division was a trading operation that imported and exported metals, primarily steel.

Fedmet focused on metals distribution. The executives said they were not fabricators and hence upward vertical diversification was not considered a viable option for the organization. Their key product was service – the service of providing the metals to customers in quantities and with the frequency of deliveries that the customer needed. Pat Eckersley, president of Drummond McCall, argued that "if you think of steel distribution as a stock market, you will go bankrupt." He said there was some friction in the pricing over a broad price band within which orders can be satisfied. He argued that they moved people up the price band by providing excellent service. When asked to define this, both he and Al Shkut, president of Russelsteel, argued that customers were willing to pay for trust and comfort. They need to trust that the metals will arrive on time, will fit their engineering specifications and will be cut to fit exactly in their manufacturing process.

Their customer base was mixed. The majority of their business was broken bundles. Mills have minimum quantities that they are willing to sell, and thus many of their customers needed quantities of metals that were too small to be serviced by the mills directly. Some broken-bundle customers were large users of metals and normally bought from the mills and used Fedmet to fill in the gaps when they ran short of certain metals. Others needed special cutting or processing that the mills would not provide. This was primarily flat-rolled metals that were slit or cut to length. They also cut plate metal in shapes for manufacturing parts for heavy machinery. A third type of business that Fedmet's service centers were involved in was direct mill sales. In these sales, Fedmet acted as a broker for a fabricator or manufacturer who, for some reason, failed to meet all of the mills' criteria. This was not business they sought, since it tended to be low margin. Shkut and Eckersley said they spend a great deal of time trying to strengthen their relationships with their customers. Shkut argued that what they wanted to achieve was to "pull a customer into our rhythm – you know, so we just become part of their business."

In addition to strengthening their relationships with customers, Fedmet had spent a great deal of effort reaching out to their suppliers. Shkut argued that they approached the mills with a "how can we help you?" attitude. The logic was that they were part of a community of metals that will work better with cooperation, said Eckersley.

Federal Industries annually prepared a five-year strategic plan. Their plan was complete by mid-January. The four industrial groups, including Fedmet, were required to prepare a five-year plan by mid-April, and their divisions' plans were due in the middle of July. The 1989 strategic planning process for Fedmet began with a meeting of nine executives on January 23, 1989.

January 23, 1989: Warm bubbles and little arrows

The planning documents from previous years and the memo for the upcoming strategic planning day in January stressed the need to look on planning as a learning process. These three paragraphs are from the 1988-'93 strategic plan:

> *Successful companies that survive and prosper in the long run are ones that seem able to learn and adapt. Such companies have an ability to live in harmony with their business environment, to switch from a survival mode when times are turbulent to a self-development mode when the pace of change is slow. Many companies, however, do not learn to adapt or, at least, not very quickly; a full one-third of the Fortune 500 industrials listed in 1970 had vanished by 1983! Russelsteel only just survived.*

*In this context then what is planning's role in corporate learning? In a
nutshell the role of planning is to act as facilitator, catalyst and to help
accelerate the corporate learning process. The most relevant learning is
done by the people who run the business – the operators. So the real
purpose of effective planning is to facilitate the ongoing development of
the emerging strategies and thinking that the decision-makers carry in
their heads.*

*Our ability to learn faster than other players in the industry may be our
only long-run competitive edge. The tremendous improvement in the
results of recently acquired steel service centers is, to a large extent, a
result of exposure to the thinking of people in the Metals Group and the
resulting "fast learning" experienced by the management teams in the
newly acquired units.*

In preparation for the 1989 planning cycle, David Fine, vice president
of planning, circulated a memorandum. The memo had a series of
questions that were to be addressed in the meetings over the next three
months. On the first page, Fine introduced the role of planning at Fedmet.

*The planning process requires us to talk to each other on a scheduled basis
– that's about all – and then take a snapshot of our conversations.*

The all-day meeting took place in a picturesque country club several
miles from the head office. They sat around a series of tables organized in
a U-shape. The agenda was very loose.

Fine:
*Our agenda today is "Warm Bubbles and Little Arrows." The morning
session on "Warm Bubbles" is soft. We will review the visions and values
of the group and address four questions. The afternoon is a little more
focused, as we discuss the initiatives of 1988 and propose new initiatives
for 1989 and the 1990s.*

After a little more description of the stated visions and values of the
group, he put an acetate slide on the projector with four questions
preceded by Fedmet's vision statement – Every Person a Manager:

1.   What configuration of the vision and value "bubbles" do we
     envision for the Metals Group?
2.   Which ones do we feel good about?
3.   Which ones do we not feel good about?
4.   What revisions to group vision and values would we like to see?

"Let it happen" was a guiding principle of the Fedmet team. During the meeting, almost every member used the phrase repeatedly in describing what was happening or could happen in their divisions or areas of responsibility. Although the Fedmet team believed in the philosophy of "let it happen," they often struggled with its implementation, particularly in Drummond McCall. Drummond McCall and Russelsteel had been major competitors for more than 100 years. In 1987, after Federal Industries purchased Drummond McCall, it immediately became a separate division of the Fedmet group. The cultures of the two competitors were different and had resulted in a very different orientation in many dimensions of the business. Pat Eckersley became president of Drummond McCall at the time of purchase, after being with the Russelsteel organization for many years. Shkut argued that Eckersley was inculcated with the Russelsteel culture, which made the transition very difficult at times. Eckersley argued passionately about the need for the line workers to be closer to the customer to help improve the productivity of the operations. However, he was struggling with the process concept of letting it happen and the content of this idea, which he felt sure was valid.

Eckersley:
I don't think we'll ever sell the concept of quality to our people in their hermetically sealed plants, who only see steel pass through the airlock and see it come back in with a label on it that says it wasn't any good. I don't think we'll ever really crack quality until our people who are producing or working with our product have a feel for what happens to that product outside. The only way they can do that is to talk to the guys in the customers' plants who use the product. I mean our hourly guy talking to the customer's hourly guy to understand the goddamn problems they have with the product that comes out of our plant. … I can order them to do this, but that won't work, we have to let them come to the idea themselves, and want to do it and see the value in it. I am looking for an easy acceptance of a worthwhile thought but the structure of Drummond McCall is so hard-edged.

Middle management was the focus of much of the discussion. They argued that middle managers inhibit the process of "let it happen."

A key struggle the Fedmet team had during the day was the concept of the sequence of plans and actions. The team explicitly eschewed the idea that plans precede actions. They argued that a major purpose of the annual planning sessions was to reflect on the past actions and attach meaning to those events. They referred to this concept as "retrospective sessions." They institutionalized retrospective sessions for all levels of the organization, arguing that there was a significant learning process in

Aides
• *Reflection*

reflecting on the past.

The meeting concluded with Fine expressing the thought that translation of the visions and value into actions was the missing link that Fedmet needed to understand. Fine agreed to work on a summary document that would take a snapshot in words of the process and the outcomes of the meeting. They would then use the snapshot to continue in developing the concepts and material for the five-year strategic plan.

Executive pornography

The executive team of Fedmet occasionally referred to strategy as a four-letter word, an obscenity. As an example, they labeled an article in the business press that focused on chief executive officers and their strategic decision-making role in an organization as "executive pornography." The management group identified and commented on some of the pornographic words, phrases and images in this article. They appear in Exhibit 2.

At the meeting on January 23, 1989, the team discussed the article. David Hurst, executive vice president, argued that it presumed that the ideal manager is some sort of genius who can analyze reams of relevant data and use the analysis to make the key decisions that will then be implemented by the people in the organization. There are a number of facets to this image that the Fedmet team found obscene. First, they objected to the implied controller-controlled duality. Second, they objected to viewing the "people side" of the organization as one that involves "motivating people." This insinuates that there is a need and a right to manipulate people to act in the manner the CEO requires to implement his, or her, plan. It also suggests some unique personal ownership of the strategy by the CEO.

One of their central concerns about a conception of strategic management

---

Exhibit 2 Executive pornography

Pornographic words, phrases and images of the chief executive officer:

- masterminding
- maneuvering
- it's fun to move the company in the direction you want it to move
- he (or she) is expected to be above the fray, reading, thinking and developing long-term strategy
- he (or she) has got to figure out how to get the company to understand where he (or she) wants to go and to help him (or her) get there
- the challenge of motivating people
- strategic management is the absolute key element of success
- engineered a turnaround; the CEO is in control

(The "obscenities" were underlined in Hurst's copy of: "The Boss Under Fire." *Business Magazine.* Feb. 1989.)

Exhibit 3 Fedmet: Living the vision

The Vision: "Every Person a Manager"	Living Every Person a Manager: Linkage Processes	The Reality: "Every Person a Manager"
• Customer is king	• Living "60/60" person-to-person	• Front-line people, fully mobilized, flatter organization
• Small company feeling	• Living "60/60," team-on-team	• "Big company" opportunities
• Excellent supplier relations	• Living "60/60" president-to-president	• Cooperative initiatives
• An environment for free thought	• A retrospective by unit	• Goals to "get better"
• People-oriented	• Fedmet; creating and living the environment	• Magnetizing group and division offices, such as a Fedmet library
• Plans its future	• Living our plan for growth	• Growth in the 1990s
• Profit is a requirement	• Living "a federal industries company"	• Embracing the Federated Industries Ltd. employee stock ownership plan to make "RONA* never below 20" percent a reality *return on net assets

hostage to such obscene images, is the time dimension implicit in strategic thinking. They argued that an understanding of where they are and where they are going can only be grasped in retrospect. They questioned the presumed sequence of (1) analysis, followed by (2) decisions and consummated by (3) action. In the terminology of management strategy, they were not convinced that implementation follows planning or decisions. They implicitly believed in experiential learning rather than learning by analysis. Their key phrase that reflects this was "Let it happen."

The Fedmet team eschewed many traditional strategic management procedures. In particular, its members objected to the emphasis placed on developing a strategic plan. The process of planning was considered useful, but the "black marks on white paper," or the plan itself, was of significantly less value. They viewed all management as a process in which the best one can do at any point in time is to capture the process in a two-dimensional way, as in a snapshot or photograph. Fedmet labeled its 1990-'94 plan "A Series of Snapshots of the Group Planning Process." The metaphor of the snapshot permeated the document. Since a snapshot can only picture the external dimensions of a situation, visions and values, which were the critical management focus of the Fedmet team, could not be adequately captured in a snapshot.

Another dimension of the snapshot analogy is the connotation that strategy is enacted. Thus a photograph can only capture one point in time, which is over as soon as the photograph has been taken. In the 1990-'94 strategic plan they stated that a snapshot cannot capture motion and therefore is limited to portraying dynamic interaction as a static arrangement. The Fedmet team focused on the process elements and suggested that the structures or plans were merely temporary manifestations of the process.

January 24 to March 15, 1989: Living the vision

During the next two weeks, Fine worked on the concept of translating the vision into reality. Fine and Wayne Mang, CEO, met frequently to discuss the issues. Hurst was often present at these meetings. They discussed what the linkage process between the vision and the reality should be, and the conversations often centered on the need for appropriate body language or actions rather than words. There was considerable jousting in the discussions but Mang's influence was evident. More often than not, the phrases or words he suggested were included in the final chart, which can be seen in Exhibit 3.

The team reconvened on February 8 at the Fedmet offices to discuss Fine's approach. Although there was considerable discussion about the appropriateness of the approach – including concerns about the linearity of the process – all agreed to work through the ideas as the next step to develop the plan. The task was broken into five subgroups, each charged with the responsibility to investigate further the linkage and the reality of the visions and values. The first three values listed in Exhibit 3 were combined, since all dealt with the linkage process of "living 60/60." (The "60/60" concept indicates that each side in a relationship has to go more than

Exhibit 4: The seven priorities
1. Create and maintain an appropriate environment
2. Mobilize and empower front-line people
3. Capitalize on "big company" opportunities
4. Promote cooperative buying Initiatives
5. Goals to "get better"
6. Focus on earnings per share
7. Growth in the 1990s

half-way to make it work.) The other four groups each had one value to address. Fine prepared lists of questions to stimulate the discussions.

The subgroups consisted of three people, in addition to Fine who participated in all the subgroups. Each member of the executive team volunteered to work on two subgroups. The subgroups were expected to meet once for approximately half a day and to report their findings at the next strategic planning meeting on March 29, 1989.

After the five subgroups had met, David Fine prepared a draft strategic plan that was intended to reflect the subgroup discussions. In consultation with Mang and Hurst, he summarized the subgroup discussions into seven priorities. The document was circulated to the Fedmet executive team a week prior to the meeting. The draft plan used the photography analogy and presented the plan as a series of snapshots. The memo attached to the draft indicated the need to continue to challenge the document. One section of the draft dealt specifically with the subgroup discussions. The realities were outlined along with the linkage process to move the value into reality. Under each of these seven items was a blank section titled "Questions." The questions, Fine told us later, were intended to be wicked questions, in that they would be challenging and equivocal, often with a paradox or an oxymoron embedded in it.

March 29, 1989: The wicked questions

The group's priorities were the centerpiece of the day's discussion. The seven realities or priorities for the next five years are shown in Exhibit 4.

Under each reality was the list of the translation processes to convert the priority into a living process. These were essentially the summary of the subgroup meetings as Fine saw them.

After some heated debate about the document, and in particular the implications for the divisions' long-range plans, which were supposed to reflect Fedmet's plan at least to some extent, the discussion moved to the wicked questions. The rest of the day was spent discussing the linking processes before the wicked questions were finalized. Mang sat back away from the table for most of the meeting, only occasionally raising a question or reiterating someone's comment. Fine played a more active role at this meeting than at previous meetings. The deadline for completing the strategic plan was mid-April, so there were certain pressures for closure.

Aides
• *Wicked questions*

There was some discussion about how much of the document was retrospective versus future-oriented.

Shkut:
Wayne, I think your caution is, don't make it a total retrospective document. So we need to look at items six and seven on the list because

e d g e w a r e

that is where we really go forward. Are we really comfortable with that?

Hurst:

I don't agree that is where we go forward. I think all of them are forward-looking. Creating and maintaining an environment can't affect yesterday's business, but it sure as hell affects tomorrow. We will only get to [the end] point by going through points one to five.

Shkut:

OK. Yep, you're right.

Hurst:

At this instant we have a historic RONA [return on net assets] of whatever it is and the only way to affect tomorrow's RONA is through

---

Exhibit 5: The wicked questions of the seven priorities

1. Create and maintain an appropriate environment
   • Do our "body language" and our everyday actions reflect what we write?
   • Are we committed to practicing this – if so what change does this require in my own behavior?

2. Mobilize and empower front-line people
   • Are we ready to put the responsibility for the work on the shoulders of the people who do it?

3. Capitalize on "big company" opportunities
   • How can we maintain the advantages of interdivisional rivalry while also achieving all the benefits of close cooperation between divisions?

4. Promote cooperative buying initiatives
   • How can we maintain the benefits of autonomy while taking full advantage of our size?

5. Goals to get better
   • Have we learned anything from our history?

6. Focus on earnings per share
   • What needs to happen for us to say "RONA never under 20" percent is a reality?

7. Growth in the 1990s
   • Where will we find the people to achieve this growth?
   • Will FIL be able to balance its portfolio with growth in other groups to permit our growth?

the people. We can't work on the numbers directly. The numbers are a result of action, behavior. ... All we can work with is people in such a way that when the numbers are measured, the results are favorable. So we have to think about what we can do now that may affect the results later.

Eckersley:
But it is a bit of a circle, because it is looking at the numbers that leads you to think about things that would affect the numbers, so it goes round and round.

Greene:
And surely in that process you have to get as many people as possible keying in on those numbers.

They agreed that the past and the future were reflected in the seven priorities and then spent the next three hours developing the wicked questions related to each priority. The questions are noted in Exhibit 5.

Fine noted that the questions were to be presented in the strategic plan, rather than the answers, with the expectation that the divisions would address these questions and raise these and other questions with their branches. They discussed at some length the need to keep the questions both ambiguous and challenging, to create some discomfort among people at all levels in the organization. Fine argued that using questions indicated that the process is continuous. The strategic plan was viewed as a snapshot of one point in time of the ongoing process

Principles
• *Tune to the edge*

After the meeting the 1990-'94 strategic plan was written by Fine and distributed to the members the Fedmet team, the divisions and FIL. The process of preparing the plan began with a very loose, broad agenda and focus, and gradually narrowed into some specificity of actions, only to broaden and loosen again at the end with the wicked questions. The ambiguity inherent at the beginning of the process was also inherent at the end. Hurst said they trusted the process to develop the content. He said that objectives of what to do should not be clear at the beginning, rather they become clear through the process.

Reflection: *Fedmet's senior management team struggled with the traditional conception of management and of strategic planning. Both were built on clockware, predictability, intermediaries, expert knowledge and the separation in time of plans and action. Although they found these concepts invaluable for some dimensions of their work, they found them misleading and unhelpful in situations in which they needed to access the* *creativity of all 2,000 employees. Without a prior knowledge of complexity science, they intuitively created an approach to strategy that was consistent with the underlying principles of the science.*

At Fedmet, both clockware and swarmware operated simultaneously in a complementary and competitive fashion. The swarmware system was not new to Fedmet. What was new was articulating it and discussing it. They exposed the assumptions of the traditional model, which provided opportunities for finding new ways of acting and making decisions.

The wicked questions were the final stage of the strategic "plan." They were an indication to all the employees that the strategies were still emerging and they were invited to play a role. One of the unintended consequences of the wicked questions was that others in the organization began to mimic the process and ask their own questions. The concept of leader as the giver of answers was being replaced by the concept of the leader as a questioner who used inquiry to access the full potential of the system. ✺

Comparison of Strategic Processes*

	Traditional Clockware Strategic Planning	Complex Swarmware Strategic Management
Uncertainty	• absorption/reduction	• creation/expansion
Organizing principle	• controller-controlled duality	• self-organization
Role of senior executive(s)	• leader(s) • "the" strategist	• catalyst(s) • enactment of strategies by members of organization
Information (role or type)	• processing • syntactic	• creation • semantic
Human capacities	• bounded rationality	• limitless ability to create connections
Strategy and vision	• simple, explicit	• complex, implicit
Strategic sequence	• formulation first followed by implementation	• concurrent formulation and implementation
Assumption of ideology	• ideological uniformity	• counterforces
Dominant evolutionary drive	• adaptation to environment	• requisite destabilization and self-presentation

III. Tales

* This chart is adapted from: Zimmerman, Brenda. "Chaos and Nonequilibrium: The Flipside of Strategic Processes." *Organization Development Journal* 11, no. 1, 1993. The paper provides an explanation of the two approaches and the strategic management literature that links to them.

aides

Aides for complexity

Most people would call what we present here *tools* for complexity. Our problem with the word *tools* is that it conjures up a machine metaphor. Tools are reductionist in nature; discrete items that can be used in isolation. Tools are also inanimate things; not living and evolving items that are an extension of the person using them. Somehow, the word *tools* just did not seem appropriate to describe techniques that help us understand complex adaptive systems.

Principles
• *Complexity lens*
• *Clockware/ swarmware*

On the other hand, we do like the part of the tools metaphor that brings to mind such concepts as useful, practical and helpful in moving forward in a situation. "What," we asked ourselves, "would you call a living thing that is useful, practical and helps you move forward in a situation?" Our favorite word from among those brainstormed was *aide* (with an "e" on the end). An aide is a living, coevolving assistant; not a mechanical device. And that is precisely the metaphor we want you to have in mind as you use this material.

The aides for complexity described here do not come with rigid instructions. Rather, they should be used in ways that are as flexible and adaptable as the complex adaptive systems we are seeking to understand. There is no "right" way to use a particular aide, only ways that help in a given context and ways that do not help very much in that context.

Principles
• *Multiple actions*

You should also understand that an aide is an extension of yourself and your coworkers. You, the others and the aide itself are all elements of a complex adaptive system. It is therefore our intention only to explain the concepts behind the aide, give some guidance on its use and provide some tips to accelerate your learning. Exactly how you use an aide will depend on you and your context. Experiment. Reflect. Learn. Allow the aide to coevolve with you and your context.

The aides described in this chapter are only a starting point. We have selected them because we feel that they are the most generally useful and basic aides for the understanding of complexity. The many references in the Bibliography describe other aides that you will also find useful.

The minimum specifications for the aides included in this chapter are that:

- they are ubiquitous; they have multiple uses
- we know of tales that illustrate the use of the aide; that is, others have actually used them in real situations
- they are consistent with the emerging principles of complexity that we describe elsewhere in *Edgeware*

Aides
• *Minimum specs*

IV. Aides

- they provide the user with a visual summary or memorable story that can become a part of the context of a complex adaptive system
- they are likely to be new to most people.

Bibliography
• Plsek: *Creativity*

Principles
• Tune to the edge

The last item in the minimum specs – likely to be new to many people – raises an important point. There are many other aides with which people are already familiar. We do not mean to say that complexity can only be understood through the use of exotic new methods. For example, brainstorming, a tool that nearly everyone knows, helps sustain diversity in idea generation and therefore helps a group stay farther from equilibrium. Systems diagrams, popularized by Peter Senge and colleagues, are another familiar tool that obviously helps in the understanding of complex adaptive systems. The aides described here are additional aides. We are not suggesting that you discard what you already know.

How this chapter is structured

Each aide section has roughly the same outline:

The basic idea:
A one- to two- sentence description of the aide.

Potential context for use:
Some thoughts on when the aide might be especially handy.

Description:
More detail about the aide.

Reflection:
Things to think about both before and after using the aide.

Examples:
Some quick stories that feature the use of the aide, or citations to longer stories in the Tales chapter.

Facilitator's tips:
Some thoughts that may help you use the aide more effectively or avoid pitfalls.

Attachments:
Additional descriptions, examples, applications, graphics and so on that you will find helpful.

The aides are in no particular order. You should read through them all and pick out a few to try in your immediate context. Reflect on what you learn and go on to pick a few more ... or try the first ones again in a different context. Just keep reflecting and learning as you go.

We recommend that before you use an aide, you should read through the tales of complexity cited for that aide. This will give you additional insight into how you might proceed.

Finally, we also suggest that you reread this chapter and the associated tales periodically. Your context and mental models will change over time. Something that might not have been meaningful to you when you first read it, might later stand out as a key point.

Summary of the complexity aides

Establish only the very fewest requirements necessary to define something, leaving everything else to the creative evolution of the CAS.

The art of temporarily detaching oneself from a situation in order to think clearly about it, assign interpretation and meaning to the situation, and draw out deeper learnings.

Growth doesn't always mean building. Frequently, destruction is a necessary component in the lifecycle of a system – much like a forest fire that provides rich nutrients to replenish the soil. Drawing from a biological metaphor, this aide invites leaders to think about what they need to deliberately destroy or stop doing to facilitate the renewal of their work in health care – and to realize that a healthy organization has elements in all phases of the ecocylce at the same time.

Do you feel restricted in your use of a complexity approach because of a board that is unconvinced, uninterested or stuck in a command-and-control mindset? You're not alone. But rather than take a polarizing "me vs. them" approach, consider the leaders of the organization through a complexity lens ... and reflect on these tools for helping them assume the additional roles of adapting and learning.

Learning is an emergent property of a CAS. The overall system learns collectively as individual agents within the system learn. This aide summarizes some learning approaches designed to diffuse complexity principles throughout your organization.

Stacey agreement and certainty matrix[1]

Principles
- *Clockware/ swarmware*
- *Tune to the edge*
- *Complexity lens*
- *Shadow system*

The basic idea:

A method to select the appropriate management actions in a complex adaptive system based on the degree of certainty and level of agreement on the issue in question.

Tales
- *Another way to think*
- *A complexity tool box*

Potential context for use:

Bibliography
- Stacey: *Strategic Management*

- when choosing between management or leadership approaches for a specific issue or decision

- when making sense of an array of decisions (or an agenda for a group)

- when communicating with others why a particular approach is appropriate

- when innovations and creative alternatives are needed, this matrix can be used to deliberately increase the uncertainty and disagreement needed to nudge the system to the edge of chaos

[1]Stacey, Ralph. *Strategic Management and Organizational Dynamics.* London: Pitman Publishing, 1996.

Description:

The art of management and leadership is having an array of approaches and being aware of when to use which approach. Ralph Stacey proposed a matrix to help with this art by identifying management decisions on two dimensions: the degree of certainty and the level of agreement.

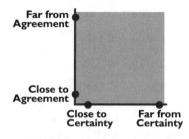

Let's take a closer look at these dimensions.

Close to certainty: Issues or decisions are close to certainty when cause-and-effect linkages can be determined. This is usually the case when a very similar issue or decision has been made in the past. One can then extrapolate from experience to predict the outcome of an action with a good degree of certainty.

Far from certainty: At the other end of the certainty continuum are decisions that are far from certainty. These situations are often unique or at least new to the decision-makers. The cause-and-effect linkages are not clear. Extrapolating from experience is not a good method to predict outcomes in the far from certainty range.

Agreement: The vertical axis measures the level of agreement about an issue or decision within the group, team or organization. As you would expect, the management or leadership function varies depending on the level of agreement surrounding an issue.

IV. Aides

The following pages examine different zones within the matrix. They are:

❶ Close to agreement, close to certainty
❷ Far from agreement, close to certainty
❸ Close to agreement, far from certainty
❹ Anarchy: far from agreement, far from certainty
❺ The edge of chaos (the zone of complexity)

❶ Close to agreement, close to certainty

Much management literature and theory addresses the region on the matrix that is close to certainty and close to agreement. In this region, we use techniques that gather data from the past and use them to predict the future. We plan specific paths of action to achieve outcomes and monitor the actual behavior by comparing it against these plans. This is sound management practice for issues and decisions that fall in this area. The goal is to repeat what works to improve efficiency and effectiveness.

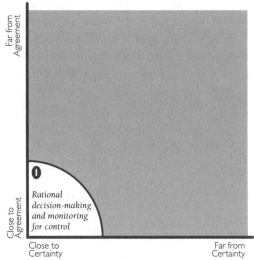

❷ Far from agreement, close to certainty

Some issues have a great deal of certainty about how outcomes are created, but high levels of disagreement about which outcomes are desirable. Neither plans nor shared mission are likely to work in this context. Instead, politics become more important. Coalition- building, negotiation and compromise are used to create the organization's agenda and direction.

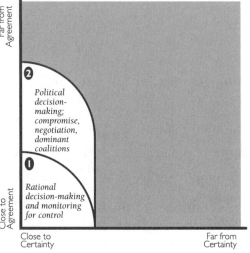

❸ Close to agreement, far from certainty

Some issues have a high level of agreement, but not much certainty as to the cause-and-effect linkages to create the desired outcomes. In these cases, monitoring against a preset plan will not work. A strong sense of shared mission or vision may substitute for a plan in these cases. Comparisons are made not against plans, but against the mission and vision for the organization. In this region, the goal is to head toward an agreed-upon future state, even though the specific paths cannot be predetermined.

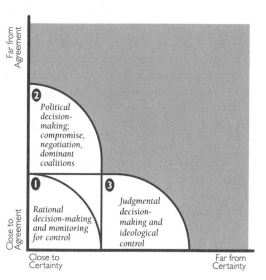

❹ Anarchy: far from agreement, far from certainty

Situations in which there are very high levels of uncertainty and disagreement often result in a breakdown or anarchy. The traditional methods of planning, visioning and negotiation are insufficient in these contexts. One personal strategy to deal with such contexts is avoidance – avoiding the issues that are highly uncertain and for which there is little disagreement. While this may be a protective strategy in the short run, it is disastrous in the long run. This is a region that organizations should avoid as much as possible.

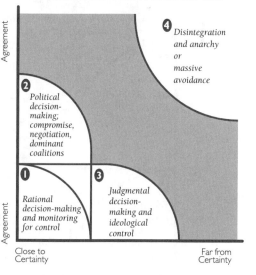

IV. Aides

❺ The edge of chaos (the zone of complexity)

There is a large area on this diagram that lies between the anarchy region and regions of the traditional management approaches. Stacey calls this large center region the zone of complexity – others call it the edge of chaos. In the zone of complexity, the traditional management approaches are not very effective, but it is the zone of high creativity, innovation and breaking with the past to create new modes of operating.

In business schools, we spend much of our time teaching and learning how to manage in areas (1), (2) and (3). In these regions, we can present models that extrapolate from past experience and thereby can be used to forecast the future. This is the hallmark of good science in the traditional mode. When we teach approaches, techniques and even merely a perspective in area (4), the models seem soft, and the lack of prediction seems problematic.

We need to reinforce that managers and leaders of organizations need to have a diversity of approaches to deal with the diversity of contexts. Stacey's matrix honors what we already have learned, but also urges us to move with more confidence into some of the areas that we understand intuitively but are hesitant to apply because they do not appear as solid.

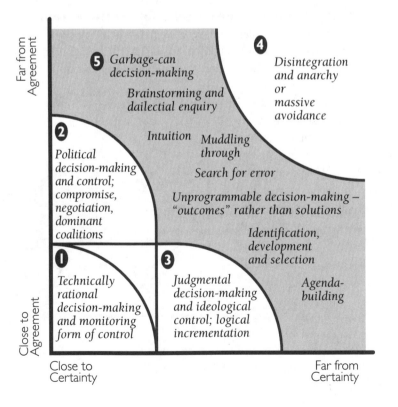

Reflection:

Before using this aide: Do you have diversity in the level of complexity (or the extent of agreement or certainty) in the issues or problems your organization faces? Do you have sufficient diversity in the approaches you take for these different contingencies?

After using this aide: How can you adapt this approach to make it your own?

Examples:

By Brenda Zimmerman

Another researcher and I were studying a not-for-profit organization in an action-learning mode. We observed and worked alongside the board during a full year of meetings. They were very keen on complexity science and its applications to their work.

After a while, my fellow researcher and I became increasingly concerned about the board's approach to issues. They seemed to complexify some very simple issues and drop some of the more challenging and fundamental issues facing the agency. Meanwhile, staff members were getting increasingly frustrated with the board and began to oversimplify issues and seemed to want to avoid any creative suggestions from the board.

Aides
• *Reflection*

At a board-staff retreat, we presented them with a simplified version of the Stacey matrix. We used only four categories of issues – *simple, complicated* and *complex* issues, which were all manageable to some extent, and *anarchy*, which was to be avoided. We divided the participants into five groups and gave them a number of sheets of plastic film on which they could write and post on the walls. We asked them to think through the

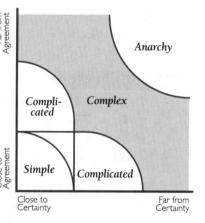

issues and decisions of the past year and sort them into three categories – simple, complicated and complex. Each issue was written on a separate page. They were then asked to post them on a wall under the three headings – simple, complicated and complex.

What we discovered was there was almost no disagreement about the issues and how they should be sorted. All of the groups came to the same (or very similar) conclusions. We then asked them to think about the management techniques or approaches they had used for each issue. After a while, we heard laughter from several of the groups. They became aware of how they had used simple approaches for complex problems and vice versa. We added to this by reading excerpts from the transcripts from some of the meetings we had attended.

Staff members began to volunteer their insights into the board's behavior and their reaction to it. The staff commented that they could now see why the board was at times trying to push them into the zone of complexity. The board could see why the staff wanted to cut off discussion and generation of new ideas on some of the simpler issues. They also commented on how the matrix did not represent a rigid landscape, rather that issues moved from one zone to another in part due to external conditions, and in part due to the participants' perspectives on an issue.

The result was an honoring of a diversity of approaches. They could see the value others added to the array of issues facing the organization.

The next stage was to ask them to do the same exercise with the coming issues or issues that they were expecting to address in the coming year. Again the exercise showed remarkable overlap between the participants as to which category an issue belonged. But they also began to question their own quick consensus. Should this issue be as simple as they had suggested? Could they be missing an opportunity by not pushing it, at least for a while, into the zone of complexity?

Aides
• *Wicked questions*

Their story is still unfolding, but it showed how the matrix was a useful aide in opening up discussion and creating opportunities for them to examine the management approaches they often took for granted.

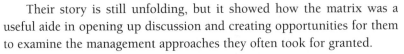

Facilitator's tips:

- Present the matrix in a layered format as shown in the Description section. This can be done with or without Stacey's words in the various regions. (For some groups, the matrix in the example may be an easier way to introduce the matrix.)

- Ask participants to identify concrete examples from their workplace for each region.

- Have the participants discuss which approaches make sense for which region, and why.

- Lead a discussion of what factors would suggest an issue is more likely to be in the zone of complexity or one of the other regions? Look for issues of how many people or institutions are connected, the time frame between the cause and potential effects, areas of higher turbulence or unpredictability, and so forth.

- Start with historical examples and then move into current or future issues.

- After the participants have worked with the matrix in a real context, have them reconvene and reflect on how they used it. Did they adapt it or change it for their own context?

Attachments:

Dr. Stephen Larned is vice president of Medical Affairs for Maine Medical Center. He has found the Stacey matrix very helpful in his work. He began by using the matrix to make sense of past events. Then he used it to help with current events. Now he has revised the matrix to make it work best for him with current and future issues.

His revision is a diagonal line through the matrix on which he has placed seven management interventions. Each of the seven approaches fits with the degree of certainty and agreement present in the context. The role of the leader shifts quite dramatically as you move along the diagonal. The matrix shown below is Larned's adaptation.

Larned's value added in this is twofold. First, he demonstrates the value of owning your own models. Second, he shows specific and concrete examples of how his management and leadership style need to vary by context.

IV. Aides

Moving from agreement and certainty

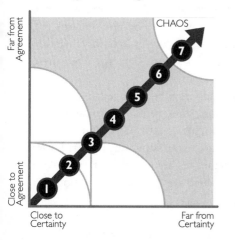

1 • *Direct workers to complete tasks*

2 • *Change work processes to facilitate self-organization*

3 • *Modify structure to increase diversity, information and connections*

4 • *Bring agents from different CASs together to intervene and seek change*

5 • *Bring agents from different CASs together to facilitate self-organization*

6 • *Examine and describe patterns that are beyond leaders' influence*

7 • *Scan the system for patterns*

Metaphor

Principles
- *Complexity lens*
- *Tune to the edge*

Tales
- *Another way to think*
- *Make it or let it*
- *Emerges from the fabric*
- *Worldwide complexity*

Bibliography
- *Morgan: Images*
- *Morgan: Imaginization*

The basic idea:

Using discussion of an analogous system as a way to help people get common and creative insights into the operation of the CAS they are in.

Potential context for use:

- Members of the group have differing, but largely unexpressed, views of the mission, purpose or method of working together.

- The group seems stuck in its approach to issues (stuck on an attractor) and needs some creative insight.

Description:

Metaphor is a tool of language in which one thing is said to be something else (or to be like something else). Exploration of the similarities and differences between the two things gives a group a way of thinking and a way of seeing a situation that can bring creative insight about ways to move forward. For example, we might say, "We want our HMO clinic teams to function as well as the NASA space shuttle team," and then explore the implications of this statement.

The predominant metaphors in use in organizations today are those of a machine and a military operation. If an organization is a machine, then we just need to specify the parts well and make sure each part does its job. If an organization is a military operation, then command, control and communication needs to be hierarchical, survival is key and sacrificial heroes are desired (although no one really wants to be one themselves). Most of today's organizational artifacts – job descriptions, organization charts, root-cause analysis, turf battles, and so on – emerge from these largely unexpressed and undiscussed metaphors.

The basic problem with these metaphors when applied to a CAS is that they ignore interaction effects among the agents, or worse, simply assume that these interactions can be tightly controlled through better (read: more) specification. While there are many situations in health care for which the machine and military metaphors are useful – for example, a code blue team or a surgical process – there are also many situations for which these metaphors are grossly inadequate.

When we use the tool of metaphor in a CAS, we are seeking to make

*explicit the metaphors that guide interactions within the system, and we
are seeking new metaphors that can provide fresh insight into the
dynamics of the system.*

Gareth Morgan suggests a number of generic metaphors that we can
use to create dialogue and shared meaning within groups. Several of
Morgan's generic metaphors are described in the attachment. A facilitator
can introduce these metaphors and challenge the group to extract key
themes that can then be applied to the real-world CAS with which the
group is concerned.

Bibliography:
• Morgan:
  Imaginization

Reflection:

Before using this aide: What metaphors is the group unconsciously
using in its current approach?

After using this aide: How will the group transform its new insight into
action? What plan do we have for keeping the new metaphor alive so that
we don't slip back into the old metaphor?

Examples:

There are several examples in the Tales chapter that illustrate the use
of metaphor to help provide new insight into common organizational
issues.

Facilitator's tips:

- Break large groups into smaller groups of two to four people.
  Encourage diversity by allowing the small groups to work on
  different metaphors, or different angles of the same metaphor.
  Quick agreement and oversimplification work against what we
  are trying to accomplish.

- Before you set the groups to work, use the examples we provide,
  or your own anecdotes, to illustrate what metaphor is intended
  to accomplish. Concrete and highly analytical thinkers will
  flounder without some guidance as to what they are supposed
  to do with the metaphors.

- Beware of taking metaphors too literally. As a facilitator, help
  the group identify key themes from the world of the metaphor,
  but then immediately pull them back into the world of the CAS
  under discussion and ask for concrete suggestions for how this

IV. Aides

theme applies in the real world. Expect to cycle back and forth several times between the world of the metaphor and that of the real CAS.

Attachments:

Some of Gareth Morgan's generic metaphors

The eight metaphors described below are just a few of the literally infinite number of useful metaphors. They are described here to pique your interest and imagination. The best metaphors are those that emerge during discourse with others within a CAS.

Spider Plants

Spider plants are commonly found in hanging baskets. There is a central plant in the basket, rooted in soil. From the basket, the plant sends out long stems a foot or so in length; "tentacles." At the ends of these tentacles are a clump of leaves. Morgan suggests drawing a picture or bringing in an actual spider plant to stimulate creative discussion about centralization vs. decentralization issues in organizations.

Example of a provocative question for a group:

- What insights from the structure of a spider plant can we apply to the issue we are discussing?

Strategic Termites

Termites are master builders. Termite mounds are intricate affairs that are the tallest structures on earth when compared to the height of their builders. But every termite mound is unique; there does not appear to be a detailed blueprint that the insects follow. Instead, Morgan points out, "The 'masterpiece' evolves from random, chaotic activity guided by what seems to be an overall sense of purpose and direction, but in an open-ended manner."

Example of a provocative question for a group:

- How would we approach strategic or financial planning if we were termites?

The Gulf

The gulf is a metaphor for the deep organizational pool into which people and issues can fall, never to emerge again. Everyone in the organization knows (or learns quickly) about the gulf. Everyone knows (or learns quickly) that venturing into the gulf is a "career limiting move." An example of an organizational gulf might be: challenging policies or programs that come down from headquarters. Even if the policies or programs are obviously flawed, and everyone seems to know it, people have learned that it is personally damaging to say anything. Silence is one of the main factors surrounding and sustaining the gulf. Morgan suggests that naming the gulf is helpful, because it breaks the silence but provides a safer, depersonalized way to discuss it.

Example of a provocative question for a group:

- Have we just entered another "gulf" here?

Political Football or Tug-of-War

Many organizational issues have important political aspects to them. Powerful groups and individuals, often with hidden agendas, are at play within the CAS. Technical or process-oriented solutions to issues can fail miserably if the political aspects of the issue are not acknowledged openly and addressed. To make the political dimension of the CAS discussible, Morgan suggests the metaphor of the issue as a political football or tug-of-war. Since the discussion is uncomfortable, several rounds of dialogue may be needed, but this aspect of the CAS becomes more potentially tractable with each such round.

Example of a provocative question for a group:

- In what ways might our issue, or the people who will be involved in its resolution, be like a political football (or tug-of-war)? Focus the discussion on: who is doing the kicking (or pulling)? In what direction? With what force? For what reasons? With what likely outcome? Who or what exactly is being kicked (or pulled)? Why can't they resist?

IV. Aides

Self-Organizing "Blobs"

Morgan suggest that images from nature such as octopi, amoebas, spiders and dandelions can help groups better visualize creative ways to organize and accomplish their purposes. All of these "blob" metaphors focus discussion on aspects of self-organization and adaptability in accomplishing a purpose.

Example of a provocative question for a group:

- The facilitator might introduce a specific metaphor for discussion and ask: How would we go about our task if we were a _____? Alternatively, the facilitator can challenge the group members to come up with their own metaphors by asking: What animal or other image from nature captures for you the essence of how we should approach our task?

Deerhunting

(Morgan attributes this metaphor to his colleague Lin Ward.) "Deerhunters set out for the forest, shoot a deer and carry it back home. Right? Well, not exactly. They carry the body back, but the essence of the living deer remains in the forest." Organizations often do the same thing when they "implement programs" such as quality management, empowerment, visioning and so on. They have the artifacts to show that they did the program, but they do not have the "living essence" of the

ideas that underlie the program. False information about a false reality spreads through the CAS of the organization degrading the chances for positive, emergent behaviors. As with the Gulf, the Deerhunting metaphor gives a name to this phenomenon and provides a means for discussing what is happening.

Example of a provocative question for a group:

- Are we just "deerhunting" here?

These final two metaphors are not strictly attributable to Gareth Morgan. Many others have suggested these, or variations.

Holograms (or Fractals)

A hologram is a three-dimensional photograph; you've seen them in shops or on credit cards. An interesting property of a hologram is that if you cut it into pieces, each piece displays the entire picture! Similarly, look at a tree. The branching structure of the tree is basically the same from the trunk all the way out to the ends of the limbs. Whether you look at the tree as a whole, or break off a branch and study it alone, the number and style of branches at a branch-point is a characteristic feature of the type of tree you are looking at. This property of a unit of structure that is replicated at various levels is a harmonious, self-organizing feature of nature.

We can use this metaphor in exploring more harmonious organizational structures by focusing on the need to build an organizational kernel and then replicate this at all levels of the organization. For example, imagine a leadership kernel consisting of a trio of a physician, nurse and administrator that accepts collective accountability for the success of whatever they are charged to oversee. Once we understand this kernel, the hologram or fractal metaphor suggests that we should establish such leadership trios at all levels of the organization. If there is a level at which these three have a separate, not collectively accountable structure, there may be discord in the CAS.

Example of a provocative question for a group:

- What is the kernel of organizational structure we need here? What are the "minimum specs" for that kernel? Are we maintaining harmony by truly using the same kernel at all levels of the organization?

Team Metaphors

"Team" is an overused and underdefined word in current organizational jargon. Everyone is forming teams; everyone knows they need to be a good "team player" to be successful. But there are many, diverse images of a good team and how it operates. Successful team behavior is very different when one is on a basketball team (where fluid flow is valued), vs. a baseball team (where roles are very clearly defined), vs. a community theater group (where all roles are important but some get more visibility than others), vs. the NASA space shuttle team (where technical expertise and detailed planning are key). In general, it is not a good assumption to image that everyone in a CAS has the same mental picture of how they should interact on a "team." Explicit discussion is very valuable.

Example of a provocative question for a group:

- What type of "team" are we?

Wicked questions
Surfacing differences

Principles
• *Complexity lens*
• *Paradox*
• *Tune to the edge*

Tales
• *Make it or let it*
• *Emerges from*
  the fabric
• *Wizards and CEOs*
• *Unleashing*
  people

The basic idea:

Wicked questions are used to expose the assumptions we hold about an issue or situation. Articulating these assumptions provides an opportunity to see the patterns of thought and bring the differences in a group to the surface. These patterns and differences can be used to discover common ground or to find creative alternatives for stubborn problems.

Wicked questions invite participation in both forming the questions and searching for solutions.

Potential context for use:

- to change the role of leadership from having the answers to having the questions

- when innovative solutions are needed for stuck problems

- when there are polarized positions in a group and there seem to only either-or answers

- to open up possibilities that are not intuitively obvious

- to bring in new information to a problem or issue by exposing the differences

- to openly contrast goals and actual circumstances

- to promote ongoing inquiry

- when the context seems overwhelming and confusing, and the group needs an approach to make sense of the patterns

- to make the "undiscussable" discussable – to articulate the assumptions held by members in a group

Description:

Wicked questions do not have an obvious answer. They are used to expose the assumptions that shape our actions and choices. They are questions that articulate the embedded and often contradictory assumptions we hold about an issue, context or organization.

Aides
• *Reflection*

A question is wicked if there is an embedded paradox or tension in the question. The embedded tension or paradox creates an opportunity to tune to the edge of chaos. This is an area of great creativity and innovation.

A wicked question is not a trick question. With a trick question, someone knows the answer. Wicked questions do not have obvious answers. Their value lies in their capacity to open up options, inquiry and bring to the surface the fundamental issues that need to be addressed.

The paradoxes or tensions are often found in the implicit assumptions we hold about a context, issue or person. Exposing these assumptions in a question is often both uncomfortable and a relief. It is uncomfortable because the myths we create to bury our assumptions often seem more acceptable and defensible. They are the right thing to say. For example, it is popular today to talk about empowered front-line people. But in many cases, these words are not really accurate. We have created policies or procedures, such as needing supervisory approval for minor expenditures, that are the antithesis of empowerment.

Wicked questions invite participation in both forming the questions and searching for solutions to address them. Leaders can create the questions that can be used to promote a search for local solutions. They can be used to create the conditions for inquiry and innovation at all levels of the organization.

Reflection:

Before using this aide: Is there sufficient trust in the group to expose assumptions? Will people feel safe to express the paradoxes and tensions that exist?

After using this aide: How will the group use the question or questions to continue the process of searching for alternatives? How will the questions be shared with others? Which questions will be explored further? Why?

IV. Aides

Examples:

One comprehensive example of using wicked questions is in the tale "Make it Happen or Let it Happen." This tale is from outside the health care field. The organization, Federal Metals (or Fedmet), is a metals distributor. The senior management team of Fedmet was concerned that traditional strategic planning did not promote continuous inquiry and challenge. Instead, they felt it limited the strategic thinking to a few senior members of the organization. To create the conditions for emergence of strategic options throughout the organization, they ended their traditional annual strategic planning document with a series of wicked questions. These questions did not have obvious answers. The wicked questions were an invitation for everyone in the organization to participate in finding solutions to complex problems.

In the tale "Emerges from the Fabric," Linda Rusch uses wicked questions as a method to make the undiscussable discussable – to articulate the issues that people are thinking but not saying to each other – at least in the official meetings.

In another organization, wicked questions were used as an ongoing process. The wicked questions were posted on a wall in a common area of the offices. They stayed up for about six weeks after the original session. Sheets of paper and markers were left by the wall and people were invited to add to the questions, move them and create their own. The wall was near the coffee area and people would chat about the questions while they were getting their coffee. People in the organization talked about the issues and shared ideas for potential action opportunities. There was no stated agenda or specific meeting times allocated to this activity. It emerged from the wall, the questions and the connections created.

Facilitator's tips:

• To see the patterns in the questions, draw three to five shapes on pieces of paper and place them high on a wall. Space the patterns out. Ask each participant or group to create two wicked questions. You can specify the context or boundaries to focus the questions, if appropriate. Participants will write their questions on two sheets of paper, which can then be taped or tacked to the wall.

• Tell the participants to put each of their questions under the shape that seems to fit their questions, but ask the participants to read the other questions on the wall as well. When they see a question that seems similar in theme to their own question, place the questions together. Questions can be moved around and regrouped by the participants.

- The idea is to have the participants see the patterns in their questions – to see the common themes, the differences, the links. When they are satisfied with the sorting of the questions, have them examine the whole wall and ask what surprised them about the questions. Use this "surprise" idea to identify areas of new information or understanding that can lead to creative options.

- You can also ask them to identify action opportunities. Focus on one of the key questions. Ask participants to state one thing they could do (or stop doing) in their work to address the question.

- One of the purposes of this technique is to identify the patterns that are beneath the surface. Use plastic easel paper called "Static Image" sheets for this purpose. The plastic sheets stick to the wall with static and can be easily moved around without the bother of tacks or tape. Cut a regular easel-size piece of paper into eight to 16 smaller pieces so they can be more easily moved about. Whiteboard markers will write on these sheets.

- Be creative in the use of this technique. Experiment with methods to promote the inquiry process behind the technique itself.

Attachments:

Goldstein describes processes of inquiry that can be used to promote creativity, information flow and self-organization. He discusses Brenda Zimmerman's analysis of the wicked questions process at Fedmet, and also provides examples of other inquiry processes. Difference questioning was originally used to deal with "stuck problems" in dysfunctional families, and can be used as a method to expose differences in organizational settings. Goldstein extends difference questioning to look at cultural difference questioning and purpose contrasting. Purpose contrasting creates a stretch between what you say your work is all about and what you actually do.

Bibliography
- Goldstein, *Unshackled*

Generative relationships

The basic idea:

When really innovative ideas are needed, when the future is highly uncertain, traditional approaches to planning are of limited utility. An alternative approach involves the use of generative relationships. In this approach, new ideas and strategies emerge from relationships inside and outside the organization. The role of the leader is to foster generative relationships and learn from the results, letting direction emerge instead of being set in advance by a central authority.

Principles
- *Tune to the edge*
- *Good-enough vision*
- *Multiple actions*

Tales
- *What we could be doing*
- *Unleashing people*
- *Wizards and CEOs*
- *A leap into uncertainty*
- *Another way to think*

Potential context for use:

- when an organization needs new, creative strategies, a different direction, when times call for a firm to be more flexible and adaptive

- when a group is searching for innovative new processes or products

Bibliography
- Lane/Maxfield: *Generative*

- when an organization is evaluating potential partners for participation in a new system or network

Description:

The developers of the concept of generative relationships, Lane and Maxfield, identify three types of future scenarios confronted by organizations: clear, complicated and complex foresight horizons. When the future is clear – simple, stable and predictable – they suggest traditional approaches to setting strategy are appropriate since an organization can identify, rationally evaluate and select alternative courses of action designed to achieve some desired end. On the other end of the spectrum, when the world is characterized by "cascades of rapid change, perpetual novelty and ambiguity," they suggest an alternative, an approach based on what they have termed generative relationships. In this process, strategy and direction (which cannot be foreseen) emerge through ongoing interactions inside and outside the firm.

Aides
- *Stacey matrix*

IV. Aides

The two key elements of their approach are:

Aides
• *Reflection*

1. making sense of what is happening in the organization and within the larger system in which it resides

2. fostering generative relationships and following the directions and ideas they produce

Making sense, according to Lane and Maxfield, entails examining what is happening inside and outside the organization, interpreting this information from many viewpoints throughout the organization, not just in headquarters, and doing this all the time. This process must unearth and challenge basic assumptions about the organization and its environment. This work is best done through conversation. It is the contention of Lane and Maxfield that these practices will help an organization better understand itself, detect changes in the structure of its environment, make sense of these shifts and, therefore, open up space for possible future actions.

With this understanding, generative relationships enter the picture. Lane and Maxfield define a relationship as generative if it produces "new sources of value that cannot be foreseen in advance." But if you can't know in advance what a relationship will create for the organization, how can you decide which relationships to build, to continue?

Complexity theory suggests some essential preconditions, some characteristics to look for or build into relationships.

Preconditions for building generative relationships:

- *aligned directedness* – agreement about a general direction or area of interest

- *heterogeneity* – differences, diversity of ideas and competencies among agents

- *mutual directedness* – interest in and ability to engage in recurring interaction

- *permissions* – implicit or explicit permission for parties to engage in explorations

- *action opportunities* – ability and willingness of the agents to engage in joint action, to do more than talk

Reflection:

Look back in time in your organization and think about how new direction actually emerged, where new program ideas came from. Were they all anticipated, set in advance in the strategic plan, or were generative relationships at work?

Notice the increasing number of strategic alliances happening in the business world. Consider whether the conditions for generativeness were in place.

Examples:

The ROLM Story

A great example of the power of generative relationships is the story of the ROLM company as told in the generative relationships article by David Lane, an economics professor at the University of Modena and a faculty member at the Santa Fe Institute, and Robert Maxfield, one of the founders of ROLM.

In the 1970s, a little computer company with a few young electrical engineers focused on making minicomputers for the military decided it needed to diversify to grow. These engineers came up with the concept of marrying the computer with the telephone switch. With a basic system in hand ROLM sought to build relationships with the executives responsible for telephone services in medium-sized firms. Many were afraid to try out this risky new technology. But some made the switch and as a result of the significant savings and better, more flexible service they were rewarded with promotions, increased responsibility and encouragement to continue their efforts to bring down phone costs. These executives, with their understanding of the computer controlled PBX concept and their relationships with the ROLM account managers, began to search for new opportunities for savings and productivity gains. The resulting conversations between these company executives and ROLM representatives led to many product enhancements that led to an entirely new conception of the PBX – an "intelligent interface between a company and outsiders," instead of just an old-fashioned phone system.

Notice that this innovation did not come from the computer or phone company giants of the time, IBM and AT&T, but a small company that happened upon the strategy of generative relationships. ROLM was acquired by AT&T for a billion dollars.

The VHA Example

One of the authors, Curt Lindberg, had the good fortune of meeting David Lane and Bob Maxfield at a session on complexity and strategy at the Santa Fe Institute. With an up-close-and-personal acquaintance with the concept of generative relationships he decided to tap this approach in his plan to bring complexity thinking to VHA member leaders. As such, he sought relationships with a wide range of complexity faculty (from biologists, to computer scientists, to organizational theorists and consultants) and VHA member leaders (physicians, CEOs, nursing execs) who were searching for new management constructs and could be categorized as "early adopters." This mix of people satisfied a number of the preconditions for generativeness – heterogeneity, aligned directedness, an interest in recurring interaction (because the researchers were looking for organizational types who would try their complexity ideas and the practitioners were looking for partners to help them understand and use complexity-inspired management approaches). After getting acquainted in a series of educational sessions and workshops, quite a number of relationships developed – between the hospital leaders and complexity faculty, among the hospital executives themselves and among the faculty. From these relationships came new sources of value, surprises, new connections and real progress on the use of complexity thinking in management and in health care organizations. For instance:

- The number of VHA hospital leaders involved in this initiative grew, mostly by word of mouth, by more than a factor of three during its first year.

- Hospital leaders began to use complexity concepts to create fresh approaches to challenging issues such as how to plan when the future is unknowable, building health care systems, learning how to collaborate with longstanding competitors and creating organizational climates that allow creativity to flourish.

- One of the world's leading science writers heard about this initiative and began interviewing some of the hospital leaders for his book on complexity and business organizations. He is now being tapped by VHA to write stories of efforts by VHA members to use complexity thinking in their work so others can learn from them.

Some relationships did not become generative; they were simply dropped.

Facilitator's tips:

- When facing a new project or needing to kick off a planning process ask whether the relevant foresight horizon is clear, complicated or complex. If it is clear or complicated, traditional management and planning processes will probably work fine. If you are in the realm of the complex, consider using the approaches suggested by complexity, including generative relationships.

Aides
• *Stacey matrix*

- Map the existing or potential relationships germane to the issue or project at hand. Examine them in light of the preconditions for generative relationships. Ask whether you can do anything about missing preconditions. For instance, can you supply the room and the permission to experiment. If you uncover relationships that lack many of the preconditions and you can't supply them, consider dropping them and spending the energy elsewhere.

- Ask whether you have a sufficient number of relationships in play. The more important the issue or challenge and the more uncertainty you face, the more relationships you should consider fostering. This will increase the probability of producing innovations and creative new ideas.

- Regularly reflect on the status of the relationships. Give the ones that seem to be producing something of value room to develop further. Watch them for surprises, unexpected consequences; you may be looking at a potentially big opportunity. When such opportunities emerge, remain ready to put aside previous plans and follow where the relationships lead.

- Find out what is happening in the shadow system. Generative relationships are forming here all the time.

Principles
• *Shadow system*

IV. Aides

edgeware

Minimum specifications

The basic idea:

Establish only those very few requirements necessary to define something, leaving everything else open to the creative evolution of the CAS.

Principles
- *Complexity lens*
- *Good-enough vision*
- *Clockware/ swarmware*
- *Multiple actions*

Potential context for use:

- when designing or planning something

- when choosing between options

Tales
- *Another way to think*
- *Worldwide complexity*
- *Emerges from the fabric*
- *Unleashing people*

Description:

One of the most remarkable findings about complex adaptive systems is that simple rules can lead to complex behaviors. The classic example of this is the "Boids" computer simulation, developed in 1987 by Craig Reynolds. The simulation consists of a collection of autonomous agents – the boids – placed in a environment with obstacles. Each agent follows three simple rules: (1) maintain a minimum distance from all other boids and objects, (2) match speed with neighboring boids and (3) move toward the center of mass of the boids in your neighborhood. Remarkably, when the simulation is run, the boids exhibit the very lifelike behavior of flying in flocks around the objects on the screen. They flock, a complex behavior pattern, even though there is no rule explicitly telling them to do so. While this does not prove that real birds use these simple rules, it does show that simple rules – minimum specifications – can lead to complex behaviors. These complex behaviors emerge from the interactions among agents, rather than being imposed upon the CAS by an outside agent.

In contrast, we often over-specify things when designing or planning new activities in our organizations. This follows from the paradigm of "organization as a machine." If you are designing a machine, you had better think of everything, because the machine cannot think for itself. Of course, in some cases, organizations do act enough like machines to justify selected use of this metaphor. For example, if a person is having their gall bladder removed, they would prefer the surgical team operate like a precision machine; save that emerging, creative behavior for another time! Maximum specifications and the elimination of variation might be appropriate in such situations.

Bibliography
- Morgan: *Images*
- Plsek: *Creativity*

IV. Aides

Most of time, however, organizations are not machines; they are complex adaptive systems. The key learning from the simulations is that in the case of a CAS, minimum specifications and purposeful variation are the way to go.

Looking closer at the boids, we see some key elements of the minimum specifications aide (the minimum specifications for "minimum specifications"):

- Don't attempt to define the outcome or behavior of the system in detail.

- Provide local rules that can be applied by individual agents, or in individual cases.

- Have only a very few such rules.

- Allow complex behavior to emerge from the bottom-up in the system through interactions among agents, or between agents and the context.

A practical approach to establishing minimum specification would be to begin with a "good-enough vision" of the desired outcome. Then brainstorm a list of rules you might reasonably expect to lead to that outcome. Follow the rules of brainstorming; no criticism allowed. Now step back from the list and challenge each proposed rule by asking, "Can we imagine a situation where we get our desired outcome even though this rule is violated?" If you can, eliminate the rule. Also cross off rules that are simply minor variations of other rules. With the list whittled down, go back through each rule again and ask, "If all the other rules are met, but this one is violated, will we certainly fail to achieve our desired outcome?" Think of each rule as unnecessarily constraining creativity. If you can imagine situations in which you still get the desired outcome even if that rule is violated, throw it out, it is not a minimum spec. Continue this process until you have only a few rules left, and all pass the test above.

Reflections:

Before using this aide: What has happened in the past when we have tried to use maximum specification and total conformance in our design and planning efforts? How has this experience contrasted with times when we have given people few rules and lots of freedom to act?

After using this aide: What creative approaches can we imagine that would still meet our minimum specifications? What can we now do to tune our organization to the edge of chaos?

Examples:

An example of establishing minimum specifications is given in the attachments. Additional examples of how we used "min specs" in designing this resource book are given in the introductions to this chapter.

Facilitator's Tips:

• Follow the process described above to get started using this aide, but do not be constrained by it. This is just one way to do it using familiar group tools such as brainstorming and group discussion. Experiment.

• Take it slow and really think as you whittle down the list to a minimum. Challenge quick-judgment statements such as, "You gotta have that." Ask, "Wait a minute, you're telling me that there is no possible way to achieve the outcome unless that rule is applied?"

• Revisit the minimum specifications from time to time as you proceed with the actual work to which the specs refer. Stress creative experimentation. Check to see that new rules (constraints on how we are thinking about what must be) have not inadvertently crept into use. Review the list and challenge each rule anew; do we really need each rule?

• When faced with a choice among options, go back to the minimum specs. Eliminate options that violate a rule (after reaffirming that the rule really is absolutely necessary). If you have multiple options that all meet the minimum specs, look for ways to try them all and let direction emerge.

IV. Aides

Generating minimum specifications for this book

As you will see in the introductions to several chapters in this book, we used minimum specifications throughout. An elaboration on one such instance will serve as an illustration of this aide.

Principles
• *Good-enough*
vision

1. At the first meeting about the book, we explored how to create learning experiences about complexity for health care leaders. After some dialogue, we had a good-enough vision: "A learning experience for innovators and early adopters that equips them to go out and generate, capture, reflect on and understand complexity stories." We also noted that we wanted the learning experience to be living; that is, we hoped that individuals and groups that took part in the experience would be able to go out and reproduce it with others.

2. We then brainstormed specifications for this learning experience. Every idea was boarded for consideration – no judgment at this phase of the effort.

3. After several minutes of brainstorming we felt that we had exhausted our ideas. We then went back through the list asking, "Do we really need that spec, can't we still have a good learning experience without it?" One rule that was easily eliminated was that participants should be teams from an organization. We could easily imagine a good learning experience for an individual. Indeed, our initial complexity learning group was composed almost entirely of individuals. Several other rules were similarly eliminated, or were removed as being redundant with other rules.

4. We now had a list of seven specifications for the learning experience we hoped to create:
    •   everyone has enough content to enable intelligent conversation
    •   actions during the experience should be consistent with complexity theory
    •   all agree to be complementary learners; committed to

continuous awareness and open, honest, safe reflection, both individually and collectively
- good-enough diversity, ever-changing (as much as practical and possible to avoid inbreeding)
- participants have the capacity, permission, and responsibility to take action in their home CASs
- enough time together for rich information flow (to enable and allow reproduction)
- a safe container for reflection

5. While this looks like a nice, logical, short list, we then went back through it one more time to challenge whether it really was a minimum list. Considering each rule a potentially unnecessary restriction on our creativity, we took them one at a time and asked, "If all the other rules are met, but this one is violated, do we really risk not achieving our desired outcome?"

In this process, we eliminated the second item in number four above, "actions during the experience should be consistent with complexity theory." On the surface, this seemed an obvious rule. Surely, if we were going to help others understand complexity, we must model it consistently in our behavior at all times. But on reflection, we realized that actions that were inconsistent with theory could actually enhance the learning experience. If participants were really learning, then they should be able to point out these inconsistencies. The reflection and discussion that followed could be very rich. Besides, removing this specification takes away the burden on everyone to always be unnaturally perfect.

The six remaining rules are the minimum specifications for the learning experiences of this book.

Reflection

The basic idea:

The art of temporarily detaching oneself from a situation in order to think clearly about it, assign interpretation and meaning to the situation, and draw out deeper learnings.

Principles
• *Complexity lens*
• *Clockware/ swarmware*
• *Tune to the edge*
• *Paradox*
• *Shadow system*

Potential context for use:

• Literally, anytime. This is the most ubiquitous aide. It is useful to reflect before you do anything, and after you do anything.

Tales
• *Learn as you go*
• *Another way to think*
• *Make it or let it*
• *Worldwide complexity*

Description:

Reflection is a natural part of any learning. Whether we think about it or not, things happen all around us, and will simply continue to happen. However, if we think about them – reflect on them, learn from them – we might see patterns in the events around us that help us better understand what is going on. Without reflection, we remain hapless victims (or, if we are lucky, hapless beneficiaries) of events. With reflection, we can begin to modify our actions and expectations and, potentially, have a more constructive effect on future events. While it could be argued that reflection is what everyone does naturally every minute of the day, what we are talking about here is a conscious and purposeful effort that builds capacity for more effective action on the part of the individual or group participating in the reflection.

Bibliography
• Schon: *Reflective*

The basic action of reflection is to ask questions such as:

• What do we think is going on here?

• What did we intend to happen? What did happen?

• How is what I am observing connected with deeper theories about how things work?

• Here is my view and how I arrived at it; how do others see it?

• What assumptions are we making?

• What pressures seem to be at play in the system?

IV. Aides

- What role am I playing?

- What am I thinking and feeling?

- What leads me to think and feel the way I do?

- What am I going to do with my insight?

> The goal of this inquiry is to become more aware
> of one's own thinking and reasoning.

As a matter of style, some people prefer to reflect by themselves, while others prefer to reflect in conversation with others. Both modes are useful and neither should be used to the exclusion of the other. Individuals who prefer to reflect by themselves will benefit greatly from seeing the points of view and mental models of others. On the other hand, those who can only reflect in conversation with others may not be developing sufficient self-reflective skills for use in situations when immediate action is needed.

Three kinds of reflection

We can speak of at least three different types of reflection:

- *Hindsight reflection* involves looking back on events, possibly reinterpreting them, and drawing out lessons learned.

- *Foresight reflection* involves imaginatively playing out events into the future for the purpose of understanding more about what to do in the present and what signals to monitor for direction.

- *Insight reflection* is the most subtle skill in that it involves simultaneously being both in a present situation and detached from that situation; simultaneously participating in a situation, interpreting the situation, adjusting the situation and learning from the situation.

The modern concept of reflective learning can be traced to philosopher John Dewey, and was further developed by several others. For example, reflection is the "Study" phase of the Shewhart-Deming cycle of Plan-Do-Study-Act.

Examples:

The entire Tales chapter is an illustration of reflection. There are examples of all three types of reflection, as well as both individual and group reflection. Some of the tales also directly illustrate the value of multiple lenses, in that various people have offered their reflections. The tales cited in the margin illustrate the direct use of this aide as part of an evolving context.

Facilitator's Tips:

- Be a good model of reflection yourself. Balance your own private and group reflection. Make it known that you keep a journal, or at least make time for private reflection. When you ask questions in groups, don't look for a particular right answer, and don't always feel that you have to supply an answer or have the last word. Be comfortable with silence. Be careful of your own defensive reactions. Honor others' points of view as true for them and an important part of the coevolving CAS.

- Stress the need for diversity of reflection. Challenge too easy consensus and oversimplified labels. Ask, "That's one way of seeing it, what are others? How do you think (a specific person or group) would see that?"

- Remember that reflection is only one phase of a cycle of learning that also involves doing something. Always ask the "So what?" question. "What have we learned from this? What are we going to do now?"

edgeware

From lifecycle to ecocycle
Renewal through destruction and encouraging diversity for sustainability

The basic idea:

The evolution and sustainability of complex adaptive systems includes the natural and necessary processes of *destruction* and *renewal*. The ecocycle framework invites leaders to think about what they need to deliberately destroy or stop doing to facilitate the renewal of their work in health care.

Drawing from biological systems, the ecocycle also suggests a need for a healthy organization or system to have parts (or aspects) of the organization in every phase of the ecocycle. Diversity in the phases of ecocycle is crucial for the sustainability of a complex adaptive system.

Principles
• *Complexity lens*
• *Clockware/ swarmware*
• *Tune to the edge*
• *Cooperation/ competition*
• *Multiple actions*

Bibliography
• Hurst and Zimmerman: *Lifecycle to ecocycle*
• Hurst: *Crisis and renewal*

Potential context for use:

- to identify things to stop doing to support the renewal of the work or of health care

- to recognize when you are complicit in perpetuating the very things you know need to be stopped

- to redirect energy and reallocate resources to activities that support renewal and change

- to determine the skills and attributes needed for a management team, board of directors or project team

- as a contingency framework, to determine which techniques or approaches are needed for different phases of work

IV. Aides

- to encourage diversity in the stages of the ecocycle by recognizing that healthy organizations or systems exhibit all phases of renewal, birth, maturity and destruction

In this aide, the description section gives some background to the ecocycle concept. The facilitator's tips section outlines four ways to use the ecocycle in organizations. The examples section follows the facilitator's tips and provides two situations for which deliberate use of the model have been helpful for organizations facing major changes in their environments. For a more complete description of the ecocycle model, read Hurst and Zimmerman, "From Life Cycle to Ecocycle: A New Perspective on the Growth, Maturity, Destruction and Renewal of Complex Systems," Journal of Management Inquiry, Vol. 3, No. 4, pp. 339-354.

Description:

The lifecycle model of organizations has proven useful to understand the growth and maturity of industries and organizations. It has been called the S curve in business schools. It depicts the birth, growth and maturity of a business or industry.

However, the S curve has failed to address other aspects of living systems: their death and conception, in other words the phases of destruction and renewal. The model is silent on these aspects of a true lifecycle. The ecocycle extends the lifecycle concept to incorporate these dimensions. The evolution and sustainability of complex adaptive systems includes the natural and necessary roles of destruction and renewal. The paradox is that renewal and long-term viability require destruction.

The ecocycle concept is used in biology and depicted as an infinity loop. In this case, the S curve of the business school lifecycle model is complemented by a reverse S curve. It is the reverse S curve, shown on the following page with the dotted line, that represents the death and conception of living systems. In our depiction of the model, we call these stages creative destruction and renewal. The importance of the infinity loop is that it shows there is no beginning or end. The stages are

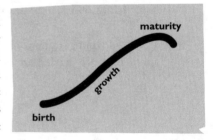

all connected to each other. Hence renewal and destruction are part of an ongoing process.

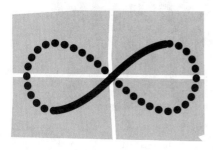

Being an infinity cycle, there is no obvious start or end to the cycle. Let us begin our examination of the stages at the beginning of the traditional S curve. We will begin each phase by using the biological example of a forest and then look at the analogous phase in human organizations.

The lower left quadrant is the birth and early stage of life phase. This may be an open patch in a forest. This state is characterized by a wide variety of species all competing for the resources. There is usually not one dominant species. There are a lot of births in this stage, but many of the new births do not reach maturity.

Principles
• *Multiple actions*
• *Competition/ cooperation*

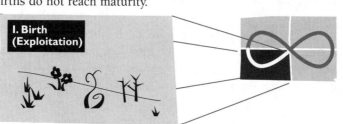

In human organizations, this is the early entrepreneurial phase of an industry or organization. This is a period of high energy, lots of new ideas and trial-and-error learning. Resources are spread over a variety of projects or activities.

In the forest, after a while the open space becomes crowded, competition starts to require efficiency. Fewer species are supported as the resources become consolidated or conserved in a few trees that begin to dominate the space. This maturity or conservation phase is the upper right quadrant on the ecocycle.

In human organizations, travelling up the S curve from the lower quadrant to the upper right quadrant has been the mainstay of business wisdom for the past 50 years. Strategic planning, budgeting and most control systems are designed for this process of consolidation and improving efficiency. Streamlining operations and allocating resources with more predictable returns is good management as you move through this phase.

We now move to the reverse S curve as we move to the lower right

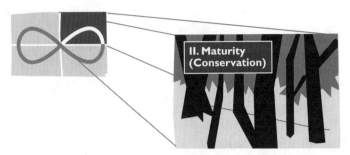

quadrant. This is the phase of creative destruction, or in our forest analogy, the forest fire. The system is not fully destroyed. But this is not obvious to the naked eye. The burning of the trees and dead wood releases nutrients and genetic material into the soil to create the conditions for new growth.

In human organizations, the creative destruction phase may require dismantling systems and structures that have become too rigid, have too little variety and are not responsive to the current needs of the community (or market). An additional level of difficulty in human organizations is the consciousness of the participants who may cling to the old ways because they were the keys to success as they moved up the S curve. This can be a very disturbing, unsettling time for organizations as assumptions need to be exposed and re-examined in light of changing needs and environments. However, the creative aspect of the creative destruction phase also indicates the potential for this to be a period of high innovation and new insights.

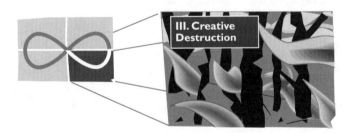

The quadrant in the upper left completes the reverse S curve and the ecocycle. This is the mobilization and renewal phase. In a forest, this is the phase after the fire in which open spaces have now been created. The soil is rich with nutrients and the number of possibilities of how these nutrients will be recombined is very great. It is rich with potential but it is not at all clear what combinations will be most successful.

In organizational terms, this is a phase in which the needs of the organization are not about increasing efficiency or even effectiveness. Instead, this is a stage of creating connections, mobilizing resources and skills to create the next generation of effective (and eventually efficient) goods and services.

As these brief descriptions show, the role of the manager and of the leader change radically when moving up the S curve as opposed to travelling the reverse S curve. The lessons from complexity science are highly relevant to travelling the reverse S curve.

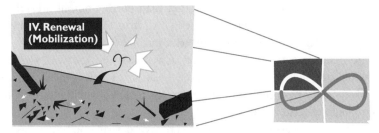

Looking at a forest analogy, we learn several things about the ecocycle. First, a healthy forest exhibits patch dynamics. In other words, a healthy forest has all parts of the ecocycle in evidence. Some parts of the forest are dense with mature trees. Other parts are open patches in which life is not obvious to the naked eye. A healthy forest will have areas of new growth with many species. Finally, there are parts of the forest that are in periods of destruction perhaps through a fire, flood or disease.

Patch dynamics are healthy for forests. Yet they look untidy and a bit disorganized. From an aerial view, the unbroken blanket of mature trees may be more aesthetically appealing, but history has shown that a forest in this state is brittle and can be completely devastated by, for example, a fire. Here is the paradox. The forest needs occasional fires (or other forms of creative destruction) to renew itself. However, a massive fire can actually damage not only the trees but also the soil. What this aide is

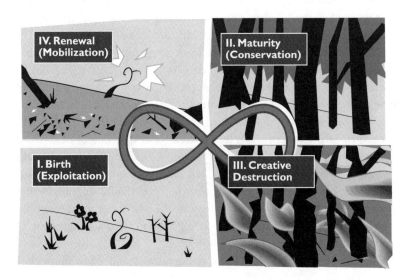

advocating is not a "scorched earth" policy of wanton destruction. Rather fires or their equivalent in organizations, can be beneficial if they break down the structures without damaging the soil.

With no firebreaks in the forest, there is nothing to stop the path of destruction caused by a fire. Firefighters discovered this in the late 1970s and have since changed strategies. Rather than putting out all fires, they look for situations in which they can let a fire burn. They also deliberately set fires at times. Fire serves as a powerful form of creative destruction in forests. It burns away the dead wood, it replaces the soil with needed nutrients and sets the context for the creation of new generations of growth or even new species. A forest needs to have patchiness to it to ensure its long-term viability.

The ecocycle uses the concept of creative destruction and crisis to explain the necessary destruction of forms and structures periodically to maintain the long-term viability of the overall system. The word crisis is derived from the Greek *krinein,* meaning "to sift." In the ecocycle model, we think about crises as opportunities to sift so that the unnecessary forms and structures are removed to enable the substance to be renewed and continue to evolve.

What does this mean for organizations or human systems? Forms and structures that no longer support the work or the mission of an organization or system need to be destroyed in a manner that does not destroy the substance. It is a substance over form distinction. Forms and structures are necessary to enable the work to be accomplished, but they are not the essence of the work. In health care, this has become a major issue. The substance of health care is not the structures of hospitals, clinics or even the professions of physicians and nurses. Rather these are forms that have enabled health care work. As enablers, they are crucial, but they are not the substance of the work. Forms and structures must be seen as ephemeral. They support the work, but are not the work itself.

Why should health care leaders learn about this concept? It sounds quite threatening to the medical professions and institutions. This is a fair assessment, yet this appears to be happening anyway and it is preferable to be a player in the process to ensure the substance of health care is not lost, but renewed in this period of change. We return to the paradox mentioned earlier that fires can lead to creative destruction or devastation. Creative destruction is positive and is not synonymous with devastation that destroys forms and structures, but substance as well. In a forest, a devastating fire has the potential to destroy the trees and the soil. In these situations, it can take generations before the soil can nurture new life. Creative destruction is designed to release the nutrients so that new life can indeed emerge.

In addition, leaders of health care organizations need to think about whether their organizations exhibit patch dynamics. Is there enough diversity in the organization to prevent a single match from setting fire to the whole system? Are there firebreaks in the organization? Firebreaks may take the form of diversity in funding sources so that one funding source cannot determine the survival or demise of the organization. Firebreaks may also be the "skunk works" in the organization – the parts of the organization that are trying out new ideas and approaches uninhibited by the "way things are done here." This is insurance for situations when the community, the funders, the patients or other key constituents no longer support the way things are done here.

Reflection

Before using this aide:
- Will the group be comfortable using biological metaphors (such as a forest) to reflect the issues in your organization?

- Will the group see this as an unethical approach? Will they trust that this is a process of honest reflection? Can you demonstrate this by applying the model first to your own context before exposing others to the model?

After using this aide:
- How can you move the intellectual discussion of application of the metaphor and model into meaningful action?

Facilitator's Tips:

Stop doing and complicity exercise
- After a description of the ecocycle, post on a flip chart these two questions:

  What do you need to stop doing to focus on (the nutrients or) the substance of your work?

  In what ways are you complicit in perpetuating what you say you must stop doing?

- Direct the participants to spend 10 minutes addressing these questions on their own. Then direct them to spend 10 minutes

IV. Aides

sharing answers with their group. For very large groups, you will need to break them into smaller groups. Have each group post on the flipchart the two "best" answers – one for what you must stop doing, and one for how you are complicit.

- The definition of "best" has to satisfy the "whoa" test. In other words, what made you sit back and go "whoa"? You don't have to agree with the "best," you simply have to find one that took you by surprise. Maybe it is controversial, maybe it is gut wrenching and maybe it is challenging or outrageous.

- Post the flipchart on the wall when you are finished. Use these for discussion purposes and coming to some agreement on what the group will stop doing.

- It is crucial that the complicity side of the exercise be completed. Without it, it is too easy to say that what must be stopped or changed is someone else's responsibility or domain. The purpose of the exercise is to uncover how your own actions need to change to enhance the renewal of the work. Recognizing your own complicity in maintaining the status quo is a critical first step.

Substance over form exercise

- Suggest individual work for 20 minutes. Because they will not be sharing this with others, they can be brutally honest with themselves.

- Draw a vertical line down the middle of a piece of paper. On one side of the line write, "form" and on the other write "substance."

- Think about your work. What aspects of your work are form and what aspects are substance? As you enter something on the substance side of the page, ask yourself if there is any way this could be form. Could there be something more substantive that underlies it (try to go as deep as you can on the substance side).

- Ask yourself what forms or structures need to be abandoned to focus on the core substance or purpose of your work?

Patch dynamics exercise

- After a reading of the ecocycle article or a discussion of the need for patch dynamics in the organization, ask the participants to map the various activities of the organization on an ecocycle diagram.

- One way to do this is to identify some of the key activities, programs or projects of the group. Have participants put the activities on sticky notes. On a large flipchart, draw the ecocycle as background. Post the flipchart on a wall. Direct participants to place their sticky notes on the diagram.

- The differences can open up conversations about how people view different programs, their implicit assumptions about the environment and strategic directions.

- Have people listen to each other's ideas and move their sticky notes if their perspectives have changed.

- After the discussion has taken its course, say 30 to 60 minutes, look at the map drawn. Is there a sense of healthy patch dynamics in the organization? Does the map show areas where there is little emphasis? Does this indicate the need to redirect energy and resources in these areas?

- Often what happens in this exercise is that an organization will be depicted with a dominance in the mature or conservation phase of the ecocycle. In those cases, it is often useful to reiterate the argument about firebreaks and the need for them as protection against massive devastation. Ask the participants to identify the firebreaks that exist in the system. Then ask them how they can put more firebreaks into their system. Ideally, you would like them to identify where these firebreaks are most needed and suggest next steps to implementing them.

Choosing the management method to suit the ecocycle stage

- One of the messages of the ecocycle is that the dominant management models, tools and techniques are highly relevant for the S curve of the ecocycle but are inappropriate to address the reverse S side. It suggests a contingency approach for management. When on the S curve, use the traditional strategic

Aides
• *Stacey matrix*

planning and management approaches. When on the reverse S, use methods or aides that fit an edge-of-chaos mode.

- The problem is that what made an organization or system successful on the rise from birth to maturity often is the opposite of what is needed for the creative destruction and renewal phases. The expression "nothing fails like success" fits here if the management and leadership do not adjust for the change in the stage of the ecocycle that the organization is facing.

- As a facilitator, ask participants to identify some of their most successful programs or services. Ask them to map them on the ecocycle. Direct the participants to explain the critical success factors of the program or programs. Then ask them how these critical success factors could become critical failure factors if the environment changed. Is this happening now? Where? What does this suggest for alternative management and leadership approaches? (If the alternatives needed are for more work on the reverse S of the curve, then look to other aides in Edgeware for guidance or suggestions.)

- The purpose of this exercise is to explore how the success factors of the past can blind you to the needs of the future.

Examples:

(Told by Brenda Zimmerman.)

In this section, I provide two examples of the Ecocycle aide in practice. The first relates to leaders of organizations who, using the stop doing and complicity exercise, became "unstuck" in their leadership role. The second example tells the story of how a board realized that it needed more capacity for creative destruction and renewal and deliberately recruited new board members to fulfill this need.

Example 1: Leaders of social service agencies stop doing and get moving

In late November 1996, I facilitated a meeting with close to 100 leaders of social service agencies. We did the "stop doing and complicity exercise." These organizations were in similar contexts of decreasing government support, increasing demand for their services and exhausted employees.

In response to "what should we stop doing," a few of their answers were:

- practicing impression management

- taking control of everything

- fighting with funding sources (especially on how to implement programs)

- reacting to negative energy

- being seduced by matters of false importance such as paper work, putting out brush fires, negative thinking and old greivances

There was a strong sense in the meeting that these were common issues across the agencies. Before doing the complicity side of the exercise, several of the CEOs expressed frustration that these realities were unchangeable by them.

I then asked them to think carefully about the lists that had been generated and take a hard look in the mirror to reveal ways they had been complicit in perpetuating the problems.

In response, they generated long lists of ideas, some of which were:

- rescuing or protecting others from change

- taking things personally

- feeding into negative energy by not countering with something positive

- condoning negativity with silence

- avoiding talking about the real issues

- assuming too much responsibility

- keeping information to ourselves

- believing they are indispensable to the organization

When we debriefed the exercise, participants commented that there was a paradox in the complicity part of the exercise. Recognizing one's complicity in the problems was humbling but at the same time energizing. The leaders were all comfortable taking action and yet had felt frozen in many ways. By recognizing their own part in the problems, they had specific things they could change. In addition, they commented on how it was great to be thinking about what they had to stop doing rather than adding to their to-do lists.

Since then, several of them have spoken to me about the changes they have made. They commented that they are far more selective about what meetings to attend. They said they find negative energy far less threatening because they felt they didn't need to own it or work with it. They also found their role as leaders had both expanded in scope at the same time as they were more willing to delegate real responsibility.

Example 2: An organization brings creative destruction and renewal to its board

A board of a not-for-profit organization worked with the ecocycle to reveal what management and governance practices were needed to address changes in their context. The organization was facing competition for its services from all three sectors: other not-for-profit organizations, government agencies and for-profit businesses. The organization needed to rethink its identity and role in a context of increasing competition for a shrinking pool of financial resources and increasing demand for its services in the community.

Realizing that the organization's success to date had been due to skills at riding up the S curve, the board saw that its current needs were radically different. One of the changes it made was to change the criteria for board members. To go through the creative destruction and renewal phase, board members needed skills in the areas of building generative relationships (often with organizations and sectors with which they had not previously interacted to any great extent), thinking about the issues systemically and making sense of complex information. The organization looked for board members who were diverse in backgrounds and experience, shared a passion for the mission of the organization, but were not committed to the institution itself. These new board members were willing and able to make connections with people and organizations to rethink how the substance of the work should be done. In essence, the organization brought the capacity for creative destruction and renewal into the board.

Aides
• *Generative relationships*

About three years into this process, the board was faced with a 25 percent cut to its funding. With the help of the board and with the explicit use of complex adaptive systems thinking, the organization survived and has now, almost three years later, returned to its original size. However, the organization is radically different in form than its predecessor. What was once one organization is now two linked organizations. The tasks and programs for the most part are substantially changed from those offered six years ago. What has remained unchanged is the focus and passion for child welfare and prevention of social, economic and health problems for children.

One interesting footnote to this story is the organization in question found CAS thinking so valuable for its own purposes, that one of its new services is a consulting practice for other not-for-profit organizations based on the principles of CAS.

IV. Aides

Board of trustees
Evaluation and appreciation

James B. Webber

Introduction:

"Complexity is about reframing our understanding of many systems by using a metaphor associated with life and living systems rather than machines or mechanical systems" (Primer chapter, page 18).

Most trustee evaluation schemes were designed for the machine age, for stable worlds characterized by predictable futures, planning as prescriptive intent, being in control and short-term fiduciary responsibility. The oversight of conformance and performance is a necessary role, but one that is insufficient in a world of unpredictable change.

In a world in which strategy becomes emergent, where being somewhat out of control is desirable and where leadership is asked to absorb and amplify uncertainty rather than protect the institution from it, the board, along with the rest of the organization, must assume the additional role of adapting and learning. The three approaches outlined in this section are designed to help with this, and can be used with the board and any other leadership group within the organization. The approaches are:

1. Board evaluation using the complexity lens
2. Board evaluation using "slow learning"
3. Celebrating our CASness

Principles
- *Complexity lens*
- *Clockware/ swarmware*

Bibliography
- Stacey: *Strategic management*

IV. Aides

1. *Board evaluation using the complexity lens*

The basic idea:

Complexity criteria drawn from *Edgeware* materials are used to assess and appreciate the role of the board in creating conditions of adaptability and learning among board members and within the institution and its leadership.

Potential context for use:

- when there is a sense that change is overwhelming the institution

- when there are complaints of lack of responsiveness and lack of nimbleness

- when the *Conforming* and *Performing* roles of the board seem to be in good shape, but there is a serious, intuitive concern for long-term viability

- when the CEO is trying to introduce a complexity perspective into the leadership approach of the organization and needs the support, understanding and wisdom of the trustees to do so

- when board members need a step-by-step approach to exploring complexity (in spite of our reservations about explicit tools)

Background:

Board evaluation systems under conditions of both stability and change should involve the search for both efficiency and adaptability.

Both "A" Stable World, Search for Efficiency	And "B" Unstable World, Search for Adaptability
Board Role: *Conforming* and *Performing*	Board Role: *Adapting* and *Evolving*
Short-term fiduciary responsibility	Long-term fiduciary responsibility
An orderly world. Protect from and dampen uncertainty and change.	*A disorderly world. Absorb and learn from uncertainty and change.*
Board self-assessment topics: • Governance • Planning oversight • Quality oversight • Community oversight • Financial oversight • Management oversight • Board effectiveness • Individual assessment	Board self-assessment topics: (From: *Edgeware: Complexity Resources for Health Care Leaders*) • A Complexity Science Primer "[An invitation] to examine the *unpredictable*, disorderly and unstable aspects of organizations." • Nine Emerging, Connected Organizational and Leadership Principles – The lens of complexity – Good-enough vision – Clockware/swarmware – Tune to the edge – Uncover paradox and tension – Multiple actions, let directions emerge – Listen to the shadow system – Grow complex systems through chunking – Mix cooperation and competition •Aides for Complexity •Tales of Complexity

There are many examples of health care organizations
that did a fine job in column "A," but missed the boat in column "B." They
performed, but did not evolve.

IV. Aides

Description:

1. Complexity criteria (see sample criteria in the next sections) are first identified, reviewed and discussed for understanding, using the resources in *Edgeware*.

2. The board then rates the relevance of the criteria to the organization's situation using a simple scale, say, from 1 (low) to 3 (high).

Aides
• *Reflection*

3. Given highly relevant criteria, how is the board and the institution doing? Use a simple scale, say, from 1 (low) to 10 (high). Evaluate and discuss the extent the organization or board meets each relevant criteria.

4. Explore what actions are suggested by the results of the evaluation. How can the board or the organization act more like a living system and less like a machine? In what ways can the organization's leadership create conditions that will promote organizational learning, adaptability and responsiveness?

Reflection: This process helps boards spend time discussing long-term viability rather than concentrating on shorter-term operating and conformance matters. Board members make their wisdom explicit by searching for and testing complexity criteria, and by applying the relevant criteria to the situation at hand.

Examples:

A. In a retreat setting, trustees, management and medical staff members of a community hospital developed a set of complexity criteria to provide a basis for evaluating management performance in an uncertain future. The need for the complexity criteria arose when the CEO convinced board members that adaptability of the organization was as important as current operating efficiency. After a brief primer on complex adaptive systems using a chart similar to "Both 'A' and 'B'" above, and Stacey's Agreement and Certainty Matrix, participants were asked to evaluate the relevance of a set of complexity criteria. Small groups were formed to evaluate which characteristics were most applicable to the hospital's future governance using a scale of 1 (low) to 3 (high). The group work was tallied, discussed and a consensus was reached by the full group. The results were a set of institutional expectations for the board in creating conditions for greater adaptability. A portion of the results are shown here.

Aides
• *Stacey matrix*

Adaptability Criteria	Group Ratings 1 (low) – 3 (high)	Comments
• extent leadership is aware of and tries to be one step ahead of emerging trends	2.8	• but not too far out front
• appreciation of experiments and learning	2.7	• *innovation* is a better term than *experiments*
• do incentives support adaptability?	2.3	• need reinforcement to walk on the edge
• exploratory thinking before strategic planning	2.0	• need a balance between the two
• membership diversity of all kinds	2.7	• it takes all kinds, but no quotas
• web of connections of board members – breadth and depth of community connections	2.8	• web masters wanted!
• balanced scorecard for the hospital, adding innovation, adaptability and personal development to conventional financial performance and activity measures	1.5	• no comments
• acceptance of ambiguities, paradoxes and dilemmas at the top	2.2	• it is the reality; calls for wisdom

IV. Aides

B. The board of directors of a state hospital association used this method to evaluate their effectiveness under conditions of disruptive industry change. The project was initiated by the president of the organization, who felt the board was spending its time on minutia and missing the need for industry restructuring and association redesign. In evaluating themselves against a set of complexity criteria, they found that they were spending too much time on routine and short-term matters and were dodging their long-term fiduciary responsibility for creating the conditions for hospital and association change.

Specifically, the criteria used were clustered into four groups similar to those listed here, and an overall rating was given to the board's performance for each. The results were:

Criteria	Group Ratings 1 (low) – 5 (high)	Comments
• evolutionary promise	1.6	• virtually no time spent or consideration given to adaptability, emergence, learning, boundary stretching; too busy to do so
• analytical creativity	1.7	• few assumptions challenged, no exploratory thinking, some consideration of market value migrating away from hospitals
• political savvy	3.1	• in dealing with the state, yes; in terms of our membership, a lack of diversity on the board; political channels seem clogged
• relational competence	4.1	• have created and maintained a diverse set of relationships, could use them in a more generative fashion

Sample criteria (see also the Primer, Principles and Tales chapters of this book):

Overall: Health care organizations, like all living systems, are viewed as complex adaptive systems, always in the process of evolving, changing and becoming in an unpredictable world. In this view, the leader sees the organization through the complexity lens.

Evolutionary Promise:

- Consciously encourages living on the edge to stimulate complex learning and knowledge creation. Amplifies fluctuations to see what can be learned. Focuses on contradictions and paradoxes as signals of potential emergence to higher levels of performance.

- Allows innovative fringe activity and protects such activity from hidebound traditions, institutional memory and bureaucratic relapse. Searches for the patterns that emerge from boundary-stretching activities.

- Thinks in terms of learning, evolving, adapting, resiliency, nimbleness, redundancies, building blocks, organizational slack, the possibility of quantum leaps and individual variety that leads to perpetual novelty.

- Views the future as always unfolding and transitioning and never fixed in spite of pundits' prognostications at industry conferences.

- Thinks of long-term societal legitimacy and ecological sustainability as a source of opportunity.

- Values the notion of coevolution, the coordinated and interdependent evolution of two or more parties, when partnering with others.

Emergent Planning:

- Ensures that open, exploratory, conceptual discussions precede any strategy-making effort. Searches for emergent strategies. Views planning as a discovery process, not as predetermined decision-making.

- Is sensitive to how data and information are handled. Are assumptions challenged, and filters surfaced and questioned? Sees management as creators, not just processors of information.

- Encourages competing for share of future, emergent opportunities (opportunity share) as well as performance in existing markets (market share).

- Ensures that the board as well as the organization as a whole enjoys abundant, shared information.

- Measures and monitors the rate of development and the contribution of new service and product initiatives, those that have been launched in the last three to five years.

- Thinks in terms of a healthy degree of diversity, anxiety and information flow when creative strategies are needed.

- Spends time encouraging and learning from multiple small experiments, searches for patterns in these endeavors and helps along those that are growing.

- Is comfortable setting a few minimum specifications to define a desired approach, leaving everything else open to creative emergence.

- Encourages examination of contradictions in current practice and challenges to orthodoxy from which new directions emerge.

- Uncovers and works with differences in viewpoints rather than suppressing them.

Relational Competence:
- Promotes distributed control, understanding that it, not centralized control, leads to adaptability.

- Ensures diversity on the board and the leadership team by including different leadership styles, personality types, learning styles and demographic backgrounds. Tolerates "loose cannons" and unorthodox thinkers in the organization.

- Prides oneself on, and continues to develop the breadth, depth and diversity of its network of connections in relevant communities.

- Ensures that the right people come together for future-oriented, generative relationships. Encourages such relationships. Understands that opportunities arise from generative relationships.

- Concerns self with the energy, mood and spirit of the organization since human relationships are central to viability, sustainability and health.

Facilitator's Tips:

With lists, weighting and evaluation, this aide is designed to appeal to concrete, rational thinkers. Many CEOs and board members like this approach. However, members of governing bodies often have substantial life experience and have been selected for their hard-earned wisdom. Such members may be affronted by linear evaluation schemes. If this is the case, use the next aide, which is much more artful and emphasizes wisdom informed by complexity principles.

2. Board evaluation using "slow learning"

The basic idea:

Wisdom of board members is built through the slow and unconscious learning processes of rumination, osmosis and contemplation. Wisdom as a group emerges from collective reflection, appreciation and sense-making. To the extent that the complexity way of thinking and seeing is inherent in all living systems, wise board members already know it. The purpose of this aide is to help make this understanding explicit and in doing so, to enhance the governance of adaptability.

Potential context for use:

- when there is little faith in the cause-and-effect relationships between effective governance and lists of criteria in the first method

- when board members are sophisticated and value the wisdom they bring to the table

- when the board has time to be reflective, to ruminate, to let their intuition come forth, "to know better by thinking slower" (Claxton, 1997)

- when a more explicit evaluation would trigger political battles or finger a specific board member

Description:

Gain a general feel for the complexity lens by discussing various chapters of *Edgeware* – especially the Tales chapter.

Aides
• *Reflection*

- Then with complexity in mind, apply reflectivity.

- Then with complexity in mind, apply collective sense-making. Sense-making definition: The leader helps others in various settings make retrospective sense of the situations in which they find themselves, and through reflection and progressive clarification create a sense of the reality they face. "What is real is up for grabs" (adapted from Weick, 1995). The leader as a sense-maker. ...

- Uses Weick's principles of a sense-making meeting, including: suspect old answers; encourage multiple interpretations; target ambiguity, not uncertainty reduction through information; understand that ambiguity collects at the top; mobilize requisite variety at meetings; and beware of norms that stress obedience and prevent embarrassment.

- Works on creating new meaning though expressive techniques such as analogies, metaphors, imaging, signs, symbols, myths, rituals, games and paradox.

- Uses verbs to capture the action that lays down the path for sense-making, "organizing" vs. organized, "integrating" vs. integrated.

- Uses storytelling about joint experiences to make sense of things.

• Then with complexity in mind, apply appreciative inquiry principles. Focus on what is working rather than what is wrong. See what it would take to amplify the positives and discuss what kind of future might be constructed based on them (see Cooperrider).

• Then with complexity in mind, apply the slow-learning processes that builds unconscious intelligence, refreshes intuition and informs wisdom. Learn complexity through osmosis. Boards are the trustees of wisdom for the institution. "Wisdom is practical; it involves seeing through the apparent issue to the real issue that underlies it; it is in touch with the simple truths that animate almost everyone; it is good judgment in hard times. To have wisdom is to possess a broad and well-developed repertoire of ways of knowing, and to deploy them appropriately. Wise persons soak up experience of complex domains, and extract the subtle, contingent pattern that are latent in it. Allowing oneself time to be wise is vital" (adapted from Claxton, 1997, Chapter 12). Slow knowing, the building of unconscious intelligence through reflection, contemplation and the exercise of curiosity is crowded out in popular management culture such as those worshiped in the magazine *Fast Company*. Managers, according to Claxton, typically look for solutions rather than examining questions, treat perception as unproblematic, base action on conscious understanding, value explanation over observation, like plans that are reasonable rather than intuitive, seek clarity rather than value confusion, and operate with a sense of impatience. Boards must counteract these tendencies and take time to cultivate a feel for complexity through slow learning and reflection.

Reflection:

Wisdom-building is not for the faint of heart.

References:

- Claxton, Guy. *Hare Brain Tortoise Mind, Why Intelligence Increases When You Think Less.* London: Fourth Estate (1997).

- Cooperrider, David L. and Suresh Srivastva. "Appreciative Inquiry in Organizational Life" *Research on Organizational Change and Development*, edited by Woodman and Passmore. Vol. 1, JAI Press (1987).

- Weick, Karl. *Sensemaking in Organizations.* Thousand Oaks: Sage Publications (1995).

3. Celebrating our CASness

The basic idea:

The board is a CAS nested within the institution as a complex adaptive system. Let's recognize and enhance it. Living under conditions of complexity is a normal fact of life. Most of us have learned how to hedge our bets as we face an uncertain future.

Potential context for use:

- when the board has learned enough about complexity to be able to recognize the reality that the board, the institution and the community are all complex systems

- when it is inappropriate to emphasize the distinction between CAS thinking and normal management thinking

- when searching for new ways of looking at things

Description:

Try some of the following:

- Relate experiences to the Nine Emerging and Connected Organizational and Leadership Principles in Chapter II. Review the general tenets of complexity emphasizing the real life nature of the perspective. Ask how a city works. Who is in overall charge? What role does comprehensive planning play in the future of a city?

- Explore the nine principles and some complexity aides, and invite participants to chose one or more that helps them interpret a particular situation. Ask them to describe the interpreted experience in story form.

    - For instance, examining the generative relationships aide might bring up a story about how an idea for a new service emerged from a relationship and extended conversations with a group of current clientele.

Aides
- *Generative relationships*

Principles
• *Chunking*

- Another example, talk about the "Grow complex systems by chunking" principle. Review John H. Holland's idea that a set of building blocks can be adapted and recombined to build a great number of new concepts. To illustrate this principle ask how many words there are in the English language (more than 460,000 in Webster's Third Edition). Then point out that these words are all based on simple building blocks, the 24 letters in the alphabet. Now apply the principle to the health care setting – think of the basic building blocks of a hospital, of a health care system. Think in terms of physician specialties or core competencies and relate these building blocks to the vast array of diseases treated.

• The limited ability of management to predict, prepare and control under conditions of dynamic change.

  – Think of recent examples of corporations that failed to adapt to changing markets such as Eastman Kodak Corp., IBM in 1991, Digital Equipment Corp., Montgomery Ward, General Motors and Levi Strauss. Did their leaders value "prediction and control toward a predetermined outcome" as the way to run a company? Were they trapped by a management mindset that valued efficiency over adaptability? Why did they miss the fundamental shifts in their markets?

  – The "butterfly effect" suggests that a small change in a nonlinear system can result in a large change. In fact, there are consulting firms that specialize in minimalist interventions. Take the beginning of World War I as an example. The assassination of Archduke Franz Ferdinand by a young Serbian student was the triggering event. What other examples of small changes having huge effects come to mind? What small changes in healthcare regulations have affected the industry in a major way? Think about the various rises and falls of Hospital Corp. of America and Columbia/HCA Healthcare Corp.

Reflection:

All of these approaches help board members become comfortable with the complexity lens. They come to recognize what they have always known that linearity – direct cause and effect – is relatively rare in human affairs.

Reference:

- Stacey, Ralph. *Strategic Management and Organizational Dynamics*. 2d ed. London: Pitman Publishing (1996).

Learning exercises

The basic idea:

Learning is an emergent property of a CAS. The overall system learns collectively as individual agents within the system learn. This is not an activity that can be dictated and controlled ... but it can be encouraged and facilitated. We can't force learning, but we can take actions that make learning more likely to occur. This aide summarizes some learning approaches designed to diffuse complexity principles throughout your organization.

Potential context for use:

- when agents within the CAS lack clear understanding of the basic lessons of complexity

- when you wish to facilitate the diffusion of a complexity approach throughout the system

- any time you desire activities to illustrate complexity principles

Description:

Learning approach	Aids learning about ...
1. Applying the principles	The nine emerging complexity principles
2. Exploring tales	Reflection, application of concepts
3. Reading club	Deep knowledge of complexity science
4. Mind grooving	Mental models and their effect on us
5. Multiple perspectives	A specific CAS and the role of mental models
6. Thumb wrestling	Power of cooperation and tit-for-tat strategy
7. Paper tear	Min specs, and the futility of max specs
8. Complexity journal	Reflection in a real, local, personal CAS

Learning Exercise:
1. *Applying the nine emerging and connected organizational and leadership principles*

Synopsis:	Group discussion about the practical consequences of the application of complexity principles in health care organizations.
When to use:	Early in your explorations of CAS.
Group considerations:	Appropriate for any group. Break up large groups into smaller groups of four to eight people to encourage more active conversation.
Learning styles:	The various elements of the discussion should appeal to all learning styles. People who like active interaction can jump right into the discussion. Quiet thinkers can read the principles beforehand and collect their thoughts. Opportunities for connections abound for those who like seeing these, and discussion of real situations will appeal to the more concrete thinkers in the group. Beware that some people may get bored repeating this exercise for each of the principles. Provide variety for them by reshuffling small groups, rephrasing the questions and so on.
The leader:	Needs to be comfortable with facilitating dialogue that does not have to go in any particular direction nor come to any conclusion. Remember, be a colearner.
Supplies needed:	Copies of the Principles chapter of this book. Share these beforehand so that those who like to prepare can do so. You may want to have easel pads for groups to record their thoughts, but avoid the impression that there is a "right answer" or that the output will be critiqued.

IV. Aides

Details:

Select a principle, provide about three to five minutes of explanation about it so that everyone is clear what it means, and give the discussion group these three activities to do:

- Make a list of three or four traditions in health care that seem counter to this principle.

- Tell stories from your past that seem to illustrate this principle (either positively or negatively).

- Pick a current issue and discuss how you might approach it with this principle in mind.

Have a large group discussion of key insights from each group.

Let the pace and intensity of the discussion be your guide regarding how long to spend on this. Fruitful discussion can be had in as few as 10 minutes and as much as an hour. The first time you use it, set a time limit of 15 minutes, announce time checks every five minutes, and ask the groups to move on to the next item to be sure they cover them all. See how it goes and adjust the time accordingly for the next principle you discuss.

You might cover several principles in a one- to two-hour session and save the rest for another time. Trying to cover all nine principles in one session is probably too much.

A peek behind the activity

The structure of the questions is intended to contain anxiety. Participants can first engage the principle at arm's length by looking at general traditions that others in health care typically follow. They next tell stories from the perspective of hindsight, from which wisdom is always more easily drawn. But, in the end, they are drawn into a discussion of some issue that is close to home for them.

The structure of the questions also creates some healthy tension for change, social support and skills for more-effective action.

Finally, the questions move from abstract, conceptual analysis to concrete action in the here and now; something for all learning styles.

Extensions of the activity

The three questions are a nice fractal for discussion of any new concept, not just the formally stated principles of complexity. For example, you could explain the minimum specifications aide and then go on to group discussion using basically these same three items.

IV. Aides

Learning Exercise:

2. *Exploring the tales of complexity*

Synopsis:	Provide your own interpretations and lens on the stories in the Tales chapter.
When to use:	Early in your explorations of CASs, but after you and your group have enough knowledge about CAS concepts to have a fruitful discussion. You might start with the tales that have explicit reflections included already, and then move on to tales that simply relate events and leave the interpretations up to you.
Group considerations:	Appropriate for any group. Consider breaking large groups into smaller groups of four to eight people to encourage more active conversation. But if you do, pay attention to providing appropriate diversity in the groups to assure a variety of viewpoints. Make sure also that there is enough knowledge in each group to assure good reflections from a complexity viewpoint.
Learning styles:	People who enjoy seeing patterns, will like doing this exercise. Extroverted people will like it if there is plenty of opportunity for interaction with others and if the discussion is kept open-ended and free from the "right answer syndrome." Practical, concrete thinkers may have difficulty seeing the relevance to their reality and current problems. If you have a lot of these sorts of people, choose the tales carefully for their value as analogous to current issues in your organization.
The leader:	Needs to be able to state a point of view without having others take it as the correct answer. Needs to be comfortable actively honoring other interpretations of events. Be a colearner.

Supplies needed: Copies of the Tales chapter of this book. Consider sharing the specific tales you will be discussing beforehand so that those who like to prepare can do so (see more about this in the Details section, below). You may want to ask people to capture thoughts on easel pads, but avoid the impression that there is a "right answer" or that the output will be critiqued.

Details:

Select a tale that you feel illustrates a concept that you want to discuss, or is particularly analogous to a situation that your organization is facing. Or, if you do not have too many strongly concrete thinkers who must see immediate relevance in order to learn, select a tale at random.

You can either have everyone read the tale in its entirety before beginning the discussion, or you can read through it one section at a time. Experiment with both options and see what your group likes best. If you use the one-section-at-a-time method, you may have to hand out the tale one-page-at-a-time if people cannot resist reading ahead. Talk about this beforehand so that everyone understands that this is not a game of "can you guess what happened next?" It is simply being done to maintain the group's focus. Also, be aware that this approach may be hard for those who prefer to have time to think and prepare before they participate.

To get more involvement and action, consider acting out the tale instead of simply reading it. This, of course, must be thought through beforehand, but it can be lots of fun and very stimulating, especially if you have lots of extroverts in your group. You could even modify some of the details to make the relevance more clear.

Regardless of the method of getting the tale out before the group, the point is to reflect on it. Consider questions and comments such as these to stimulate discussion:

- What principles, concepts, aides and so on from complexity do you see in this story?

- Does the story seem real or contrived to you? Explain. Listen to others explain their points of view and pay attention to the effect that this has on the learning group.

- What insights do you have when you view this story with the complexity lens?

- Interpret the story through other traditional lenses and contrast that with the complexity lens view.

- What would you do in this situation? How do you think it would have turned out? Why do you feel that way? What mental model are you applying?

- What mental models and metaphors do the people in the story appear to be holding?

- If you could talk to the people in the story, what would you like to ask them? Why?

- How do you think the various people in the story feel about the events of the story? What does this tell you about your own mental models and feelings?

- Does this story make you think of stories from your own experience? If so, please share the stories and the connections you see.

- How might we use the insights gained from this story to apply to our own context?

- Write a one-line moral of the story. Force yourself to distill it down to just one line. Now share with the group. What insights do you get about yourself and the others within the group through comparing and contrasting your summary statements?

The questions above are in no particular order, nor are they meant to be comprehensive. You will never fully explore all aspect of a story, so let the discussion go where it will and use your intuition for direction. Let the pace and intensity of the discussion be your guide regarding how long to spend on a story. Fruitful discussion can be had in as few as 10 minutes and as much as an hour. A good rule of thumb is to try to end the discussion and move on to some other activity just a little before most people are ready to quit. The thinking will continue on.

A peek behind the activity

Reflection is a key skill in understanding CASs. Here we are practicing reflection at arm's length by using the experiences of others. This might be safer initially than reflecting on our own context. Use this activity to get people comfortable with reflective learning; the open-ended dialogue, the unresolved diversity of opinion, the drawing out of lessons, the recognition of patterns and so on.

Think also about how this exercise helps participants develop learning style flexibility. Discuss this openly. Pragmatic, concrete thinkers need to learn how to theorize a bit and see patterns, even if they are not immediately relevant. Abstract, conceptual thinkers need to come down from the clouds and address the "so what?" question. Those who would prefer more time for quiet, private reflection need to practice thinking on their feet because it will help them handle real situations in which immediate action is needed. And those who prefer learning through activity need to learn to get something from what they might consider passive reading.

Throughout this activity, stress that the storyteller is simply telling the story from his or her point of view. What they did and what they think is not "right" in any absolute sense, it is simply what they did and thought. At the same time, point out that it is easy to be wise in hindsight and at a distance from the real events. Smugly putting down the storyteller serves no purpose.

Extensions of the activity

There is nothing magical about the stories in this book. You can, of course, use this activity with stories from other sources. Newspapers, magazines, novels, TV shows and movies may provide other stories to work with. If you are in a broader learning group with other organizations and you are keeping journals (see exercise number eight, "Keeping a complexity journal,") consider swapping stories.

IV. Aides

Learning Exercise:
3. Form a reading club using materials in the Bibliography

Synopsis:	Group discussion, or private thinking, to capture key ideas from the evolving field of CAS studies.
When to use:	After a sense of initial mastery of the basic concepts behind CASs; to develop further mastery and your own ideas about what is really important in this field.
Group considerations:	Appropriate for any group, or can be done as an individual exercise (maybe with later sharing).
Learning styles:	People who like to read and study will enjoy doing this. Those who prefer more activity and immediate application may openly revolt unless you structure the activity to meet their needs (suggestions below). Before engaging in this activity, discuss it openly and actively adapt it until everyone feels comfortable that it meets their learning needs and that the workload is fairly distributed (note: not necessarily evenly distributed, but everyone agrees that the work they have agreed to do is something that they want to do).
The leader:	Needs to enjoy learning from reading, but recognizes that not everyone feels the same. Needs to genuinely empathize with others who might find reading some of this material torturous. Needs to be active in making sure that no intellectual snobbery or cliques develop within the learning community.

Supplies needed: Copies of books and articles.

Details:

Reread the sections above and note the tone of caution. Not everybody likes to learn from reading and many of the books and articles of the topic of CAS are heavy material. Although you may be an early adopter of new ideas who has personally learned a lot on your own through reading, it is a mistake to simply assume that everyone else must go through the same process to learn what you have learned. Be respectful of others' learning styles. Have a good, honest, open, listening-oriented, no-bad-reflection-on-anyone discussion before you engage in a reading club.

Note that you can construct a reading group in a way that meets everyone's learning needs – if you abandon the idea that everyone must do equal work. You could, for example, let those who really like learning by reading take on the assignment of reading the material and presenting to the rest of the group for active discussion, reaction and application. But the presenters must agree to keep their presentations short and focused. They must agree to present what the author said so that the group can have the fun of exploring the material and coming to its own conclusions about it. They must agree not to pull intellectual rank on the group by saying things such as, "Of course, you could learn more about it if you read the book," or, "That point is covered in the book, but we don't have time to go into here."

Having said all this, reading clubs can be a great way to learn. Go through the annotated bibliography and select a few books or articles that seem interesting and relevant. Get a copy for everyone and set a plan for how you will go through it; for example, a chapter a week for a book, an article might be discussed in a single sitting. It is usually a good idea to have someone preassigned to lead the discussion. This could be a rotational assignment.

The discussion might roughly follow this outline:

- What did it say? What were the author's key points? What were the facts presented?

- What was most significant for you? What did it mean to you?

- What can we do with it? So what?

You might mix this activity with other learning activities in a single session of your learning group. Use your understanding of the learning styles of the participants to decide how much time to give to this and what do next to engage and honor those who might have struggled through it because it was not their preferred learning style.

A peek behind the activity

This is a knowledge-building activity, pure and simple. It provides more concepts and a deeper understanding that can be used later in reflection on the contexts of the learning group and its members.

Extensions of this activity

You do not really need to be physically together to do this activity. Consider forming a reading group with like-minded colleagues in distant cities. You could share insights over the telephone or e-mail. Remember the principle of generative relations – you can never tell what might emerge when a collection of people come together for interaction.

Learning Exercise:

4. Mind grooving

Synopsis:	To illustrate the power of shared mental models and natural ways of looking at things.
When to use:	When the concept of mental models is unclear, or when members of your learning group seem to be expressing doubts that we have certain ways of looking at things based on our social groups and experiences.
Group considerations:	Appropriate for any group.
Learning styles:	These are quick exercises; they happen so fast (just a minute or two) that learning styles are not much of a consideration.
The leader:	Needs to be able to conduct the demonstration and debrief quickly, being satisfied that the point is there and available for the participants to chew on without having to be driven home. Needs to be able to avoid acting smug when the predictable result occurs.
Supplies needed:	An overhead or easel sheet preprinted with the words below.
Source:	Sweeny and Meadows. *The Systems Thinking Playbook*. (Available from Turning Point, P.O. Box 1108, Framingham, MA 01701, (508) 650-0138.)

Demonstration #1: Color, furniture and flower

Ask participants to write down the first word that comes to mind when you say each of these words: *color … furniture … flower*. You can illustrate what you mean by saying, "For example, if I say *food*, you might say *hamburger*." You can reveal the words one at a time from an easel or overhead, or just say them out loud. Participants are to cover their responses so no one will see them until ready.

IV. Aides

Ask the group: How many said *red* for the color? *Blue?*
                        How many said *chair* or *couch* for the
                        furniture?
                        How many said *rose* for the flower? *Daisy?*

With uncanny consistency, the majority of the group will have written
red, *chair* and *rose* (or one of the second choices). Ask the group why they
think this happens, given the myriad of other possible responses.

Demonstration #2: Everything but sleep

On an overhead or easel sheet, display the following 10 words
arranged randomly:

slumber	dream	bed	quiet	nap
pillow	night	blanket	pajamas	snooze

Of course, all these words are associated with sleep, but do not draw
any attention to this. Ask the group to simply look at the words but not
write anything down for the moment. After 10 seconds, switch off the
overhead projector or cover the easel sheet. Now ask the group to write
down as many of the 10 words as they can remember.

After 20 to 30 seconds, ask participants to stop writing. Ask for a
show of hands: "How many wrote down *slumber? Night? Sleep?*" After the
people who raised their hand for *sleep* have lowered their hand, show the
words again. You won't have to say much, those who thought they saw
sleep will see that it is not on the list.

Debrief

The debrief needs to explore some theory and patterns for the more
abstract thinker, and some application to the here-and-now for the more
concrete thinkers. Use the notes below to make and draw out key points
from a quick group discussion of about five to 10 minutes. Don't overdo.
Be content to know that the points are there for the taking and that
participants will mull over the demonstrations in their own ways and at
their own pace.

Though we pride ourselves on being rational individuals,
socialization and shared mental patterns are stronger than we often
realize. Red, blue, couch, chair, rose, and daisy are what we have all
unconsciously agreed are common colors, furniture and flowers. And

everyone knows that the 10 words are naturally associated with sleep. If sleep isn't on the list, it was meant to be there.

These patterns of thinking are the result of the self-organizing nature of the mind. We naturally organize the vast information in our minds into related concepts. We can think of these as the valleys or ruts in our minds. Cognitive scientists would call them neural nets. (For more about all this, see: Plsek, Paul E. *Creativity, Innovation, and Quality.* Milwaukee: ASQ Quality Press (1997).)

This organizing structure of mind is good in that it is the basis for language. For example, we can say the word "hospital" and everyone knows what we are talking about: a building, with a parking lot, an emergency room somewhere, a reception desk, an admitting department, sick people, doctors, nurses and so on.

The downside is that this mental structure can tend to lock us into seeing things only one way. We can forget that our current mental picture of what constitutes a "hospital" is simply a mental model based on what we have learned to believe constitutes a hospital. It does not have to be that way. It is not the only way to conceptualize care for the acutely ill.

To bring the point home to practical application, you might ask: "What are the current contents of our mental valleys on the concepts of a *leader* or *manager*? What do we think of when we think of *workers*? Why do we think this way? How does how we think about these words influence what leaders and managers do day-by-day in organizations?"

Remember, don't overdo it. You do not have to get people to agree to anything. The exercise can actually be more powerful if you have just enough discussion to raise provocative thoughts, and then leave it there for everyone to mull over on their own. Watch and see if the illustration doesn't come back up in group discussion weeks later.

IV. Aides

Learning Exercise:

5. *Multiple perspectives*

Synopsis:	To explore the mental models and points of view of the agents within a real, local CAS.
When to use:	When you have a real issue and a CAS that you would like to understand better.
Group considerations:	Appropriate for any group. As noted below, if the members of the discussion group are also members of the CAS under consideration, make sure the discussion will be safe for everyone. Participants must be open to learning how others see them and sharing honestly how they see others. The exercise will probably take an hour or more to conduct at an appropriate depth. The nature of the exercise is such that its value is lost if it must end prematurely. Only start it if you have plenty of time and participants will remain present (physically and mentally).
Learning styles:	Different parts of the exercise will appeal to all learning styles.
The leader:	Needs to be a true coparticipant; comfortable with open, honest discussion and able to tune the information flow, power differential and diversity of the group as needed.
Supplies needed:	Index cards on which to write descriptions of the key agents within the CAS, and enough easel sheets to capture thoughts about each of these agents.
Source:	Based loosely on suggestions by Charlotte Roberts and Jim Boswell, in *The Fifth Dimension Fieldbook*, pages 273-275.

Step 1: Setting the context and identifying the agents in the CAS

Begin with a discussion about the issue that needs analysis. Typically, this would have been agreed upon prior to the group meeting and will be an issue with which everyone is familiar. The discussion is just to make sure that everyone understands the context before delving into the exercise. For example, the issue might be "Sharing financial gains from improvement activities with physicians."

Next, agree on the key agents in the CAS. These might be specific individuals, such as the medical director, or the CEO; or they might be groups, such as cardiologists, nurses and managers. Some of the agents might actually be a part of the learning group. If so, make it clear that the ground rules are that this is a safe discussion. Participants must be open to learning how others see them, and committed to sharing honestly how they see others.

There is always some judgment needed about how many agents to identify. We do not want to make a rule here. Use your good sense and your understanding of what the phrase "key agents in the CAS" means in your context. Of course, the more agents you identify, the longer the discussion will take and the more confusing it might become. But, if you leave someone out who is truly key, you sacrifice the reality and value of the exercise.

Write the individual or group names on separate cards and put up an easel sheet for each one.

Step 2: Constructing the mental models

Shuffle the cards and pass them out. If you have more cards than participants, pass one card to each person and just keep the leftovers for the next shuffle. If you have more participants than cards, involve different people in each round such that everyone shares equally in the work.

Each person takes the card they have been dealt and goes to the easel sheet for that agent. They have two minutes to complete the sentence, "From the perspective of this agent, the critical elements within this situation are. ..." Participants are to respond as if they were the person or group on the card. In essence, we are capturing our mental models of others' mental models. No one is allowed to pass.

Participants should not be influenced by what is already written. It is OK if your response contains elements already mentioned by others. The redundancy serves to illustrate how widely held the belief is.

If you get a card, you must respond as you think that person would respond. If you are the person or a member of the group, be honest in sharing your understanding of your own mental models. But this response

IV. Aides

is not the final word. Others should honestly share their models about you, even after seeing your response.

Continue cycling through card shuffles and two-minute periods of writing until each easel sheet has at least three to six listings. If you have more cards than participants, you can remove cards from circulation at some point after the easel sheet gets full.

This period of card shuffling and writing should be very active. Make participants walk around to get to the easel sheets. Talking is OK. But keep the pace lively by holding to the two-minute rule.

Step 3: Discussion about the mental models

Now spend three to five minutes looking at each easel sheet one at a time as a full group. If practical, do this standing up, moving from sheet to sheet. Others who didn't get a chance to write on the sheet can add additional insights to the sheet if they wish.

The purpose of the discussion is to create a complex picture both of that agent's mental models, and others' mental models of that agent's mental models. The point is that in a CAS, both are relevant. Each agent's actions are influenced by what they really think, by what they think others think and by what they think others think about them. Everything on the easel sheet is therefore important. It is not necessary to sort it out nor get to some conception of "truth." It is just all there.

Throughout the discussion, the one facilitating the activity should pay attention to the need to "tune to the edge." Keep the information flowing. Stress that every bit of information is relevant, diversity of viewpoint is good. Don't allow power plays or statements that imply that someone "really knows" what the agent thinks or what they will do. Point out that anxiety is good and there is no need to resolve anything, but don't let the anxiety cause the information flow to shut down.

Step 4: Implications for systems behavior

With a loose understanding of the agents and the mental models that are active in the system, turn the group's attention now to a discussion of the potential behavior of the CAS. Point out that while it is impossible to predict the detailed behavior of a CAS, we are often able to make general observations that can give us insight.

Begin the discussion with a "Suppose we did X" scenario statement. For example, "Suppose we said we were going to offer physicians who served on improvement teams a 20 percent share of the documented cost savings from that team?" Ask for comments on what other agents might think, feel and do. Participants will likely speak up naturally for certain agents. If not, pick an agent at random and inquire about their potential actions. Play out the scenario chronologically and explore multiple "what if?" branches. From time to time, return to the base of the scenario and propose an entirely different beginning.

It is impossible to explore all the potential branches. And, of course, no one can know what will really happen. Just keep the conversation moving and go down as many diverse paths as you can in the time you have.

About 15 minutes before you must break up the group, cut off the exploration and turn attention to reflecting on what you have learned. Ask simply, "So what do we think we have learned about the issue and the CAS we have been exploring?" Anything goes here. There may be thoughts about the need to better understand some of the agents. There may be ideas about new options to explore. The group may see the need for more information or more dialogue with key agents before taking any action. Capture the group's thoughts on an easel sheet.

The group and the person who organized the session must, in the end, use some intuition about what to do next. It may be important to note for the group that taking no next steps is doing something from the perspective of the CAS. The CAS will react to no new action. The system will keep on happening, whether we like it or not.

This is a complex learning exercise. It requires a high degree of dialogue skills and tolerance for anxiety. However, it can profoundly deepen participants' understanding of the specific CAS under consideration, and CASs in general.

IV. Aides

Learning Exercise:

6. *Thumb wrestling*

Synopsis:	Uses a common children's game to illustrate the power of cooperation and the tit-for-tat strategy.
When to use:	When people are having trouble seeing the power of cooperation over competition, or trouble in understanding the tit-for-tat strategy. You might use this exercise as a way of introducing the tit-for-tat strategy, before you even describe what it is.
Group considerations:	Appropriate for any size group. You will be pairing up, so you need an even number of participants. If you have an odd number, the leader can participate (see notes in the Details section).
Learning styles:	As with the mind grooving exercise, this is quick and, therefore, learning styles are not much of a consideration.
The leader:	Needs to be able to conduct the demonstration and debrief quickly, being satisfied that the point is there and available for the participants to chew on without having to be driven home.
Supplies needed:	None, unless you want to give some candy or something as a prize.
Source:	Sweeny and Meadows. *The Systems Thinking Playbook.* (Available from Turning Point, P.O. Box 1108, Framingham, MA 01701, (508) 650-0138.)

Details:

Ask participants to pair up quickly. If you have an odd number, the leader can participate. If the leader participates, he or she should follow the tit-for-tat strategy letting the partner take the lead; if the partner competes in the game, compete back furiously, if the partner suggests cooperation, cooperate.

Ask the group if they have ever done thumb wrestling before. Most people have. Have someone demonstrate for those who don't know.

In thumb wrestling, participants hold the thumb of their right hand pointing up and gently curl the remaining four fingers. These fingers are then locked into the similar curl of the partner's fingers so that the two hands are grasped with both thumbs pointing up. The wrestling occurs as the two thumbs wriggle around until one is pinned by the other. The thumb on top wins a point. Each person keeps track of his or her score.

When everyone is clear what thumb wrestling is, clearly explain that the goal is to "collect as many points as possible in one minute." Say it just like that. Be careful not to set the partners up as competitors. If anyone asks, just repeat the goal using the exact same words. If you are offering a prize, announce it. Do a quick warm-up by asking every pair to tap their thumbs down three times as you count *one – two – three*, then say "Go!" and start timing.

Call time and ask how many points participants have collected. Most people will have from one to five points, but one or two pairs will inevitably call out 20 to 30 points. This will cause cries of "foul," but ask the pairs to explain. Typically the pair has found a cooperative strategy in which one person allows his or her thumb to be pinned repeatedly, followed by switching where the other person's thumb is pinned. If there are protests, simply repeat clearly the goal of the exercise and point out that you said nothing about how they should do it.

Debrief

The debrief needs to explore some theory and patterns for the more abstract thinker, and some application to the here-and-now for the more concrete thinker. Draw out key points from a quick group discussion of about five to 10 minutes.

Ask, "What mental model was conjured up by the phrase *Thumb Wrestling?*" Obviously, a model of competition. This will be especially strong among people who played the game often as a child with a sibling or peers. Then it was about winners and losers, and not ever being beaten. Point out that the cooperative strategy that produces the best performance relative to the goal just does not seem natural. Reflect back to the group that the cooperative strategy of the winning pairs felt to others like "cheating." The mental model of competition is strong.

Bring the point home by asking, "What mental models are conjured up by some of the words and phrases we commonly use in leading an organization? Words such as *strategy, competitive benchmarking, market share, report cards* and so on." Again, it's largely about competition and is filled with school, sports and military metaphors. (This might start a discussion about gender differences. You can go down that path if you wish. Or you can simply point out that regardless of gender, we all learn a lot about competition in most organizational activities.)

Now shift the discussion to the tit-for-tat strategy. Ask one of the pairs with a high score how they decided on the strategy they used. Typically, one person in the pair proposed it. Ask, "What would have happened if the partner would have stayed with the competitive mental model?" Of course, allowing oneself to be pinned would not have worked. Now, staying with the tit-for-tat strategy, ask, "What would then have been the best course for the person who originally suggested the cooperation?" Beating the snot out of the partner! Followed up, perhaps, with a repeat of the offer for cooperation. This may have actually happened in one of the pairs.

Finally, bring this point home to application by selecting some organizational issue and asking, "What would the tit-for-tat strategy look like for this issue?" Think in advance about the issue you are going to use so that you can provide a clear tit-for-tat scenario if the group is still unable to see it. Don't overdo it. You do not have to get people to agree to anything. Just raise the provocative thoughts, and leave it there for everyone to mull over on their own.

Learning Exercise:

7. Paper tear

Synopsis:	Show the futility of trying to provide maximum specifications to guide desired performance on even a simple task.
When to use:	When you need to illustrate minimum specifications and highlight the contrast with traditional approaches.
Group considerations:	Appropriate for any size group, although larger is better.
Learning styles:	Another quick exercise for which learning styles are not much of a consideration.
The leader:	Needs to be able to conduct the demonstration and debrief quickly, being satisfied that the point is there and available for the participants to chew on without having to be driven home.
Supplies needed:	Several sheets of 8.5" x 11" paper for each participant.
Source:	Sweeny and Meadows. *The Systems Thinking Playbook.* (Available from Turning Point, P.O. Box 1108, Framingham, MA 01701, (508) 650-0138.)

IV. Aides

Details:

Give several (three or four) sheets of paper to each participant and keep one for yourself. Ask everyone to pick up one sheet.

Explain these rules: no talking; everyone is to close their eyes throughout the exercise and listen closely to the directions that will be given; everyone is to follow the directions exactly. State that the goal is for everyone to produce identical patterns with their pieces of paper.

When everyone's eyes are closed, read the directions below slowly and carefully. If anyone asks for clarification or opens their eyes to see what to do, remind them sternly of the rules of no talking and eyes closed. Simply reread the last direction and continue.

- Fold your paper in half and tear off the bottom right corner of the paper. (Pause to allow the group to do this.)

- Fold the paper in half again and tear off the upper right corner. (Pause)

- Fold the paper in half again and tear off the lower left corner. (Pause)

- Open your eyes, unfold you paper and hold it up for all to see.

These directions produce many different patterns, depending on the choices one makes at each "fold-in-half" point. You could stop here and go into a quick debrief about how hard it is to truly specify how even the simplest task should be done. Some people may think that you manipulated them with the directions. So do a few more rounds. Let anyone who wishes to be the leader come forward. Read the rules again: eyes shut, no talking, do what you're told. Restate the goal: identical patterns.

Ask the volunteer to turn his or her back to the group, or to shut their eyes. Then let the volunteer take over and give directions. They can use your directions or make up their own. The only constraint is that it must involve at least three steps, each with a fold and a tear. Enforce the rules throughout.

Typically, the volunteer uses a lot more words than you did (i.e., they go in the direction of increasing the specifications.) They might get lucky and get identical patterns if the group is small, but the chances of success are not great. Nearly always, there is at least one pattern that is different from the rest. Repeat the exercise with another volunteer if one is willing.

Debrief

The point of the exercise is reasonably easy to see. Specifications simply do not always result in consistent output. The key point is that there is a natural (learned) instinct to increase the specification when the initial specifications fail to produce the desired result.

Ask, "What would help us get the desired result of identical patterns?" Describing the desired output simply and leaving the method up to the person, allowing more information flow (talking, being able to see what others are doing), the flexibility to alter the directions based on feedback about what happened with the last direction, and so on. Point out that all of these suggestions are consistent with the theory of CASs.

To bring the ideas down to application, start a discussion around one or more of these items:

- Can you think of cases in the past for which we maybe applied maximum specifications and still failed to get the result we were looking for?

- Have we ever had success with something like minimum specifications; where we have supplied minimum directions and maximum freedom? Explain.

- Are there any currently open issues for which it might be a good idea to try minimum specifications and see what will happen?

You might want to refer participants to the minimum specifications section in the aides chapter of this book.

Learning Exercise:

8. Keeping a complexity journal

Synopsis:	Group discussion, or private thinking, using the reflection aide, to keep a record of some series of real events as seen through a complexity lens.
When to use:	After a sense of initial mastery of the basic concepts behind CAS; to sharpen your skills at seeing the world through a complexity lens. It will be helpful to have read through the Tales chapter in this book to get an idea about how to reflect and how to record stories.
Group considerations:	Appropriate for any group, or can be done as an individual exercise (maybe with later sharing).
Learning styles:	People who enjoy seeing patterns, will like doing this. Extroverts will like it if there is plenty of opportunity for interaction with others. But people who tend to judge or see the world on concrete terms might wonder, "Why are we doing this?" Discuss this openly, point out that things are seldom as black and white as we would like, and include in-sight and foresight reflection by asking, "OK, so what action should we take next in this evolving story?"
The leader:	Needs to be able to state a point of view without having others take it as the correct answer. Needs to be comfortable actively honoring other interpretations of events. Needs to be a role model and set an example by keeping her or his own personal reflection journal.
Supplies needed:	Bound, blank journals; spiral notebooks; or ring binders.

Details:

Select a situation with which you are actively involved. Again, you might agree on this as a group, or you might just do it by yourself.

Begin capturing the story by writing just a paragraph or two of relevant background information. Be concise. Think of Joe Friday on "Dragnet": "Just the facts, ma'am." But recognize that the "facts" in this case include the feelings and mental models of the agents in the CAS.

Reflect on the background information using the questions provided in the Reflection aide of this chapter. Capture your thoughts as they flow. Be explicit about the lens you are using to see the events; what do you see when you search explicitly for illustrations of things that you have learned from the study of CASs? What do you see when you adopt the viewpoint of the organization as machine or military unit?

A bullet list is fine; don't let the structure of grammatical writing interfere with your thinking process. You can always clean up the language later, but you don't really need to. The point is to learn, not to win a Pulitzer Prize.

Repeat the fact-capturing and reflection described above for the events of the present and recent past. Where is the story right now? What decisions are being made? What actions are being taken? Then, what reflections do we have about it all?

Now put the journal away. Let some time pass. How much time is hard to say. It will depend on the speed with which events are emerging in the system you are exploring. Use your common sense and intuition as a guide.

When, in your intuitive judgment, an appropriate time period has passed, open the journal and complete another cycle of fact-capturing and reflection. Begin by rereading the story and your reflections up to this point. It is OK to edit past entries in the light of new events, but you might want to do this in a different color or a highlighted font. You want to remember that you didn't see it before and you want to reflect on this as well. But, in the end, you do want to be able to tell the story in a coherent fashion.

As the story progresses, you want to include more insight and foresight reflection in addition to your hindsight reflections. Commit honestly to your thoughts about what you think you should do next. If you write them down, then you can learn by comparison when you reopen the journal later and record what actually happened. You should be doing this in a safe environment; no "gotchas" or snickers at naiveté allowed.

At some point, the story will seem to you to have reached a conclusion. Of course, this is arbitrary, as every story in a CAS leads into and becomes part of another story. But, use your common sense and declare a stop at some practical point. Reread the story and record your final reflections and thoughts (again, refer to the questions of the reflection aide in this chapter). Go on for as long as you like. Really explore the entire story and your insights from it. If you haven't been doing so up to this point, try summarizing insights and lessons from multiple points of view. If you have been doing this alone so far, now might be a good time to sit down with a few other people and share the whole story to get their points of view.

A peek behind the activity

Reflection is a key skill in understanding CASs. The point of keeping a journal is to practice reflection, not simply to keep a journal. So, of course, you can use any modern technology that helps reduce the time needed for this activity. You could record you thoughts in freeform on a tape recorder. You could type the notes, or have someone do it for you, on a word processor. Or, you might just prefer to stop with the tape recording. The point is that thinking is what it is all about, not writing. The idea is to slow down to think things through, and to capture your thoughts in some way so you can compare them to the future, unfolding reality.

edgeware

bibliography

edgeware

Annotated bibliography and resource guide

This guide contains recommended learning material on the science of complexity and its implications for organizations, management and health care. The material is organized into these sections:

- a starter collection

- annotated bibliography

- recommended journals

- Web site suggestions

This guide has been built to serve as a resource for health care leaders involved in bringing to life promising new leadership, organizational, and health care concepts.

A starter collection

If you are interested in building a basic collection of books that cover, in an approachable way, the basics of the science of complexity and organizational and management implications, these works are recommended. They are presented in alphabetical order by the author:

- *Fractals: The Patterns of Chaos*, by John Briggs

- *Competing on the Edge: Strategy as Structured Chaos*, by Shona Brown and Kathleen M. Eisenhardt

- *The Unshackled Organization: Facing the Challenge of Unpredictability Through Spontaneous Reorganization*, by Jeffrey Goldstein

- *Out of Control: The Rise of Neo-Biological Civilization*, by Kevin Kelly

- *Images of Organization* (chapters 4 and 8), by Gareth Morgan

- *Managing the Unknowable*, by Ralph Stacey

- *Complexity: The Emerging Science at the Edge of Order and Chaos*, by M. Mitchell Waldrop

Annotated bibliography

Note that to help you find publications of interest, resources in this bibliography have been organized into these categories:

- Introductions to complexity
- The science of complexity
- Complexity and organizations
- Complexity, medicine and health care
- Related organizational works
- General interest

Annotations are provided for all works. Those shown in quotations are from the annotated bibliography in *Out of Control*, by Kevin Kelly.

Introductions to complexity

These are works for the general reader interested in learning about the basics of complexity. Most are written by journalists.

- Briggs, John. *Fractals: The Patterns of Chaos*. New York: Simon & Schuster (1992).
  This beautiful book is the visual way into chaos theory and nonlinear dynamics. It tells the story with wonderful fractal images from artists, computers, nature, space and physiology. The matching prose covers basic concepts of the science in an engaging, elegant manner. You will definitely be glad you added this to your collection.

- Capra, Fritjof. *The Web of Life: A New Scientific Understanding of Living Systems*. New York: Doubleday (1996).
  Tom Petzinger: "Excellent layman's overview, with much less anti-industrial ideology than in Capra's earlier *The Turning Point*."

- Gleick, J. *Chaos*. New York: Viking Penguin (1987).
  "This bestseller hardly needs an introduction. It's a model of science writing, both in form and content. Although a small industry of chaos books has followed its worldwide success, this one is still worth rereading as a delightful way to glimpse the implications of complex systems."

- Kelly, K. *Out of Control: The Rise of Neo-Biological Civilization*. Reading, Mass.: Addison-Wesley (1994).
  This popular, insightful and wide-ranging work pulls important new pattern-building findings from fields as diverse as computer science, biology, physics and economics, relates them to the new worlds of complexity, chaos theory and post-Darwin evolution, and lays out the implications for creating complex organizations and systems of all types. Many of his findings are contrary to management traditions and practices.

- Lewin, Roger. *Complexity: Life At The Edge Of Chaos*. New York: Collier Books (1992).

  One of the best introductions to complexity told by one of the best science writers around. This work chronicles the author's search for deep understanding of this developing field through fascinating conversations with leading scientists in many fields – biology, computer science, psychology, ecology, physics. Don't miss it.

- Waldrop, M. M. *Complexity: The Emerging Science at the Edge of Order and Chaos*. New York: Simon & Schuster (1992).

  This is one of the finest introductions to complexity. Told through the stories of some of the leading contributors to this new science – engineer and psychologist John Holland, economist Brian Arthur, biologist Stuart Kauffman, computer scientist Chris Langton. These contributors come from a variety of disciplines and have come together through the Santa Fe Institute.

The science of complexity

These are works by complexity scientists that go deeper than the introductory books and articles. Still, they are accessible (with some work) to most readers.

- Brockman, John. *The Third Culture: Beyond the Scientific Revolution*. New York: Simon & Schuster (1995).
  Recommended by Jeffrey Goldstein. A very good compendium of leading complexity (and other) approaches. Chapters by Stuart Kauffman, "Order for Free"; Christopher Langton, "A Dynamical Pattern"; Doyne Farmer, "The Second Law of Organization"; Murray Gell-Mann, "Plectics"; Brian Goodwin, "Biology Is Just a Dance."

- Axelrod, R. *The Evolution of Cooperation*. New York: BasicBooks (1984).
  This classic work was the first to suggest a guided mix of cooperative and competitive behavior. Puts forth the tit-for-tat strategy and establishes robust reciprocity as a key to long-term organizational viability. Don't miss it!

- Gell-Mann, Murray. *The Quark and the Jaguar: Adventures in the Simple and Complex*. New York: W.H. Freeman and Company (1994).
  The story of complexity from one of its founders, a Nobel Prize winner in physics and member of the Santa Fe Institute faculty.

- Goertzel, Ben. *The Evolving Mind*. Langhorne, Penn.: Gordon and Breach (1993).
  Written by a mathematician and computer scientist, this book presents some highly original interpretations of complex systems cutting across several disciplines but winding up in a complexity theory of cognitive processes and brain functioning. Highly technical mathematical constructs are put at the end of each chapter in a special appendix, thereby making the book accessible to the nonmathematician. Recommended not only for its discussion of many areas of complexity science, but also for its capacity in inspiring the reader to see complex and nonlinear systems in a new way.

- Goodwin, Brian. *How the Leopard Changed Its Spots: The Evolution of Complexity.* New York: Touchstone (1994).
  Tom Petzinger: "A layman's guide to how complexity science may explain the forms and structures of life."

- Guastello, Stephen. *Chaos, Catastrophe, and Human Affairs: Applications of Nonlinear Dynamics to Work, Organizations, and Social Evolution.* Mahway, N.J.: Lawrence Erlbaum Associates (1995).
  Stephen Guastello, a professor of psychology internationally known for his pioneering work in the application of nonlinear dynamics to psychological research in a host of different areas including organizational psychology, leadership and design, offers a very useful review of his major research. Some of the material requires some element of mathematical and research methodology sophistication.

- Holland, John H. *Emergence: From Chaos to Order,* Reading, Mass.: Helix Books (1998).
  The latest book by one of the founders of complexity demonstrates how a small number of rules can generate systems of great complexity and novelty. In understanding the patterns generated, as in board games such as chess, Holland shows how we can gain deeper understanding of complex systems in life.

- Holland, John H. *Hidden Order: How Adaptation Builds Complexity.* Reading, Mass.: Helix Books (1995).
  Tom Petzinger: "This book is pure science – no history, no flag-waving – but it is startlingly clear and thoughtfully concise at 172 pages. John Holland is the father of genetic algorithms ... you'll find much more here that explains how systems adapt in both nature and the manmade world."

- Kauffman, S. A. "Antichaos and Adaptation." *Scientific American* (August, 1991).
  "A very accessible summation of Kauffman's important major ideas, with nary an equation in it. Read this one first."

- Kauffman, Stuart. *At Home in the Universe*. New York and Oxford, England: Oxford University Press (1995).
  The lay person's version of *The Origins of Order* – fresh insights into strategy-making, system-building from nature's viewpoint.
  Tom Petzinger: "A bit daunting in spots, it goes further than other books in exploring what complexity theory might mean for the future of economics and organizations. And Kauffman's speculations on the origins of life are thrilling."

- Kaye, Brian. *A Random Walk Through Fractal Dimensions*. New York: VCH (1989).
  Probably the best introduction to the fascinating world of fractals. Moreover, it doesn't demand a mathematical background at all. Wittily written, Kaye sprinkles his book with fascinating tidbits of word etymology that spur creative ideas in the reader.

- Lorenz, Edward. *The Essence of Chaos*. Seattle, Wash.: University of Washington Press (1993).
  Written by metereologist Edward Lorenz who first discovered what later was termed "chaos." Looking at chaotic systems from a unique and creative perspective, Lorenz draws out the meaning of such characteristics of chaotic systems as sensitive dependence on initial conditions, strange attractors, aperiodicity and stability/instability. Although, this book is written for a nonmathematical audience, it does require careful reading and thought. Highly recommended as a work from the original "chaologist," as well as for the creative and original way Lorenz describes chaos.

- Merry, Uri. *Coping with Uncertainty: Insights from the New Sciences of Chaos, Self-Organization, and Complexity*. Westport, Conn.: Praeger Publishing (1995).
  Tom Petzinger: "Extremely approachable overview."

- Peak, David and Michael Frame. *Chaos Under Control: The Art and Science of Complexity*. New York: W.H. Freeman (1994).
  One of the best introductions to complexity sciences covering the whole gamut of the field including complex adaptive systems, nonlinear dynamics and chaos, fractals, cellular automata, neural nets and genetic algorithms. This book is extremely clear and well-written, but it does require college

level mathematics. Probably has the best description of the logistic map, fractals and cellular automata in the literature.

- Prigogine, Ilya, and Isabelle Stengers. *Order Out of Chaos: Man's New Dialogue with Nature*. New York: Bantam Books (1984).
  Tom Petzinger: "A compelling historical account of the limitations of Newtonian science and the dynamics of complexity by a Nobel laureate in chemistry, with an emphasis on thermodynamics and dissipative structures."
  For the scientists in the crowd, this is one of the works that triggered the development of the science of complexity. A must read for those interested in the phenomena of self-organizing systems.

Complexity and organizations

These works explore the implications of complexity for organizational theory, management and leadership.

- Arthur, W. B. "Increasing Returns and the Two Worlds of Business." *Harvard Business Review* (July-Aug. 1996): 100-109.
  There are two worlds of business: The decreasing-returns world is the processing of bulk goods (the "Halls of Production") and products with little incorporated knowledge; the increasing-returns business has to do with knowledge-based industry (the "Casino of Technology") and interlinked webs of technologies. This award-winning author argues that different organizational orientations, skills and approaches to planning are required for these two worlds.

- Brown, Shona L. and Kathleen M. Eisenhardt. *Competing on the Edge: Strategy as Structured Chaos.* Boston, Mass.: Harvard Business School Press (1998).
  A new book by a Stanford University professor and a McKinsey consultant that explores a "competing on the edge" management strategy. Introduces concepts such as edge of time, the improvisational edge and time pacing, and includes lots of real company examples. Worth a look!

- Caulkin, Simon. "Chaos Inc." *Across The Board* (July-Aug. 1996): 32-36.
  An easy-to-read introductory article on complexity and potential uses within organizations. Written for business executives.

- de Geus, Arie. "The Living Company." *Harvard Business Review* (March-April 1997): 51-59.
  Has the makings of classic article. Arie de Geus explores what nature can teach executives about narrowing the large gap "between the average and maximum life expectancies of the corporate species." Argues for supporting ideas at the margins, giving people space and freedom to explore, building communities within organizations, fostering collaborative learning. A book by the same name, *The Living Company*, was published in 1997 by the Harvard Business School Press, Boston.

- Dooley, K. "A Complex Adaptive Systems Model of Organizational Change." *Nonlinear Dynamics, Psychology, & Life Sciences* 1 (1997): 69-97.

  A highly readable and informative exploration of how organizational change can be understood in terms of complex adaptive systems theory. Moreover, the author brings together the essential theories touching on CASs in terms of organizational change including autopoiesis, system dynamics, chaos and self-organization (dissipative systems). Then the author presents a model of change based on a complexity framework derived from work in cellular automata.

- Dooley, Kevin and Timothy L. Johnson. "TQM, Chaos and Complexity." *Human Systems Management* 14 (1995): 287-302.

  A superb article that explores what chaos and complexity theory offer to traditional thinking about quality improvement. Includes a comprehensive set of references.

- Eoyang, Glenda. *Coping with Chaos: Seven Simple Tools.* Cheyenne, WY: Lagumo Corp. (1997).

  At long last, an eminently practical book for how leaders throughout all levels of organizations can apply main findings from chaos and complexity theories. An organizational complexity practitioner and owner of her own computer company, Glenda Eoyang provides jargon-free explanations, as well as specific pointers for various situations facing managers based on seven principles of complex systems: 1. the Butterfly Effect; 2. Boundaries; 3. Feedback Loops; 4. Fractals; 5. Attractors; 6. Self-Organization; and 7. Coupling.

- Gersick, Connie. "Revolutionary Change Theory: A Multilevel Exploration of the Punctuated Equilibrium Paradigm." *Academy of Management Review* 16, no. 1 (1992): 10-36.

  The idea that a deep structure enhances system stability over time gives a novel approach to understanding resistance to change. Packaging periods of major change into compact revolutions allows for isolation of events for research and intervention. These paradigm changes are being observed in several different areas.

V. Bibliography

- Goldstein, Jeffrey. *The Unshackled Organization: Facing the Challenge of Unpredictability Through Spontaneous Reorganization.* Portland, Ore.: Productivity Press (1994).
  This is one of the few management books on the implications of complexity and nonlinear systems theory for the management of organizations. It is well done and offers the self-organization approach to major change in contrast to more conventional approaches.

- Huber, G.P. and W.H. Glick, ed. *Organizational Change and Redesign: Ideas and Insights for Improving Performance.* New York: Oxford Press (1993).
  Sound ideas for improving managerial performance under conditions of accelerating change. Weick's chapter "Organization Redesign as Improvisation" is a classic. The "Downsizing and Redesigning Organizations" chapter by Cameron, Freeman and Mishra presents some of the first research results on downsizing and redesign. A number of the findings are consistent with complexity principles. This work should be on your ready-reference shelf.

- Hurst, David K., and Brenda J. Zimmerman."From Life Cycle to Ecocycle: A New Perspective on the Growth, Maturity, Destruction, and Renewal of Complex Systems." *Journal of Management Inquiry* 3, no. 4 (Dec. 1994): 339-354.
  A fresh view of cycles of development and decline of organizations that goes beyond the S-curve concept. The authors, using the complexity framework, explore strategies for helping organizations adapt and remain relevant in light of the ecocycle metaphor.

- Hurst, David K. *Crisis & Renewal: Meeting the Challenge of Organizational Change.* Boston, Mass.: Harvard Business School Press (1995).
  Tom Petzinger: "Fresh and insightful look at corporate change through the lens of complexity, enriched with revealing historical research."

- Katel, Peter. "Bordering on Chaos." *Wired* (July, 1997): 98-107.
  The article tells the story of a Mexican cement company, Cemex, which has put complexity theory in action and has grown over 10 years to become the world's third-largest cement company, with more than 20,000 employees and 486 plants.

- Lane, D. and R. Maxfield. "Strategy Under Complexity: Fostering Generative Relationships." *Long Range Planning* 29 (April, 1996): 215-231.

  Strategy in the face of complex foresight horizons is an ongoing web of practices that interpret and construct the relationships that comprise the world in which the organization acts. Strategy and the future are discovered through generative relationships – those that produce unforeseen value and new possibilities. Authors provide guidance on where to look and how to foster productive generative relationships. The hunch is that this article will become a classic in management literature.

- Lewin, Roger. "It's a Jungle Out There." *New Scientist* (Nov. 29, 1997): 30-34.
  A view of businesses, markets and economies as ecosystems and complex systems presented by a well-known science writer. This perspective, supported by examples from the business world, helps us see differently.

- Lindberg, Curt and James Taylor. "From the Science of Complexity to Leading in Uncertain Times." *Journal of Innovative Management* (Summer, 1997): 22-34.
  An article that introduces the science of complexity to managers and explores the implications of the science for leadership and the role of the executive.

- Maguire, Steve. "Strategy as Design: A Fitness Landscape Framework." *Cahier de Recherche*. CETAI (Centre D'Etudes en Administration Internationale). HEC (Ecole des Hautes Etudes Commerciales). Montreal: Universite de Montreal (1997). Another version will appear in Y. Bar-Yam (Ed.), Proceedings of the International Conference on Complex Systems, Boston, Mass.: New England Complex Systems Institute (In Press).
  An excellent application of Kauffman's N/K Model, including the concept of fitness landscapes to corporate strategy and

planning. The author presents strategy as a design problem in which fitness landscapes can be of assistance in evaluating the adaptive value of specific strategic initiatives. The article, although technical at times, is very accessible to the nonspecialist.

- McMaster, Michael D. *The Intelligence Advantage: Organizing for Complexity.* Douglas, Isle of Man: Knowledge Based Development Co., Ltd. (1995).

  "Intelligence is the source of an organization's capacity for survival." This book combines complexity theory and postmodern thought to describe a new era of leadership as we move away from the "iron cage" of Newtonian thinking.

- Nohira, Nitin and James D. Berkley. "An Action Perspective: The Crux of the New Management." *California Management Review* 36, no. 4 (Summer, 1994): 70-92.

  The search for rational, linear designs is not the point in a nonlinear world. The identification and reliance on pragmatic action will suggest the direction of future actions. Designs are a part of action but are not given special privilege. This article compares and contrasts the design and action perspectives.

- Petzinger, Thomas Jr. Various short pieces, such as "How Creativity Can Take Wing At Edge of Chaos," "This Company Uses Sound Business Rules From Mother Nature," "At Deere They Know A Mad Scientist May Be A Firm's Biggest Asset," "Self-Organization Will Free Employees To Act Like Bosses," "How Lynn Mercer Manages a Factory That Manages Itself," "June Holley Brings a Touch of Italy to Appalachian Effort,""The Rise Of The Small, And Other Trends To Watch This Year." From the column "The Front Lines." *The Wall Street Journal,* July 12, 1996, Oct. 18, 1996, Jan. 3, 1997, March 7, 1997, Oct. 24, 1997, Nov. 21, 1997, Jan. 9, 1998, and other dates.

  This fine journalist from *The Wall Street Journal* is closely following the business implications of complexity; and we're lucky he is because he is uncovering many useful examples and stories of complexity at work.

- Stacey, Ralph D. *Managing the Unknowable: Strategic Boundaries Between Order and Chaos in Organizations.* San Francisco: Jossey-Bass Publishers (1992).

  Stacey maintains that the old maps are no good because we are sailing through uncharted waters. It is impossible to predict long-term changes in the future of a system. Answers and direction emerge.

- Stacey, Ralph D. *Complexity and Creativity in Organizations.* San Francisco: Berrett-Koehler Publishers (1996).
  New frameworks for sense-making in organizational life from the new sciences. Operate on the edge of chaos to be a creative organization. One of the best works on the management and leadership implications arising from the science of complexity. Emphasizes the human dimension.

- Stacey, Ralph D. "Emerging Strategies for a Chaotic Environment." *Long Range Planning* 16 (April, 1996): 182-189.
  A new look at planning from a complexity perspective.

- Waldrop, M. Mitchell. "The Trillion-Dollar Vision of Dee Hock." *Fast Company* (Oct.-Nov. 1996): 75-86.

  Fascinating article about Dee Hock and how he used the principles of distributed control, a mix of collaboration and competition, simple rules and diversity in the organization of VISA and his current drive to help social, environmental and community organizations use the concepts from complexity and chaos theory.

- Wheatley, Margaret J. *Leadership and the New Science: Learning About Organization from an Orderly Universe.* San Francisco: Berrett-Koehler Publishers (1992).
  An examination of science and the ways it affects what we know about the world and organizations; helped usher in a much greater appreciation for what nature and modern science can teach us about management.

- Zimmerman, Brenda J. "Chaos and Nonequilibrium: The Flip Side of Strategic Processes." *Organization Development Journal* (Spring, 1994): 31-38.

  A paper that contrasts the assumptions of equilibrium and nonequilibrium, or chaos theory, and develops the implications of the two world views for strategic management.

- Zimmerman, Brenda J. and David K. Hurst. "Breaking The Boundaries: The Fractal Organization" *Journal of Management Inquiry* (Dec. 1993): 334-355.

  The presentation of a fractal framework for understanding organizations, in theory and practice.

Complexity, medicine and health care

These writings deal with what a complexity perspective offers medicine and health care.

- Dandik, Irving I. "The Origin of Disease and Health, Heart Waves: The Single Solution to Heart Rate Variability and Ichemic Preconditioning." *Frontier Perspectives* 6, no. 2 (Spring/Summer, 1997): 18-32

  A provocative new theory about health and illness suggests that an increase in heart rate variability is the cause of health, while a decrease in heart rate variability (or heart wave range) is the ultimate underlying cause of chronic disorders.

- Goldberger, Ary L. "Non-linear dynamics for clinicians: chaos theory, fractals, and complexity at the bedside." *Lancet* 347 (May 11, 1996): 1312-1314.

  A wonderful introductory article for medical personnel by a physician who has delved deeply into human health and physiology from the complexity and chaos perspectives. Suggests new definitions for health and ill-health, and new diagnostic and therapeutic approaches. Contains comprehensive reference list of other medically related articles.

- Goldberger, A.L., D.R. Rigney and B.J. West. "Chaos and Fractals in Human Physiology," *Scientific American* 262: 42-49.
  This pioneering work was the first to suggest how developments in nonlinear dynamics and chaos theory could lead to advances in our understanding of human physiology.

- Goodwin, James S. "Chaos and the Limits of Modern Medicine." *The Journal of the American Medical Association* 278, no. 17 (November 5, 1997): 1399-1400.

  A provocative short piece that suggests that chaos and complexity theory can contribute to advancing the practice of

medicine by viewing people as complex systems and going
beyond traditional scientific medicine.

• Lindberg, Curt, Alfred Herzog, Martin Merry and Jeffrey.
  Goldstein. "Life at the Edge of Chaos – Health Care
  Applications of Complexity Science." *The Physician Executive*
  (Jan.-Feb. 1998): 6-20.
     This article seeks to introduce health care practitioners to the
     science of complexity and show how it can be helpful in
     dealing with both medical and health care organizational
     issues.

• Lipsitz, L.A., A.L. Goldberger. "Loss of 'Complexity' and Aging:
  Potential Applications of Fractals and Chaos Theory to
  Senescence." *The Journal of the American Medical Association*
  267 (1992): 1806-1809.
     New views of the aging process by two leading researchers
     suggest that aging is related to the loss of complex patterns in
     physiologic systems.

Related organizational works

Writings that do not stem from strictly a complexity perspective, but that are consistent with such a perspective.

- Fishman, Charles. "Change: The 10 Laws of Change That Never Change." *Fast Company* (April-May, 1997): 64-75.
  An article that offers some lessons on organizational change primarily from the perspective of the change agent. Provides a number of company examples. Many of the 10 laws (such as: "create tension, there is information in opposition, the informal network is as powerful as the formal chain of command, and you get to design your informal network") are consistent with complexity theory.

- Hamel, Gary. "Killer Strategies That Make Shareholders Rich." *Fortune* (June 23, 1997): 70-84.
  A well-known business consultant is now writing about the need for genetic diversity, novel experiences, many connections inside and outside the company and multiple experiments as keys to successful strategies.

- Morgan Gareth. *Images of Organization* 2d ed. Thousand Oaks, Calif.: Sage Publications (1997).
  The newly revised edition of this classic work in the management literature demonstrates through metaphors the multiple ways, realities and dimensions of organizations. The new edition contains expanded chapters, "Unfolding Logics of Change – Organization as Flux and Transformation" and "Learning and Self-Organization: Organizations as Brains," which deal with chaos and complexity theory in organizations.

Highly recommended

- Morgan, Gareth. *Imaginization:The Art of Creative Management.* Newbury Park, Calif.: Sage Publications (1993).
  Using a variety of images and metaphors (i.e. strategic termites, spider plants) the author shows how they can become powerful allies in fostering innovation and real change. He makes wonderful contributions to moving current organizational theory into practice.

Highly recommended

V. Bibliography

- Plsek, P.E. *Creativity, Innovation, and Quality*. Milwaukee, Wis.: ASQC Quality Press (1997).

  Though not written explicitly from a complexity perspective, you will find complexity concepts throughout. The book introduces Directed Creativity, taking the reader all the way from first principles to application.

- Pfeffer, Jeffrey *The Human Equation: Building Profits by Putting People First*. Boston: Harvard Business School Press (1998).

  This Stanford Business School professor lays out the research that demonstrates that long-term organizational success (including profits) is tied to management concern for employees. He cites troubling evidence that conventional management wisdom is often wrong and contrary to this research (excessive organizational focus on costs and rewarding short-term financial results rather than people management). Pfeffer believes that it takes courage for corporate leaders to abandon conventional wisdom and design strategies centered on employees, because this means abandoning the crowd.

- Schon, D.A. *The Reflective Practitioner*. New York: BasicBooks (1983).

  In this classic text, adult learning and change expert Donald Schon lays out his basic theories about how professionals develop new skills through purposeful reflection.

- Stacey, Ralph D. *Strategic Management and Organisational Dynamics*. London: Pitman Publishing (1993).

  A comprehensive management text book that traces the development of the field and also presents some of the author's work on complexity, including the helpful certainty and agreement matrix.

- Wenger, Etienne. "Communities of Practice: The Social Fabric of a Learning Organization." *Healthcare Forum Journal* (July-Aug. 1996): 20-26.

  Some fresh ideas about how to foster genuine learning in organizations. Many of the suggestions are consistent with complexity principles.

General interest

These works by scientists underpin some aspects of complexity.

- Bohm, David. *Wholeness and the Implicate Order.* London: Routledge (1980).

   Tom Petzinger: "The great quantum physicist delves into the holistic structure of everything. A powerful (if mathematically daunting, in parts) book."

- Csikszentmihalyi, Mihaly. *Flow: The Psychology of Optimal Experience.* New York: HarperCollins (1990).

   Tom Petzinger: "A wondrous examination of consciousness and happiness as emergent phenomena, based on research by the University of Chicago psychologist. The only self-help book I recommend."

- Hoagland, Jahlon and Bert Bo Dodson. *The Way Life Works: Everything You Need to Know About the Way All Life Grows, Develops, Reproduces and Gets Along* (1995).

   An authors' note sums up this work well: "When we – biologist and artist – first met in 1988, we discovered that we shared a fascination with the unity of life – how, deep down, all living creatures from bacteria to humans use the same materials and ways of doing things. We began exploring ways we might share our wonder with others, and came to believe we could achieve our purpose through an intimate merging of science and art. In the process, we hoped to persuade our audience that a deeper understanding of nature would enhance their appreciations of its beauty – and thereby enrich their lives."

- Smoot, George. *Wrinkles In Time.* New York: Avon (1994).
   A story, by perhaps the greatest living cosmologist, of his discovery, which Stephen Hawking called the "most important of the century, if not of all time," confirming the big bang theory and leading to an understanding that matter is not distributed uniformly throughout the universe. As he traces the development of the universe from the moment of creation until the present, he outlines some of the most basic principles of life, such as phase transitions and the increasing complexity of life's systems, which undoubtedly manifest themselves in organizations.

- Volk, Tyler. *Metapatterns: Across Space, Time, and Mind.* New York: Columbia University Press (1995).

  Not specifically arising out of complexity science per se, this book offers a remarkable journey through "metapatterns" of nature and society that are in many ways congruent with similar patterns being revealed in complexity theory. A very exciting and inspiring read!

- Wilson, Edward O. *The Diversity of Life.* Cambridge, Mass.: Harvard University Press (1992).

  This world-famous biologist and Pulitzer Prize-winner explores the fundamental role played by diversity in earth's living systems.

- Wilson, Edward O. *Naturalist.* Washington, D.C.: Shearwater Books (1994).

  Edward Wilson tells the story of his life and his many path-breaking scientific discoveries, a number of which (self-organization, simple rules, biodiversity) were central to the development of the science of complexity.

- Wilson, Edward O. *Consilience: Unity of Knowledge.* New York: Alfred A. Knopf (1998).

  Another groundbreaking endeavor by one of the most respected and broadest-thinking scientists of our time. This Pulitzer Prize-winning author and world-famous biologist showcases his argument for what he calls consilience – proof that everything in our world is governed by a small number of fundamental natural laws.

Recommended journals

A number of journals pay particular attention to the science of complexity or its implications for organizations and health care.

- *Complexity*. John Wiley & Sons Inc., 605 Third Ave., New York, N.Y. 10158-0012; phone: (800) 825-7550; email: *subinfo@wiley.com*.
  This journal, connected with the Santa Fe Institute, is a bimonthly publication that focuses on the science of complex adaptive systems.

- *Complexity and Chaos in Nursing*. Department of Nursing, Southern Connecticut State University, 501 Crescent St., New Haven, Conn. 06512; phone: (203) 392-6488; email: *vicenzi@scsu.ctstateu.edu*.
  This journal is devoted to examining the implications of chaos theory and complexity for nursing. It is published by the Department of Nursing, Southern Connecticut State University.

- *Fast Company*. P.O. Box 52760, Boulder, Colo. 80321-2760; phone: (800) 688-1545; Web site: *http://www.fastcompany.com*.
  This accessible journal covers new ideas in business and organizations. Articles on complexity in organizations appear quite frequently.

- *Nonlinear Dynamics, Psychology, and Life Sciences*. Human Resources Press, 233 Spring St., New York, N.Y. 10013-1578; phone: (212) 807-1047.
  This is the journal of the Society for Chaos Theory in Psychology & Life Sciences. It is published quarterly and periodically contains articles with an organizational orientation.

V. Bibliography

Web site suggestions

You will find a wealth of resources on the World Wide Web. We recommend the ones listed below. These URL addresses were current at the time of writing. For an up-to-date listing of complexity Web sites, visit http://www.vha.com.

http://www.vha.com – VHA's Web site contains an online library of the contents of this book, including additional tales and resources, and news of upcoming events.

http://www.bionomics.org – This is the site of the Bionomics Institute, a not-for-profit educational organization devoted to helping people understand the economy as a complex adaptive system. Resources from this institution's journal, conferences and the writings of founder Michael Rothchild are contained here.

http://www.brint.com/systems.htm – This site is the work of a University of Pittsburgh doctoral candidate. It contains a host of references, papers on business applications, and links to other Web sites.

http://www.calresco.force9.co.uk – This is the site of a not-for-profit organization, CALResCo, dedicated to promoting understanding of complex system sciences. It is full of useful information including a glossary, images, tutorials, introductions to related topics (genetic algorithms, self-organizing systems, artificial life, nonlinear science), links to other sites and papers. The welcome page contains this warning: "Take care – this site is conceptually demanding, once bitten you may never be quite the same again."

http://www.santafe.edu – This is the site maintained by The Santa Fe Institute, the acknowledged center of the science of complexity. You can access the scientific work, educational offerings and background on SFI, its faculty and Business Network.

http://www.imaginiz.com – This is Gareth Morgan's Web site. He is the highly respected organizational researcher and teacher from York University and the author of the newly revised management classic, *Images of Organization.*

http://www.industrialstreet.com/chaos/metalink.htm – A wide array of general complexity and chaos offerings are found here – from bibliographies to pictorial representations of the Mandelbrot set, to general educational offerings on chaos and complexity.

http://www.lissack.com/writings/ – A number of papers written by Michael Lissak on the implications of complexity for knowledge development and management are found on this site.

http://www.vanderbilt.ed.sci/chaos/cspls.html – This is the site of the Society for Chaos Theory in Psychology and the Life Sciences. It offers educational material, information on the society and other conferences, membership details and links to other sites. The society has wide interest in complexity, nonlinear dynamics, self-organization, chaos theory and has membership from many disciplines, including management, biology, psychology and philosophy.

http://sprott.physics.wisc.edu/lectures.htm- A site by Clint Sprott, including a PowerPoint presentation that was delivered to the VHA Leadership Network at its gathering on December 3, 1997.

http://www.eas.asu.edu/kdooley/index.html – A site maintained by Kevin Dooley. It includes a number of references to the area of quality management and assurance. A strong set of links and a nice section on creativity are also included.

http://www.DirectedCreativity.com/pages/ComplexityWP.html – Paul Plsek's creativity site. Contains a working paper: "Some emerging Principles for Managers of Complex Adaptive Systems (CAS)."

http://HOME.EASE.LSOFT.COM/archives/complex-m.html – This is the Complex-M mailing list, an e-mail-based discussion group for people interested in topics of complexity science, management, sense-making and the relations among them. There is a link on this page to join the dialogue.

glossary

A Nonlinear Dynamics and Complexity Glossary

Jeffrey Goldstein

Adaptation:

In Darwinian evolution, adaptation refers to the ongoing process whereby an organism becomes fit or adapted to a changing environment. Adaptation is brought about through modifications of an organism that prove helpful for survival. These modifications can result from random mutations as well as recombinations of genetic material (such as by means of sexual reproduction). In general, through the mechanism of natural selection, those modifications that aid in species survival are maintained. However, insights from the study of complex adaptive systems are suggesting that natural selection operates on systems that already contain a great deal of order simply as a result of self-organizing processes following the internal dynamics of a system (Kauffman "order for free"). Indeed, a fundamental characteristic of complex adaptive systems is their capacity to adapt by changing the rules of interaction among their component agents. In that way, adaptation can consist of learning new rules.

Algorithm:

A well-defined method or systematic procedure to solve a problem. In mathematics, an algorithm is a set of rules for performing a calculation or solving a mathematical problem. An example is Euclid's algorithm for finding the highest common factor of two numbers (the highest common factor of 1,365 and 3,654 is 21). In the case of computers and artificial intelligence, an algorithm refers to a routine(s) in a computer program used to calculate or solve a particular type of problem. In general, an algorithm is a formalized method for solving a problem.

Attractor:

The evolution of a nonlinear, dynamical, complex system can be marked by a series of phases, each of which constrains the behavior of the system to be in consonance with a reigning attractor(s). Such phases and their attractors are roughly analogous to the stages of human development: infancy, childhood, adolescence and so on. Each developmental stage has its own characteristic set of behaviors, developmental tasks, cognitive patterns, emotional issues and attitudes (although, of course, there is some variation among different people). Though a child may sometimes behave like an adult (and vice versa), the long-term behavior is what falls under the sway of the attractor operating within a specific developmental phase. Technically, in a dynamical system, an attractor is a pattern in phase or state space called a phase portrait to which values of variables settle into after transients die out. More generally, an attractor can be considered a circumscribed or constrained range in a system that seemingly underlies and attracts how a system is functioning within particular environmental (internal and external) conditions. The dynamics of the system, as well as current conditions, determine the system's attractors. When attractors change, the behavior in the system changes because it is operating under a different set of governing principles. The change of attractors is called bifurcation, and is brought about from far-from-equilibrium conditions that can be considered as a change in parameter values toward a critical threshold.

Types of Attractors:

Fixed-Point Attractor: An attractor depicted by a specific point in phase space, sometimes called an equilibrium point. Since it is only a point, this kind of attractor represents only a very limited range of possible behaviors in the system. For example, in a pendulum, a fixed-point attractor represents the pendulum when the bob is at rest. This state of rest attracts the system because of gravity and friction. In an organization a fixed-point attractor would be a metaphor for describing when the organization is "stuck" in a narrow range of possible actions.

Periodic (Limit Cycle) Attractor: An attractor that consists of a periodic movement back and forth between two or more values. The periodic attractor represents more possibilities for system behavior than the fixed point attractor. An example of a period two attractor is the oscillating movement of a metronome. In an organization, a periodic attractor might be when the general activity level oscillates from one extreme to another. Or, an example from psychiatry might be bi-polar disorder where a person's mood shifts back and forth from elation to depression.

Strange Attractor: An attractor of a chaotic system which is bound within a circumscribed region of phase space yet is aperiodic, meaning the exact behavior in the system never repeats. The structure of a strange attractor is fractal. A strange attractor can serve as a metaphor for creative activities in an organization in which innovation is possible yet there is a boundary to the activities determined by the core competencies of the organization as well as its resources and the environmental factors effecting the organization. A strange attractor portrays the characteristic of sensitive dependence on initial conditions (the butterfly effect) found in chaos.

Bifurcation:

The emergence of a new attractor(s) in a dynamical, complex system that occurs when some parameter reaches a critical level (sometimes called a "far-from-equilibrium condition"). For example, in the logistic equation or map system, bifurcation and the emergence of new attractors take place when the parameter representing birth and death rates in a population reaches a critical value. More generally, a bifurcation is when a system shows an abrupt change in typical behavior or functioning that lasts over time. For example, a change of an organizational policy or practice that results in a long-term change of the business' or institution's behavior can be considered a bifurcation.

Boundaries (Containers):

Processes of self-organization and emergence occur within bounded regions. An example is a chemical vessel or container holding Benard liquid, which keeps the liquid intact as it undergoes far-from-equilibrium conditions. In cellular automata, the container is the electronic network itself, which is wrapped around, in the sense that cells at the outskirts of the field are hooked back into the field. These boundaries or containers act to demarcate a system from its environment, and thereby maintain the identity of a system as it changes. Furthermore, boundaries channel the nonlinear processes at work during self-organization. In human systems, boundaries can refer to the actual physical plant, organizational policies, rules of interaction and whatever serves to underlie an organization's identity, and that distinguishes an organization from its boundaries. Boundaries need to be both permeable in the sense that they allow exchange between a system and its environments, as well as impermeable insofar as they circumscribe the identity of a system in contrast with its environments.

Butterfly Effect:

A popular image portraying the property of sensitive dependence on initial conditions in chaotic systems, i.e., a small change having a huge effect, such as a butterfly flapping its wings in South America eventually leading to a thunderstorm in North America. It has been suggested that the term refers to the butterfly-like shape of the phase portrait of the chaotic attractor discovered by the meteorologist Edward Lorenz when he first identified "chaos" in his computerized calculations of weather dynamics. The Butterfly Effect introduces a great amount of unpredictability into a system, since seemingly negligible causes may be amplified and lead to a drastically different outcome than expected. However, since chaotic attractors are not random, but operate within a circumscribed region of phase or state space, there still exists a certain amount of predictability associated with chaotic systems. Thus, a particular state of the weather may be unpredictable more than a few days in advance; nevertheless, climate and season reduce the range of possible states of the weather, thereby adding some degree of predictability even into chaotic systems.

Cellular Automata:

Computer arrays composed of a grid of cells connected to neighboring cells according to certain rules (a cell might be on if its four neighbor cells, east, west, north, and south, are also on). The entire array can self-organize into global patterns that may move around the screen. These emergent patterns can be quite complex, although they emerge from very simple rules governing the connections among the cells. Cellular automata were originally conceived by the late, eminent mathematicians John von Neumann and Stanislaw Ulam, and were realized more recently by the equally eminent living mathematician John Conway in his famous "Game of Life." Today, the study of cellular automata often goes under the name "Artificial Life" (or A-Life) because the exploration of cellular automata and their patterns (at such places as the Santa Fe Institute) is revealing a "life-like" behavior of these complex systems, and has, accordingly, led to insights into the way structure is built up in biological and other complex systems. Businesses and institutions can be modeled by cellular automata to the extent they are made up of interaction among people, equipment and supplies. For example, the strength, number and quality of connectivities among people or groups can be modeled by cells and rules among cells, leading to possibilities for investigating how changing the rules influences the emergence of new patterns.

Chaos:

A type of system behavior which, while appearing random and unpredictable, is actually deterministic and contains a hidden order. Chaos can be found in certain nonlinear dynamical systems when control parameters surpass certain critical levels. The emergence of chaos suggests that simple rules can lead to complex results. Such systems are constituted by nonlinear, interactive, feedback types of relationships among the variables, components or processes in the system. Chaotic time series of data from measurements of a system can be reconstructed or graphed in phase or state space as a chaotic attractor with a fractal structure. Chaotic attractors are characterized by sensitive dependence on initial conditions so that although the behavior is constrained within a range, the future behavior of the system is largely unpredictable. However, there is some measure of predictability due to the way the attractor of the system is constrained to a particular region of phase space. For example, if the weather is a chaotic system, particular states of the weather are unpredictable, yet the range of those states is predictable.

Chunking:

A term coined by journalist Kevin Kelly to describe how nature constructs complex systems from the bottom up with building blocks (systems) that have proven themselves able to work on their own. This concept is widely appreciated by evolutionary biologists and has been highlighted by complexity pioneer John Holland as a key feature of complex adaptive systems. He used the image of children's building blocks, of different shapes and sizes, combined in a variety of ways to yield new creations such as castles and palaces.

Coevolution:

The coordinated and interdependent evolution of two

or more systems within a larger ecological system. There is feedback among the systems in terms of competition or cooperation and different utilization of the same limited resources. For example, Kauffman and Macready give as examples of coevolution the way in which alterations in a predator will alter the adaptive possibilities of the prey. Businesses or institutions can coevolve in various ways with their suppliers, receivers, markets, communities, even competitors. For instance, the many joint ventures that are emerging can be considered a kind of coevolution.

Complexity:
A description of the complex phenomena demonstrated in systems characterized by nonlinear interactive components, emergent phenomena, continuous and discontinuous change, and unpredictable outcomes. Although there is at no one accepted definition of complexity, the term can be applied across a range of different yet related system behaviors such as chaos, self-organized criticality, complex adaptive systems, neural nets, nonlinear dynamics, far-from-equilibrium conditions and so on. Complexity is usually understood in contrast to simple, linear and equilibrium-based systems. Measures of complexity include algorithmic complexity, fractal dimensionality, Lyapunov exponents, Gell-Mann's effective complexity and Bennett's logical depth.

Complex Adaptive System:
A complex, nonlinear, interactive system that has the ability to adapt to a changing environment. Such systems are characterized by the potential for self-organization in a nonequilibrium environment. CAS evolve by random mutation, self-organization, the transformation of their internal models of the environment and natural selection. Examples include living organisms, the nervous system, the immune system, the economy, corporations, societies and so on. In a CAS, semi-autonomous agents interact according to certain rules of interaction, evolving to maximize some measure such as fitness. The agents are diverse in both form and capability, and they adapt by changing their rules and, hence, behavior, as they gain experience. Complex adaptive systems evolve historically, meaning their past or history (their experience), is added onto them and determines their future trajectory. Their adaptability can either be increased or decreased by the rules shaping their interaction. Moreover, unanticipated, emergent structures can play a determining role in the evolution of such systems, which is why such systems show a great deal of unpredictability. However, it is also the case that a CAS has the potential of a great deal of creativity that was not programmed into them from the beginning. Considering an organization such as a hospital, as a CAS shifts how change is enacted. For example, change can be understood as a kind of self-organization resulting from enhanced internal connectivity as well as increased connectivity to the environment, the cultivation of diversity of viewpoint of

organizational members, and
experimenting with alternative
rules and structures.

Concept of 15 Percent:

The organizational theorist Gareth
Morgan's concept for the amount
of discretionary influence a
manager has in influencing
change processes. One of Morgan's
points is that this 15 percent can
accomplish a great deal in a
nonlinear, complex system. For
example, nonlinearity means that
a small change can have a huge
outcome. Therefore, although
one's discretionary efficacy may
only be 15 percent, there can still
be a large influence resulting from
these discretionary efforts.

Deterministic System:

A system in which the later states
of the system follow from or are
determined by the earlier ones.
Such a system is described in
contrast to the stochastic or
random system in which future
states are not determined from
previous ones. An example of a
stochastic system would be the
sequence of heads or tails of an
unbiased coin toss, or radioactive
decay. If a system is deterministic,
this doesn't necessarily entail that
later states of the system are
predictable from knowledge of the
earlier ones. For example, chaos
has been termed "deterministic
chaos" since, although it is
determined by simple rules, its
property of sensitive dependence
on initial conditions makes it
largely unpredictable.

Difference Questioning:

A group-process technique
developed by the organizational
and complexity theorist Jeffrey

Goldstein that facilitates self-
organization by generating far-
from-equilibrium conditions in a
work group. The process consists
of several methods whereby
information is amplified by
highlighting the differences in
perception, idea, opinion and
attitude among group members.
Difference questioning does not
aim at increasing or generating
conflict, but instead, tries to
uncover the already differing
standpoints that have been
suppressed due to pressures for
group conformity. Moreover, the
process takes place within
boundaries that ensure the self-
organization is channeled in
constructive directions. Difference
questioning aims at interrupting
the tendency toward social
conformity that robs groups of
their creative idea-generating and
decision-making potential. In
other words, it strives to allow a
greater flow of information among
the group members, which has
been shown to be correlated with
a far-from-equilibrium condition,
a condition in which self-
organizing change can take place.

Dynamical System:

A complex, interactive system
evolving over time through
multiple modes of behavior, i.e.,
attractors. Instead, therefore, of
conceiving of entities or events as
static occurrences, the perspective
of a dynamical system is of a
changing, evolving process
following certain rules and
exhibiting an increase of
complexity. This evolution can
show transformations of behavior
as new attractors emerge. The
changes in system organization
and behavior are called

bifurcations. Dynamical systems are deterministic systems, although they can be influenced by random events. Time series data of dynamical systems can be graphed as phase portraits in phase space to indicate the qualitative properties of the system and its attractor(s). Various physiological systems can be conceptualized as dynamical systems, such as the heart. Seeing physiological systems as dynamical systems opens up the possibility of studying various attractor regimes. Moreover, certain diseases can be understood now as dynamical diseases meaning that their temporal phasing can be a key to understanding pathological conditions.

Edge of Chaos:

A term made popular by researchers at the Santa Fe Institute to indicate a particularly critical phase in the evolution of a dynamical, complex system when the possibility for the emergence of new, more-adaptive patterns is supposedly at a maximum. The edge of chaos is conceived as the zone between too much rigidity and too much laxity. There is controversy whether natural systems have a tendency to evolve into edge-of-chaos conditions. The edge of chaos can also be considered as roughly analogous to far-from-equilibrium conditions in that they both represent critical thresholds in which self-organization and emergence are heightened. Organizational applications involve encouraging organizational innovation and adaptation by facilitating edge of chaos-like conditions.

Emergence:

The arising of new, unexpected structures, patterns, properties or processes in a self-organizing system. These emergent phenomena can be understood as existing on a higher level than the lower-level components from which the emergents emerged. Emergent phenomena seem to have a life of their own with their own rules, laws and possibilities unlike the lower-level components. The term was first used by the 19th-century philosopher G.H. Lewes and came into greater currency in the scientific and philosophical movement known as Emergent Evolutionism in the 1920s and 1930s. In an important respect, the work connected with the Santa Fe Institute, the New England Complex Systems Institute and similar facilities represents a more powerful way of investigating emergent phenomena. In organizations, emergent phenomena are occurring all the time yet their significance can be downplayed by control mechanisms generated by the officially sanctioned corporate hierarchy. Two key challenges facing leaders is how to facilitate new emergent structures as well as take advantage of the ones that occur spontaneously.

Equilibrium:

Equilibrium is a term indicating a rest state of a system. For example, when a dynamical system is under the sway of a fixed or periodic attractor. The concept originated in Ancient Greece when the great mathematician Archimedes experimented with levers in balance, literally "equilibrium." The idea was elaborated upon through the Middle Ages, the Renaissance and the Birth of Modern Mathematics and Physics in the 17th and 18th centuries. "Equilibrium" has come to mean pretty much the same thing as stability, a system that is largely unaffected by internal or external changes since it easily returns to its original condition after being perturbed (such as a balanced lever on a fulcrum – a child's a see-saw). More generally, equilibrium suggests a system that tends to remain at status quo.

Far-From-Equilibrium:
The term used by the Prigogine School for conditions leading to self-organization and the emergence of dissipative structures. Far-from-equilibrium conditions move the system away from its equilibrium state activating, so to speak, the nonlinearity inherent in the system. Far-from-equilibrium conditions are another way of talking about the changes in the values of parameters leading-up to a bifurcation and the emergence of new attractor(s) in a dynamical system. They are also analogous to edge-of-chaos conditions.

Feedback:
The mutually reciprocal effect of one system or subsystem on another. Negative feedback is when two subsystems act to dampen the output of the other. For example, the relation of predators and prey can be described by a negative feedback loop since an increase in predators leads to a decline in the population of prey, but when the

amount of prey decrease too much, so does the population of predators since they have less to eat. Positive feedback means that two subsystems are amplifying each other's outputs, such as the screech heard in a public address system when the mike is too close to the speaker. The microphone amplifies the sound from the speaker, which in turn, amplifies the signal from the microphone, and around and around. Feedback is a way of talking about the nonlinear interaction among the elements or components in a system and can be modeled by nonlinear differential or difference equations as well as by the activity of cells in a cellular automata array. The idea of feedback forms the basis of System Dynamics, a way of diagraming the flow of work in an organization founded by Jay Forrester and made popular by Peter Senge.

Fitness Landscape:
A graphical way to measure and explore the adaptive (fitness) value of different configurations of system characteristics or traits. Each configuration and its neighbor configurations (or the slight modifications of it) are graphed as lower or higher peaks on a landscape-like surface. High fitness is portrayed as mountain-like peaks, and low fitness is depicted as lower peaks or valleys. Such a display provides an indication of the degree to which various combinations add or detract from the system's survivability or sustainability. The use of fitness landscapes in understanding complex adaptive systems has been pioneered by Stuart Kauffman.

Fractal:

A geometrical pattern, structure or set of points that is self-similar (exhibiting an identical or similar pattern) on different scales. For example, Benoit Mandelbrot, the discoverer of fractal geometry, describes the coast of England as a fractal, because, as it is observed from closer and closer points of view (changing the scale), it keeps showing a self-similar kind of irregularity. Another example is the structure of a tree with its self-similarity of branching patterns on different scales of observation, or the structure o the lungs in which self-similar branching provides a greater area for oxygen to be absorbed into the blood. Strange attractors in chaos theory have a fractal structure. The imagery of fractals has been popularized by the fascinating graphical representations of fractals in the form of Mandelbrot and Julia Sets on a computer screen.

Generative Relationships:

A concept developed by complexity researchers David Lane and Robert Maxfield. They define a human relationship as generative if it produces new sources of value that cannot be foreseen in advance. Their contention is that organizations, in times of turbulence and change, need to foster multiple generative relationships, within and outside the organization, as a means of discovering new strategies and directions. Fostering such relationships as well as preconditions for their success, they suggest, is a key responsibility of leaders.

Genetic Algorithm:

A type of evolving computer program developed by computer scientist John Holland, whose strategy of arriving at solutions is based on principles taken from genetics. Basically, the genetic algorithm uses the mixing of genetic information in sexual reproduction, random mutations and natural selection to arrive at solutions. In an analogous manner to the way a genetic algorithm learns better solutions through the mixing of patterns and an openness to random or chance events, a complex, adaptive system can adapt to a changing environment through the mixing of previous internal models of their environment. Thus, genetic algorithm can provide insight into the creative process of problem-solving or decision-making in a complex organization.

Initial Conditions:

The state of a system at the beginning of a period of observing or measuring it. The initial conditions are what is assessed at any particular time, and to which one can compare any later observation, measurement or assessment of the system as it evolves over time. For example, chaotic systems demonstrate sensitive dependence on initial conditions, meaning that the nonlinearity strongly amplifies slight differences in initial conditions, thereby rendering impossible the predictability of later states of the system.

Instability:

The condition of a system when it is easily disturbed by internal or external forces or events, in contrast to a stable system, which will return to its previous condition when disturbed. A pencil resting vertically on its eraser or a coin resting on its edge are examples of systems that have the property of instability since they easily fall over at the slightest breeze or movement of the surface they are resting on. An unstable system is one whose attractors can change, thus instability is a characteristic of a system at bifurcation (or far-from-equilibrium).

Internal Models:

In complex adaptive systems theory, a system functions according to its internal representation or model of its environment. This internal model is encoded in a set of internal mechanisms or processes (for example, memory structures). For a system to adapt to a changing environment, the internal models must have a means for changing as well. Thus, one of the most important functions of change agents in a business or institution is to expedite reconsiderations of an organization's internal models of its environment.

Interactive:

The mutual effect of components or subsystems or systems on each other. This interaction can be thought of as feedback between the components as there is a reciprocal influence. In contrast, the effect of a pool cue on a cue ball is not interactive, since the cue ball's movement doesn't significantly effect the pool cue itself. In cellular automata, it is the programmed rules that shape the kind of interaction occurring

among neighboring cells. Complex adaptive systems are nonlinear, interactive systems.

Linear System:

Technically, any system whose change of values of its variables can be represented as a series of points suggesting a straight line on a coordinate plane – hence, "linear" for line. More generally, a linear system is one in which small changes result in small effects, and large changes in large effects. In a linear system, the components are isolated and non-interactive. Linear systems are rare in nature, since living organisms and their components are not isolated and do interact.

Mental Models:

Images, representations or thought schemes of how we perceive and cognize the world around us. We follow our mental models in getting about in the world, but can become trapped in limiting behaviors by being overly attached to certain mental models. That is why we need occasionally to be jogged out of the ruts of our dominant mental models by investigating new ways of looking at things. Complexity science has the promise of being a powerful tool to get us to look at our work and organizations in a new way, thereby changing our mental models of how to go about our business in the most effective manner.

Minimum Specifications:

The management theorist Gareth Morgan's term for processes encouraging self-organization by avoiding a overly top-down, imposed design on an organization or work group. These processes can include such elements as mission statements, guiding principles, boundaries, creative challenges and so on. The key is for leadership to provide the minimum specifications, whereas the work group itself is given a creative space to accomplish the work. Minimum specifications are analogous to the simple rules governing interactions in complex systems.

Nonlinear System:

Technically, any system for which the data points derived from the measurement of the values of its variables can be represented as a curvilinear pattern on a coordinate plane, hence "nonlinear" for not-a-line. More generally, a system in which small changes can result in large effects, and large changes in small effects. Thus, sensitive dependence on initial conditions (the butterfly effect) in chaotic systems illustrates the extreme nonlinearity of these systems. In a nonlinear system, the components are interactive, interdependent and exhibit feedback effects. Complex adaptive systems are nonlinear systems.

Novelty (Innovation):

One of the defining characteristics of emergent patterns arising from self-organizing processes is their novelty or innovative character. Indeed, that is why such phenomena are termed "emergent"– they introduce new qualities into the system that were not pre-existing. An example is the novel nature of the dissipative structures that arise in nonlinear systems at far-from-equilibrium conditions. This novelty is neither

expected, predictable nor deducible from the pre-existing components. Moreover, this novelty is not reducible to the lower-level components without losing its essential characteristics. An issue, therefore, for practitioners working with complex systems, is to determine what system processes are necessary for the emergence of novelty. Novel outcomes demand novel processes.

Order for Free:

The complexity researcher Stuart Kauffman's term for the way the internal dynamics of a system generate order spontaneously under the right conditions. This order is "for free" in the sense that it does not need to be imposed or imported from outside the system. It is Kauffman's conjecture that natural selection during the course of evolution takes place on already self-organized order. An implication is that particular biological adaptations may result from constraints on possible designs due to the inherent mathematical dynamics of a system. In terms of organizations, spontaneously emerging structures may also prove adaptive.

Schema:

A term referring to the internal models of a complex adaptive system. The idea of a schema is related to how the term is used in cognitive psychology to refer to a way information is organized and thought about. Our perceptions are determined by a combination of external stimuli and internal schema.

Self-Fulfilling Prophecy:

In a social system, a self-fulfilling prophecy is a vicious circle that takes place when an expectation (prophecy, belief, mental model) leads to actions culminating in results that serve to confirm the validity of the original expectation. An example is when a bank collapses because depositors expect (or prophecize) that the bank will fail, leading to the behavior of a large-scale withdrawal of funds, and thereby fostering the eventual failure of the bank. Self-fulfilling prophecies serve to keep out information that is contradictory to the original expectations operating on the system. The circular feedback between expectation, actions and results can serve to keep organizations locked in particular constrained types of behavior. As such, a self-fulfilling prophecy can act as an attractor in an organization. Far-from-equilibrium conditions can be used to disrupt the status quo effect of self-fulfilling prophecies.

Self-Organization:

A process in a complex system whereby new emergent structures, patterns and properties arise without being externally imposed on the system. Not controlled by a centralized, hierarchical command-and-control center, self-organization is usually distributed throughout a system. Self-organization requires a complex, nonlinear system under appropriate conditions, variously described as "far-from-equilibrium," critical values of control parameters leading to "bifurcation," or the "edge of chaos." First studied in physical systems by Ilya Prigogine and his followers, as well as the Synergetics School founded by Hermann Haken, self-organization is now studied primarily through computer simulations such as cellular automata, boolean networks and other types of artificial life. Self-organization is now recognized as a crucial way for understanding emergent, collective behavior in a large variety of systems including: the economy, the brain and nervous system, the immune system, ecosystems and the modern large corporation or institution.

Sensitive Dependence on Initial Conditions, or SIC

The property of chaotic systems in which a small change in initial conditions can have a hugely disproportionate effect on outcome. SIC is popularly captured by the image of the butterfly effect. SIC makes chaotic systems largely unpredictable because measurements at initial conditions always will contain some amount of error, and SIC exponentially increases this error.

Shadow Organization:

Management and complexity theorist Ralph Stacey's term for the set of informal relationships or networks among people in an organization that exists in tandem with the official and legitimate network or hierarchy. The shadow organization is not focused on the same stabilizing objective as the official organization, so it is a ripe ground for the instability required for self-organization and the emergence of more adaptable organizational structures and processes. Effective leaders take into consideration both the mainstream and the shadow systems, even capitalizing, according to Stacey, on the potential friction between them.

Stability:
The opposite of instability, therefore the property of a system that stays pretty much the same after being disturbed by internal or external forces or events. For example, the deeper the keel of a sailboat, the more stable it is regarding the wind and currents. A running gyroscope is stable with respect to changes affecting its centrifugally determined level plane. Stability is sometimes used as synonymous with equilibrium or with the state of a system trapped within a particular attractor regime.

Swarmware and Clockware:
Two terms coined by the editor of *Wired* magazine, Kevin Kelly, for two antithetical management processes. Clockware are rational, standardized, controlled, measured processes; whereas Swarmware are processes including experimentation, trial-and-error, risk-taking, autonomy of agents. Clockware processes are seen in linear systems, whereas swarmware is what happens in complex systems undergoing self-organization as a result of the nonlinear interaction among components.

Wicked Questions:
Management and complexity theorist Brenda Zimmerman's term for the kind of hard-hitting challenges to which managers need to subject their plans and organizing schemes. Wicked questions serve to dislodge self-fulfilling prophecies, open the ground for new experimental possibilities and increase information in a system, thereby facilitating far-from-equilibrium conditions and self-organization.

e d g e w a r e